POOR WOMEN AND THEIR FAMILIES

SUNY Series in American Labor History

Robert Asher and Amy Kesselman, Editors

Other books in this series include:

Charles Stephenson and Robert Asher (eds.), *Life and Labor: Dimensions of American Working-Class History*

Joyce Shaw Peterson, *American Automobile Workers, 1900–1933*

Daniel Rosenberg, *New Orleans Dockworkers: Race, Labor, and Unionism 1892–1923*

Martin Halpern, *UAW Politics in the Cold War Era*

Michael Cassity, *Defending a Way of Life: An American Community in the Nineteenth Century*

Craig Phelan, *William Green: Biography of a Labor Leader*

Salvatore Salerno, *Red November, Black November: Culture and Community in the Industrial Workers of the World*

Richard W. Judd, *Socialist Cities: Municipal Politics and the Grass Roots of American Socialism*

Gerald Meyer, *Vito Marcantonio: Radical Politician, 1902–1954*

Howard B. Rock (ed.), *The New York City Artisan, 1789–1825: A Documentary History*

Robert Asher and Charles Stephenson (eds.), *Labor Divided: Race and Ethnicity in United States Labor Struggles, 1835–1960*

Eugene V. Dennett, *Agitprop: The Life of an American Working-Class Radical: The Autobiography of Eugene V. Dennett*

Amy Kesselman, *Fleeting Opportunities: Women Shipyard Workers in Portland and Vancouver During World War II and Reconversion*

Michael Marmo, *More Profile Than Courage: The New York City Transit Strike of 1966*

POOR WOMEN AND THEIR FAMILIES

Hard Working Charity Cases, 1900–1930

BEVERLY STADUM

State University of New York Press

Grateful acknowledgment is made to the following: the Minnesota Historical Society for permission to reprint in Chapter 2 material that originally appeared in "Says There's Nothing Like Home": Family Casework with the Minneapolis Poor, 1900-1930," Beverly Stadum, *Minnesota History* 51/2 (Summer 1988), 42-54; and the *Journal of Sociology and Social Welfare* for permission to reprint in Chapter 5 material that originally appeared in "A Critique of Family Case Workers 1900-1930: Women Working with Women," Beverly Stadum, *Journal of Sociology and Social Welfare* 17/3 (September 1990), 73-100.

Published by
State University of New York Press, Albany

Printed in the United States of America

For information, address the State University of New York Press,
State University Plaza, Albany, NY 12246

Library of Congress Cataloging-in-Publication Data

Stadum, Beverly Ann.
Poor women and their families : hard working charity cases. 1900–1930 / Beverly Stadum.
p. .cm. — (SUNY series in American labor history)
Includes bibliographical references and index.
ISBN 0-7914-0751-9 (CH : acid-free). — ISBN 0-7914-0752-7 (PB : acid-free)
1. Poor women—Minnesota—Minneapolis—History—20th century. 2. Social work with women—Minnesota—Minneapolis—History—20th century. 3. Poor—Minnesota—Minneapolis—History—20th century. I. Title. II. Series.
HV1447.M56S73 1992
362.83′086942—dc20 90-46559
CIP

10 9 8 7 6 5 4 3 2 1

For

Women on the south side of Columbus, Ohio

Contents

Tables

Preface

Respect for the struggles of poor women was a lesson I began to learn two decades ago when I left an American Studies graduate program to join VISTA (Volunteers in Service to America). The recruiting posters that had drawn me to this federal program encouraged applicants to be "part of the solution," not "part of the problem." I was sent to work with others at the South Side Settlement House in Columbus, Ohio, an agency that was established initially to provide services to Eastern European immigrants at the turn of the century. In 1969 the surrounding neighborhood was a racially mixed target area of the local Community Action Program. Regardless of the demise of Lyndon Johnson's War on Poverty, Settlement staff understood the struggle for social and economic justice to be ongoing and essential.

The agency was then located in an old building off Parsons Avenue and going there had been a family habit for three generations of black and white households in the neighborhood. Working-class homes with backyard gardens lined some streets; the deteriorating property of absentee landlords filled others. Both coexisted with a mix of stores, heavy industry, light manufacturing, and railroad tracks. For ten years South Side Settlement and the adjacent streets served as my intellectual home where I invested both energy and affection. During this same time, I also enrolled in the master's program in Social Work at Ohio State University.

Frequently the Settlement was full of laughing and shouting children, the youngest ones oblivious to the fact that they were an integral part of the national statistics on poverty. The clearest picture in my mind, however, is of women, black and white, young and old, talking during weekly sessions around a long table, planning what they could do about community problems, organizing ways to learn about the world, and also to have fun together. Many of these women managed to maintain households and raise children with a public assistance income that left them living far below the poverty line. They welcomed Settlement staff into their homes and when they could, invested personal resources in the South Side program and philosophy that advocated a just and caring interracial society.

The behavior of these women—both their strengths and weaknesses—enabled me to recognize and let go of middle-class assumptions about women, homemaking, and America. Alarmed by the persisting fact of poverty in this country and wondering how families on the south side—and more like them elsewhere—fit into American's past, I returned to graduate school to get a Ph.D. in American History at the University of Minnesota.

The Social Welfare History Archives is an important resource at that institution, which enables one to consider social problems in an historical context, and to study the organized responses of agencies such as settlement houses and of people within the social work profession. Among its collections, the archives has thousands of case records based on social workers' experiences with poor families who came for assistance to the Minneapolis charity organization society, which evolved into the present-day Family and Children's Service agency. In the stories of women from that city, 1900–1930, I recognized families from the Columbus Settlement House, 1969–79, and I first used the case records for a paper on sisterly kin networks in a women's history seminar with Sara Evans. At that time, and later, when the material became the basis of my dissertation, she raised important questions that pushed me to focus more clearly on what women were saying about themselves amid social workers' judgments.

This book examines the multiple roles of poor women and the hard work they did in both public and private sectors in order to care for their families. To the extent possible I have tried to let women speak for themselves, but just as my recollections of Columbus' south end are skewed by whom I am and the passage of time, the records I have used here are only a partial picture of the truth. For those women long ago whose names I have omitted or changed owing to the confidentiality of their case records, and to south end women whose names I knew well, I am in debt.

This research has been possible because Family and Children's Service of Minneapolis allowed me access to these confidential case records from the past and the History faculty at the university supported my application for a fellowship, allowing me to read records on microfilm at the archives. David Klaassen, archivist of the center, provided me—as he so freely gives all researchers—a glad welcome and a learned interest in the work I was doing. He shared his own writing about the history of this agency and always was on the lookout for additional sources for me.

The History Department also provided user time in the Social Science Research Facility at the University's Computer Center; this opportunity for quantitative analysis might have come to naught but for the patience of Karl Krohn who guided the data entry process. Jo Engelhardt at Concordia College in Moorhead, Minnesota, is a friend who encouraged me as she skillfully turned my sheets of dissertation into floppy disk. Roger Maltais of the Social Science Computer Lab at St. Cloud State University assisted me in developing my own proficiency on a microcomputer.

Clarke Chambers is too much of an egalitarian to enjoy the label of mentor, but since my first discovery of the richness of these case records, he has read, criticized, and supported me as I worked through multiple drafts. He has done this generously as an educator and historian who takes learning seriously, and as a human being deeply concerned about poverty and the plight of women.

Ironically I also have to acknowledge that if Richard Nixon had not been elected on 5 November 1968, I would not have felt so obliged to speak to the VISTA recruiter as my notion of an antidote the next day, surely would never have gone to the South Side Settlement House as a volunteer, and perhaps not have had personal experiences compelling me to learn about poverty as part of American history.

Introduction

A Mrs. Nordheim wrote to the Associated Charities/Family Welfare Association (AC/FWA) of Minneapolis in 1927 asking for help as she explained in broken sentences that "the Mr." had just gone back to work after a long period of unemployment but would not be getting paid for a while, and the landlord had threatened eviction owing to unpaid rent. She was trying to pack their things, but the baby due shortly made lifting difficult, and the cupboards held no food with which to quiet her other whining children. Mrs. Nordheim wrote that she could not "stand all this suffering" and then said in despair that someone else should try to care for the youngsters on nothing as she had attempted to do. She only hoped that the powerful but unknown "they" might see and "appreciate what I done and struggled."[1]

This woman knew that those who publicly meted out most of the "appreciation" and material goods in society came from a different class than those who "done and struggled." But consistent with so many women in situations like her own, Mrs. Nordheim just kept struggling. She made do with little and periodically found work cleaning buildings at night to bring home wages when her husband failed to do so. What was unusual was her written request that others respect the daily work she did. Over half a century has passed since Mrs. Nordheim wrote this note, but the hardships of poor mothers continue at increasing variance with the material consumption and broad opportunities that are theoretically available to all Americans. Respect for what the poor struggle to do in shaping their own survival is still not common practice; for most people in this country women like Mrs. Nordheim are invisible.

Early in the century the vigor of industrialism and urban growth led successful entrepreneurs to praise America's good fortune, but the prosperity they enjoyed did not extend to the lower class whose survival meant devising and implementing strategies the middle and upper class could ignore. Gender, however, as well as class, altered what one had to do, and this book is about the efforts of three hundred poor wives and mothers like Mrs. Nordheim who lived in Minneapolis, Minnesota, between 1900 and 1930. While poverty in the country's largest urban areas has been documented, much less has been known about impoverished families in mid-size Mid-western cities. Fragments of women's lives are pieced together here in an interpretive synthesis that speaks of these women as a blunt aggregate, but also reveals how individuals persisted in maintaining their lives with children and with men. Knowledge of their experiences exists because at different points all of them came to be known at the city's largest charity agency where social workers amassed family details in longitudinal case records. While the activities examined here are circumscribed by what social workers chose to record, it becomes obvious that the role of the charity/social work agency was temporary and families worked diligently to create their own welfare. The social history scholarship referred to in the notes suggests more about the relationship between income and female roles that frames the lives of this particular group of women.

Encouraged by economic changes in the nineteenth century, social conventions redefined the "family" and separated expectations for women and men into rigid categories of activity in the privacy of home versus that in the public world of work. Definition of women's proper behavior not only meant marriage and motherhood as it had for centuries, but grew to include reliance on a husband for financial support. In middle-class homes the food and clothing women had traditionally created through household production became superfluous and considered second-rate compared to goods available in the growing market economy of urban areas.[2] While the public perceived an idle wife as a reflection of an economically successful husband, most women at home increasingly took on the "work" involved in raising children. Among the lower class, concern for household well-being forced wives into additional activities beyond that of being a parent or "helpmate" to a husband. Yet the narrow definitions of separate gender roles and the assertion that female dependency was appropriate, moved across class lines as a national ethos.[3] Among those who were financially secure, the principle simultaneously flourished that opportunities to succeed existed for *all* men in the United States. Failure to get ahead was taken as a reflection of inferior character.

In his book, *From the Depths, The Discovery of Poverty in the United States*, the historian Robert Bremner was the first to interpret how and why certain social critics in the late nineteenth and early twentieth century began to question assertions about opportunity and to identify the social and economic inequities underlying impoverishment.[4] The indictment that people were responsible for their poverty began to lose ground to the realization that modern industrialism and urbanization demanded and maintained laborers who had little choice but to compete for meager wages in irregular employment and to raise their children in unhealthy conditions. Through labor unions, workers objected strenuously to low pay and exploitation, and studies at the time confirmed the inadequacy of working-class wages.[5] Reformers rallied around social welfare initiatives expected to advance family security and social stability, and they advocated the adoption of a "family wage" that recognized a worker's need to support others besides himself.[6] The wage rates that continued to prevail, however, failed to give the working class security, although many in the public persisted in their assumption that any employment created sufficient income.

Actual "need" in a family varied with the number and age of dependents, invalidating the possibility that a standard wage could provide the same security in every household. In many industries unregulated employment cycles and frequent industrial accidents deprived families of both wages and wage earners. A pay envelope that was adequate for half the year might be entirely absent the next few months, and as a result many wives and children had little choice but to seek work to subsidize the household budget.[7] Yet employers advanced the assumptions that men were providers and women's true job was at home in order to justify paying female employees at an even lower rate than males. And male-dominated labor unions often collaborated in supporting the idea of women's work at home for that served to limit the labor pool contending for jobs.[8]

In addition to these myths about the sufficiency of wages and the inappropriateness of women in the workplace, another myth concealed the true state of family life in many households. The domestic ethos pictured women and children acting in complementary fashion under the protection of a male as household head. However, men could and some did violate their role as protector by inflicting physical and sexual abuse on both wives and children. The pain and repercussion of such actions are described in this study as a dilemma that women faced; unfortunately, the nature of the records allowed little insight into women's own abuse of children. However, the historian Linda Gordon interprets the full context of violent family relations in *Heroes of Their Own Lives, The Politics and History of Family Violence, Boston 1880–1960.* As her primary source she uses nineteenth- and twentieth-century case records from child welfare agencies whose clients were in large part poor.

Gordon rejects the notion that members in a family share a single interest in political terms. Instead, their differences in sex, age, and class give them varying access to personal and social resources. Violence in a home often reflects these contending interests and is a real struggle over power. At times, women and children have sought outsiders for protection or to mediate the conflict—as in calling upon social welfare agencies. But while society has often been anxious about the deviation of lower-class families from supposed "norms," willingness to intervene in the home regarding these matters has fluctuated over time in relationship to other social realities.[9]

For victims of abuse who found little safety within the home or through the action of outsiders, desertion of an offending parent or spouse and dissolution of the prior household unit could be welcome relief. But when working men abandoned economic responsibility for their families, the "dependents" of these deserters faced serious problems as to survival. All of this blurred sentimental pictures of proper family life that portrayed women's activity only within the shelter of homes provided by men.

Many poor women knew about male cruelty and the inconstancy of both husbands and wages.[10] With limited choices, most of the women who were mothers did what they had to on their own so as to provide a home for their children. Women's diverse involvement in the family unit is not new, but is associated with preindustrial agricultural societies in which survival claimed the combined labor of everyone in a "household economy." In *Women, Work and Family,* Louise A. Tilly and Joan W. Scott examine how female contributions to the household shifted when industrialization brought wage work and a cash economy to urban areas. They found that women continued to invest themselves—by way of their earnings—in the family unit and to take much of their personal identity from that participation with others.

Conflict within families is real and can have painful repercussions, but women's commitment to use themselves to maintain the family also appears to be deep. And since the early nineteenth century familial responsibility for many lower-class wives and mothers has included work for wages.[11] Some of the previous historical investigations of the working class have created a partial picture by dealing only with laboring men and male headed households. But women's labor history also can err by discussing wage work without paying attention to female workers' familial obligations and the accommodation wives and mothers have had to make between the two.[12] A tidy division of activity and responsibility into private spheres for women and public spheres for men may miss the truth in most peoples' lives, but it surely fails as a portrayal of poor women who felt the "spur of want" and who lacked the "luxury" of dependency on others.[13]

This book asserts that poor women *had* to use themselves in *many* ways, and their "work" included the paid and unpaid responsibilities they undertook as part of homemaking, child rearing, employment, marriage, and getting "help"—whether from neighbors, kin, or strangers at a charity. The study also suggests that to understand the complexity of survival, families' experiences have to be considered over time. Historians have noted differences in the implementation of survival strategies depending upon whether a household had a male or female head; for example, older widows were more likely to take in boarders than were married women or young widows. Maturation of family members also has been pointed to in explaining variations in household resources; for example, small children's demands mitigate against a woman's wage earning beyond the home, whereas adolescents' employment might enable a mother's withdrawal from the work force.[14] Census materials have helped scholars examine such patterns, but the shortcomings of that particular source are considerable for official enumeration recorded family structure and behavior at a static point in time. The day following the census taker's visit, family affairs could change, and the current means for survival might disappear. A married man held legal title as "household head," yet he could be absent or ill for long periods, or repeatedly come and go, leaving his wife with full responsibility for the home. Who then qualified as household head?

While the sum of women or families examined here shows similar needs and responses to problems, individual households were in great flux. To survive the irregularities and insecurities of early twentieth-century poverty called for flexibility and opportunism with minimal regard to boundaries between public and private venues. Resources had to be used as they came along, and survival for the poor had an even more precarious element to it than statistics suggest. In "getting along," women's attitudes and aspirations led to vital action in setting priorities and in creating resources for their families.

Design of the Book

Chapter 1 introduces three distinct and real women who like Mrs. Nordheim made their homes in Minneapolis, coping with poverty punctuated by family problems, ill health, and broken dreams. The context for daily activity and "work" was not simply the home but the city, with neighbors and kin, employers, and social workers. When considered together, the stories of these three—drawn from their case records at the local charity—suggest that personal attributes, described by social workers as "virtue" or "worth" as opposed to being "unreliable" or "stubborn," furnished no protection from the ups and downs of lower-class life. To be poor was to be vulnerable to a multitude of difficulties, including criticism from the social workers providing "help."

Following the women's individual stories, the local system of services and relief is described with attention to the development of casework practice at AC/FWA. The organization had strong connections nationally and was prominent in the local social welfare network that suggests that what happened to its client cases was neither atypical nor unusual.

More than relying on the aid of organized charities, the three women solved their problems their own ways. Chapter 1 closes with an analysis of poor women's struggles that serves as the theme that runs throughout this book. Poverty meant deprivation and insecurity. Some responses to this were creative and reflected individual strengths and aspirations, but most took on a pattern that repeated from house to house. Discouragement could easily grow out of impoverishment, but it is clear, too, that many wives and mothers had pluck and were willing to reach out and take chances.

The four chapters that follow, draw on material from the social case records of all three hundred women in my sample. Each chapter focuses on a particular element of women's "work": within a household as mother and homemaker, as a paid wage earner, as a wife, and as a charity recipient. In each of these roles tension existed between the expectations set by society as shown by agency workers who were part of the emerging social work profession, and what poor women had the fortitude, resources, and inclination to do. Thus, the reality of class differences shows itself in daily occurrences.

Chapter 2 emphasizes women's energetic efforts to raise children and maintain a household against a constant shortage of material assets. Many women and their female kin expressed agreement with social workers' definitions of desirable homemaking standards. The irregularity of income, however, translated itself into other inconsistencies and pressured women to make hard choices about what mattered most within a household. In coping with problems, they regularly turned for help to neighbors and kin networks of siblings, parents, aunts, and uncles. Gender distinguished mothers' relations with children—both young and grown, and this also was a factor in the systems of "mutual aid" that women generated with others whether related by blood or affection.

The home was not simply a space for the work of being wife and mother, but it could double as a place in which women earned cash taking in boarders or doing laundry for others. Many, however, went out and sought wage work.

Chapter 3 focuses on wives' and mothers' experiences as part of the labor market. It begins by describing the injustices of inadequate wages and irregular employment that all lower-class workers faced in the early twentieth-century urban environment. Regardless of the public's unwillingness to accept married women as full-fledged employees deserving of a "family wage," the majority of these three hundred women saw—or had seen—themselves as wage earners who often filled the humblest positions in domestic service or char work. Those employed beyond their homes juggled underpaid positions with the pressures of child care, to the detriment of their own health. Poor women knew the stress of hunting for jobs and their complaints were usually not of wages, but about the irregularity of employment. To succeed in finding and holding a position could enable someone to "save" her home.

Case records show women reacting more vehemently to their abusive treatment within marriage than to their plight as laborers. Chapter 4 illustrates how the roles of wife and mother carried an emotional importance that wage-earning lacked, although conjugal harmony was a rare experience. Added to the pressures that poverty and unemployment forced on all domestic relations, many wives were dealing with deserting, drunken and abusive husbands. As women decided what to do about their own marital situations, they often were torn between fears for their physical safety and the practical need for a man's earning ability.

In spite of material deprivation, most people in the working class never appeared at the door of a charitable institution asking aid; among those who did, many regarded relief as assistance of last resort.[15] With increasing emphasis on training and standardization of the investigation process, social work as a profession changed somewhat during the first decades of the twentieth century. Among the lower class, however, many relief and family agencies continued to be regarded as intrusive at best. Chapter 5 analyzes the complex relationship between poor women and the professional workers who intended to help them but did so within set expectations.

At a specific point in a family's life, arrangements for delivery of half a ton of coal or word about an available job could be precisely the assistance a woman felt she needed from a charity worker. But most social work policies advocated maintaining traditional family and economic structures, and the means for survival that a woman created under pressure were unlikely to match smoothly with what the staff in private agencies proposed.[16] From her vantage point in the early settlement house movement, Jane Addams described this as the "subtle problem of charity." An "incessant clashing of ethical standards" took place between the poor and middle-class social workers, each acting logically from within her own experiences, but resulting in a relationship that was less than democratic.[17]

In *Heroes of Their Own Lives,* Gordon discusses similar relations between social workers and client families in her study of family violence. The case records she used offered evidence of unfounded assumptions, intrusions, and class biases on the part of social workers. Such behavior has led some historians to see most charity and welfare programs as poorly disguised efforts at asserting social control, which denies the rights of groups whose lives may be inconsistent with middle-class mores. Gordon argues with this interpretation, however, by raising a number of issues that relate to this study. People in society (or members in a family) begin with unequal power for accomplishing things on their own. Thus, the absence of intervention by outsiders may unwittingly support the inequity of the status quo. Vulnerable people have consciously asked that others—professional and nonprofessional—step in to assist (as deserted women did who came to the Minneapolis AC seeking material relief). Gordon notes, however, that the involvement of professionals has carried no guarantee that the eventual outcome would satisfy the "clients."[18]

This book is possible because contact—of varying quality and quantity—*did* occur between needy individuals and middle-class social workers. Fortunately for historians, agency personnel were encouraged to be diligent in recording what they saw and did, usually summarizing but sometimes quoting what they heard others say. In the analysis that follows, the description of the intimacies of lower-class life appears as originally written into the case records (with only the proper names being altered). But the material is all mediated through the eyes and ears of persons outside of, rather than within, the lower-class households. In the process of keeping records on others, social workers revealed and integrated their own values and activities, making obvious the contradictions, ambiguities, and gaps in their own behavior as well as that of clients. But this is neither a book with social workers on center stage nor primarily a critique about welfare and recipiency. This study of events in Minneapolis integrates the public and private lives of a select group of poor women known to be charity recipients and illustrates how they actively constructed survival within constraints.

Primary Source for This Case Study

By the early twentieth century Minneapolis was part of the dominant metropolitan area of the Upper Northwest. The population swelled as young people from northern Europe and the region's own rural communities came in great numbers to the city looking for a chance to share in American prosperity.[19] While Minneapolis residents saw few of the "new" immigrants from southern and eastern Europe who frequently were victims of social problems in cities elsewhere, local civic leaders were sufficiently alarmed by the visible presence of a poor population that they organized to seek a solution.

Social reformers in late nineteenth-century London first formulated the concept of a Charity Organization Society (COS) as the "modern" and "scientific" corrective to the careless giving and deceptive recipiency that pauperized the poor. The COS philosophy assumed that the poor needed inspiration more than dollars and that those seeking aid could not quite be trusted to accurately report their own situations. The answer was an agency that implemented a personal approach through home visits to needy applicants combined with centralization of community goodwill efforts.[20]

First in Buffalo, in 1877 and then elsewhere in the United States, civic leaders organized to implement the COS mission.[21] Over the next few decades personnel at the COS in big cities were recognized in many circles as the nation's "experts" on poverty. Many agencies quantified the facts of human misery and narrated the particulars of deprivation into annual reports and published studies. Based on experiences at the New York City COS, Lilian Brandt compiled *Five Hundred and Seventy-Four Deserters and Their Families, A Descriptive Study of Their Characteristics and Circumstances* (1905); Edward Devine authored *Misery and Its Causes* (1909); and Joanna Colcord wrote *Broken Families* (1919). Mary Richmond gathered information on poor women from cities all over the country—including Minneapolis—for *Nine Hundred Eighty-Five Widows Known to Certain Charity Organization Societies* (1913).

Organizational meetings to authorize development of the Minneapolis COS first occurred in 1884. In 1907 this agency, called Associated Charities, enumerated the following "Articles of Faith" in its annual report:[22]

> We believe:
> 1. Pauperism can be eliminated.
> 2. Poverty is curable.
> 3. Both pauperism and poverty can be prevented.
> 4. In order to eliminate the one, cure the other, and prevent both, individual sentimentality must make way for enlightened sympathy and cooperative social effort. . . .[23]

In Minneapolis, however, as in many cities, the COS began to alter its strategies and mission.[24] Gradually agencies abandoned their intentions to direct the efforts of other programs and relied increasingly on paid staff rather than on volunteers to seek out resources and opportunities that could move families toward economic self-sufficiency. Thus professional "family casework" began to develop.[25] In Minneapolis this work with families was described with the following pithy phrases:

> We endeavor to know the condition of every dependent person in the city. We send skilled workers wherever needed. We find employment. We supply the poor with influential friends. We give relief with a plan. We improve home ideals. We furnish reports of our treatment of any case.[26]

By 1922 the COS formally acknowledged this involvement with family and home by renaming itself the Family Welfare Association of Minneapolis, and with another merger two decades later it became the present-day Family and Children's Service.[27]

Every time a new family's needs or problems brought a household to agency attention, a case record was opened. This included a first page describing family demographics and disabilities, and a series of entries with the circumstance and conversation of each contact. Extensive casework recording was offered as proof to the contributing public that important and professional efforts were underway. Likewise the record was intended to assure a supervisor that regardless of a family's outcome, appropriate measures had been tried.

Reflecting the pervasiveness of male dominance, the man originally living in a household was identified throughout the record as #1, the woman—#2, the oldest child—#3, and so on. When the agency acquired a typewriter and hired a stenographer, the case records became lengthier and more personal.[28] Initials of the last name replaced numbers for persons; a Mrs. Wilson referred to as "#2" in 1905 usually appeared as "Mrs. W." in 1920 and occasionally as "Mrs. Wilson." Numbers also had been used for community institutions and agencies with the code for this entered in the record. Later, abbreviations were substituted for these, too; for example, City Hospital, which once was known as "#45," became identified as "CH" and later as "GH" for General Hospital. Over time social workers grew to believe more and more in the importance of the social environment and they expanded on details of employment, housing conditions, neighbors, and kin. The resulting case record typically included long narratives that interspersed family history, current dilemmas, and the social worker's actions and judgments. In time, thick case files were stored in cabinets in the agency's office. These files—which were largely descriptive—provide the material used here to discover the dynamics in poor women's lives.[29]

During the thirty years covered in this study, AC/FWA was the city's largest private agency, but it periodically made agreements with the public Poor Department, later the Department of Public Welfare, and with the private Humane Society, later the Children's Protective Society, as to which particular family needs should be dealt with by each. According to some of these arrangements if a man simply lacked work, then public poor relief was the answer; if a family lacked a mother or neglect and abuse was at question, then the Humane Society should step in. AC/FWA took responsibility for fatherless homes and those where problems beyond unemployment existed. Administrative records disclose, however, that this system of delegation was not followed consistently. Referrals were made, but the agency caseload continued to represent many sorts of family situations and various agencies worked concurrently with the same family.[30]

The majority of all cases at AC/FWA *initially* resembled the family units that predominated in the general population: native-born married couples with children. But the fathers in most agency families were not winning bread as the prevailing family ethos instructed, and case statistics frequently were labeled with captions such as "man incapacitated," "man nonsupportive," "man unemployed," and "man deserted." These designations, which focused on the man's status, failed to fully acknowledge that *family status did not remain fixed*. Among the lower class, *female*-headed families—*de facto* or *de jure*—often came into being. Agency workers dealt almost exclusively with women; the process and content of case records was in great part a description of female lives.

If the agency was to "know" families, it had to be able to count them, and for a time agency reports included caseload figures, although measures and language changed from one administrative record to the next. Table 1 shows that between 1900 and 1930, AC/FWA served a total of approximately 80,000 families; yet in any single year only a fraction of the city's lower-class households were reached by charity workers. In 1900, the 915 cases equaled slightly more than 2 percent of Minneapolis households, and while this figure later hovered between 3 and 4 percent—depending on local employment conditions and agency resources—not until the Great Depression were even 5 percent of the city's families served by AC/FWA.[31]

These agency figures are imperfect—not only did the unit of measurement change from one year to the next, but service rendered in one case differed in quantity and quality from another. In the early years the agency had a Visiting Nurse Department, a Legal Aid Bureau, and an Employment Bureau that also published annual service statistics, and the overlap is unclear. In 1915 the staff began separating cases as to those with "major" and "minor" services, but available administrative records fail to explain the difference. The figures in Table 1 combine the

Table 1
Families Known to AC/FWA, 1900–1930

Year	AC Caseload	Year	AC Caseload
	1900 *Minneapolis Families = 42,536 in a Total Population of 202,718*		
1900	915 cases	1905	2,171 cases dealt with
1901	827 cases dealt with	1906	2,060 cases dealt with
1902	973 families dealt with	1907	1,940 unduplicated cases
1903	1,051 applicants dealt with	1908	2,180 unduplicated cases
1904	1,746 families dealt with	1909	2,411 unduplicated cases
	1910 *Minneapolis Families = 63,241 in a Total Population of 301,408*		
1910	2,667 unduplicated cases	1915	2,363 families seen
1911	3,226 unduplicated cases	1916	2,338 unduplicated cases
1912	3,925 unduplicated cases	1917	2,742 families served
1913	2,114 unduplicated cases	1918	2,619 families served
1914	2,381 families seen	1919	2,189 families served
	1920 *Minneapolis Families = 91,843 in a Total Population of 380,582*		
1920	2,504 families served	1925	3,583 families served
1921	3,567 families served	1926	4,179 families served
1922	4,394 families served	1927	4,632 annual caseload
1923	3,814 families served	1928	4,481 annual caseload
1924	3,410 families served	1929	4,572 annual caseload
	1930 *Minneapolis Families = 117,200 in a Total Population of 464,356*		
1930	6,348 families served		

SOURCE: AC, *Annual Reports,* 1901–16, provide figures available between those years; FWA of Minneapolis, *The Family Welfare Association in Action, 1917–1926* (Minneapolis: FWA, 1926), 24, is the only public report for later years. For 1927–30 see Rose Porter, untitled report, Table: Total Annual Caseloads Major and Minor Cases, 1915 to Date, Folder-Complete Copy Minneapolis Survey, 1937, Box 4, Minneapolis Family and Children's Service (FCS) Collection, Social Welfare History Archives, University of Minnesota, Minneapolis. Minneapolis population figures from U.S. Bureau of the Census, *12th Census of the United States, 1900,* Population II, clxii; *13th Census, 1910,* Population II, 1018; *14th Census, 1920,* Population III, 523; *15th Census, 1930,* Population VI, Families, 670. The national census defined *family* as individuals jointly occupying a dwelling or individuals living alone.

two. By 1920 efforts at AC/FWA were exclusively "family work"—health care and legal work had become independent programs; figures for the last decade, therefore, are more consistent until the Great Depression in the 1930s when multiplication of need overwhelmed the agency's ability to keep count of poverty and to adequately respond to it.

For the following reasons this study draws only on AC/FWA cases opened between 1900 and 1930. Agency histories note that the work of the 1880s and 1890s was haphazard and lacking in organization, but more importantly, a fire broke out in their first office in the late nineteenth century, destroying the bulk of case and administrative materials.[32] Thus a consistent collection of documents exists only for the twentieth century, and as a condition of obtaining access to the case records, the donating organization requested that the cases used be at least fifty years old. To stop short of the 1930s also acknowledges that in the Great Depression being "poor" engulfed a much broader group than the laboring class of prior decades. In responding to this great need, new federal government programs permanently altered the role of private local agencies such as AC/FWA.

Among cases opened in the designated thirty years, a sample of three hundred was selected as shown in Table 2. Although in many cases husbands were absent, a woman's marriage and relationships with men were fundamental in defining her access to resources, problems, obligations, and status. To examine these issues, therefore, comparing women of various marital status is important. Thus every fifth record on every fifth microfilm reel of cases was selected for inclusion in the study if the record opened with the woman fitting into one of the following categories: she was (1) in an intact marriage with husband at home; (2) divorced and alone permanently, or temporarily alone owing to desertion or other factors; or (3) widowed.

Fewer of the latter group are represented here, which reflects their decreased number in the general population and in the caseload at AC/FWA and at other charities. The sympathetic public was more apt to help widows than married or deserted women because widows were seen as the blameless victims of fate. These attitudes led to popular campaigns for "widows' pensions" paid for through county and state funds. In Minnesota by 1913, "widows, wives of incurables, and those whose husbands are imprisoned [could], receive assistance from the County."[33]

Motherhood accompanied marriage for most women, then and now. Just as a husband could add to or detract from a woman's problems and responsibilities, the presence and age of children affected the social demands she faced. Therefore the woman in every selected case record was classified by the age of her children (which suggested her own age), as well as by marital status. She was considered the mother (1) of dependent young children, (2) of young children but parent also of adolescents who might share household responsibilities, or as a mother (3) of only adolescent or grown children who were theoretically able to generate income. If a case family did not include a woman whose situation fit within these combined parameters, the record was passed over and the next one reviewed. Thus, this examination of adult women includes only those living within a family context where in some capacity for some period of time they shared resources and needs with men and children.

In addition to choosing cases based on family structure, the particular year of the case opening was considered so as to put family affairs in an historical context of social and economic elements exterior to the household. While every record in the study opened and closed between 1900 and 1930, the total three hundred were subdivided into cases opened during the decades 1900–1910 and 1920–30. With this, women's earliest experiences from 1900 to 1910 establish a "standard" that can be used to weigh the impact of multiple national changes identified with the post-World War I, 1920s decade. Among these changes were increased employment opportunities for women along with a decreased pattern of child labor. An expanded array of consumer goods went into production and were marketed as "essential" for maintaining homes and for making a presentable appearance. At the same time social critics noted the rising divorce rate and evidence of female independence and questioned if the family would even survive as an institution.[34] Social welfare agencies concurrently embraced new theories on human behavior as family casework became the dominant framework for professional activity.[35]

This study asserts that by using cases with different household structures and from different periods in time, a strong statement is possible about the "constants" of poverty that defied individual family differences and time. Real life, however, cannot neatly be placed in the precise boxes historians would desire, and some cases were repeatedly opened and closed. For example, a record begun in 1907 might close in 1909 then reopen briefly in 1914 or 1920. The agency closed 40 percent of the selected three hundred cases after no more than six months. Eighty percent ended within five years, and the remaining cases lasted longer with gaps sometimes years in length.[36] During this time a deserted woman initially designated as living alone with adolescent children could become a widow, and then remarry with a new birth to follow. Thus the quantitative material and qualitative narrative in the next few chapters refer at times to separate groups of women by the original labels designating marriage and motherhood, but often the general noun "women" is used inclusively across time and circumstance.

In the chapters to follow, these three hundred families are described interchangeably as "poor," "working class," and "lower class," reflecting the ease with which workers could slide into poverty and the fact that most laborers' wages were inadequate for more than subsistence living.[37] Persons living together with a woman—children, husband, or

Table 2
Women's Status in 300 Case Records

	150 Cases Opened, 1900–1910	150 Cases Opened, 1920–1930
Women's Status at Case Opening:— Married with husband at home and		
with young children to age 12	25	25
with young and/or only adolescent children to age 18	25	25
with adolescent and/or only grown children	10	10
Subtotal	60	60 = 120
Woman alone owing to divorce, desertion, separation, and miscellaneous cause and		
with young children to age 12	25	25
with young and/or only adolescent children to age 18	25	25
with adolescent and/or only grown children	10	10
Subtotal	60	60 = 120
Woman alone owing to death of husband and		
with young children to age 12	10	10
with young and/or only adolescent children to age 18	10	10
with adolescent and/or only grown children	10	10
Subtotal	30	30 = 60
Total	150	150 = 300

SOURCE: 300 Case Records, FCS Collection.

kin—are designated as constituting a "family" and "household." This was often a fluctuating group in the course of a woman's life cycle as children went temporarily to live with kin or grew up and left home; husbands disappeared or died; and widows remarried. *Agent* and *visitor* were the original terms for paid COS staff who gradually came to be known as "caseworkers" or "social workers." "Ladies" were the upper middle-class females engaged as volunteers in civic and social welfare concerns; they saw themselves, and others perceived them, as being in a different class than the poor women whom they sometimes aided. As used in this study, "women" are distinctly lower-class wives and mothers in an urban setting whose need led them to be known at AC/FWA and whose strenuous efforts went beyond the home into the community.

The families examined here survived because these women "worked." Case documentation shows them playing directive roles, yet because they labored under the oppression of both class and gender, they were unlikely to earn much public appreciation for what they "done and struggled."[38] Perseverance and initiative link them to poor mothers today who try to cope with daily needs and dangers while having little access to the material abundance of this nation.

1

A Profile of Three Poor Women in an Urban Setting

Case One: Mrs. Carlson

The temperature in Minneapolis had risen to 28 degrees on 10 January 1920, as the city experienced a reprieve from its usual winter weather. A female social work agent from the largest charity in the city noted the chill, however, as she found her way through a deteriorated building to the end of a dark hall where an immigrant family had rented an apartment for twelve dollars a month.[1] The Carlsons' front door opened into a space filled with kindling and coal; in the next bare room the only piece of furniture was a table carefully covered with newspapers. The family appeared to be living in a space beyond this. When the agent returned to the charity and dictated a report on her visit, she described this last room as "quite comfortable with a rug on the floor and the furniture was evidently recently bought," a suitable "home." She had gone there, however, because the Carlsons were only partially able to achieve the promise of a good life that had drawn them to America.

On arriving in the United States the Carlson family had repeated the course of many Scandinavian and German immigrants by heading to the Plains. Both husband and wife found jobs cooking for traveling crews of young Norwegian men who hired out as threshers for North Dakota farmers. Their fellow countrymen loaded the train cars carrying grain to Minneapolis, the flour-milling capital of the world. When the crop was too thin, however, a job in the city seemed a better option, and the Carlsons and their three children headed back there to compete with native-born rural residents for places to work and live. From January to November 1920 their efforts at survival were assisted and recorded by personnel at Associated Charities (AC).

A public grade school teacher had first contacted the agency about the family after seven-year-old Annie Carlson stopped attending classes. Her older brothers explained it was because she lacked winter clothing. Teachers were familiar with the combination of practicality and pride that forced poor children to stay home, particularly during winter months. Thus it was school policy to call up and ask that one of the caseworkers at AC investigate the family and make arrangements for them to receive used clothing.[2]

Not only teachers, but visiting nurses, neighborhood grocers, pastors, and doctors in the community had at times followed their own observations of pale, thin children with a similar request that AC "investigate and aid." Procuring clothing, with the exception of finding underwear and shoes that would fit, was not a difficult assignment for social workers. Almost always, however, the agency judged that further help of various sorts was needed, and a worker opened a case record and intervention began.

The Carlsons appeared to be earnest and honest and simply wanted a better place in which to raise their boys to be "good men."[3] When spring came, however, the family was still living in their first dark and damp apartment in spite of the fact that the owner had begun remodeling and other tenants had vacated. Unable to find any place as cheap, the Carlsons stayed on amid exposed walls, a kettle of tar burning in the yard, and piles of lumber strewn about; the cost of rent mattered a great deal as both parents had been intermittently unemployed. Mr. Carlson found work with an implement company and then at a tannery, but a summer strike sent him back to Dakota to work as a cook for farm laborers. This was short-lived, however, as his health broke down and he needed bed rest. Returning to the city, he eventually picked up a few hours as a restaurant cook with his sons accompanying him, an ad hoc arrangement enabling on-site child care and complimentary meals.

Mrs. Carlson, who had been employed prior to and throughout her marriage, was one of millions of immigrant—and native-born women, who found work cleaning and washing clothes for other families. In 1920 this mother scrubbed floors at the Strand Theater for eleven dollars a week, an amount considered "minimum subsistence" in a labor study at the time.[4] In the fall she switched to the B and T Laundry, and as before, she felt anxious about coming to and from work alone on the street at night. Though Mrs. Carlson was not particularly strong, her job called for strenuous lifting. The agent wrote in the case record, "[does] not present a healthful appearance." Arrangements were made for the woman to have a gallstone operation, and during this same time Mrs. Carlson also nursed her own children through a bout with diphtheria, which put the home into quarantine. Health problems, her own employment schedule, and a husband who at times worked hundreds of miles away, meant that she often had to leave the children on their own; this worried her.

One of the solutions that she—rather than the social worker—initiated, was to turn to kin for help.

Traditional patterns of chain migration among immigrants meant newcomers to America often were geographically close to relatives from the "old country." Both Mr. and Mrs. Carlson had siblings who had left Scandinavia for rural Minnesota. Early in the summer Mrs. Carlson contacted her brother inquiring if she could send the boys to live for a time on his farm away from what she called city "mischief." In the country they could do more wholesome work than the bootblack job her eleven-year-old proposed for himself. With her sons cared for temporarily, she imagined that she and her daughter Annie could travel to wherever farm work took her husband.

These seemed logical plans, but for reasons not clear in the family's case record, arrangements did not go as planned. During the period of her husband's summer absence, Mrs. Carlson had the three children with her in Minneapolis. She found a better place to live, which was within walking distance of the Pillsbury Settlement House, and the agent from AC enrolled the boys in the Settlement's summer camp. In November Mrs. Carlson and the children—all dressed up—appeared at a neighborhood celebration at Pillsbury after the boys had seen preparations underway in the afternoon and had gone home to tell their mother. In the judgment of a settlement resident, the Carlsons "seemed to be quite pleased with their reception at Pills. House and made a very favorable impression." The resident herself intended to stay in touch with them and encourage continued participation. With this positive connection to the city, AC closed the family's case record after eleven months. Personnel at various private social welfare agencies had found Mrs. Carlson "cooperative"—and never "too" dependent on others. To the contrary, this particular record shows minor agency initiative with staff primarily involved in monitoring what the family was doing for itself. The woman was quoted as saying, "She planned to keep on working [in spite of her husband having found employment again] because she really liked to work and make money herself and was feeling very well and happy."[5]

Mr. and Mrs. Carlson were a married couple—a nuclear family—and registered in agency records according to this marital status. But it was Mrs. Carlson who became known to the agency. Her ability to keep house in a dire setting and to raise well-mannered children—inculcated with the work ethic—qualified her as a "good" woman. Her hopes for family life and the problems she struggled with gave direction to the agent's efforts on her behalf. In retrospect, what stands out in the case

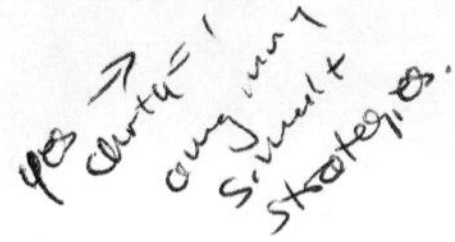

record are Mrs. Carlson's own positive efforts to take responsibility for moving her family ahead.

Case Two: Mrs. Willis

Mrs. Willis was a native-born Midwesterner. In 1907 when the Carlsons were marrying, this woman was thirty, the mother of five, already a widow, and now about to leave her second husband, a known drunkard. The corner grocer called AC to say that she soon would be on her own and would need help feeding the children. An agency worker began compiling a record that lasted for eight years with periodic entries of activity with and among the Willis family.

When the case initially opened, a worker described Mrs. Willis in a variety of positive ways: "above average" in intelligence and "pleasant with strangers." The house appeared "usually clean" and "fairly well kept in order." But the worker also sensed that the woman was "probably more quick tempered when very decided in ideas," and her "physical capac. [capacity] and endurance" were "uncertain."

Mrs. Willis not only left her second husband, but she divorced him. Initially she voiced confidence about her ability to manage; the case record quoted her saying that she "[could] get along beautifully if man will pay alimony." The judge set this at thirty-five dollars a month, but her ex-husband, who had experience as both a railroad conductor and brakeman, could not seem to stay employed. When he worked, his salary was garnisheed for debts or was spent at the local tavern, a pattern of behavior that led neighbors to say nothing good about him. Mrs. Willis had to develop her own support.

Earnings came by means of a job cleaning trolley cars with other women in an unheated barn for one dollar a day, but after developing pneumonia Mrs. Willis quit. Between 1907 and 1915 her own poor health and the cost of streetcar tickets to shuttle the children about for care, put pressure on her ability to continue gainful employment. Boarders, hand laundry, charity pensions, benevolent individuals, periodic alimony, child labor, male friends, and at least once—groceries from the Ladies Auxiliary of the Switchmen's Wives—all figured as a means to keep food and fuel in the house. At various points AC supported, and sometimes criticized, her efforts.

Early in the case, the staff at the agency wrote to her kin and those of her husband in Iowa and rural Minnesota. The form letter explained that she and the children suffered "destitute circumstances caused by the failure of Mr. Willis to pay anything toward support of his family." The agency suggested that relatives send a small amount of money to her on a monthly basis. Her brother and his sister both wrote back saying that their own situations were financially insecure; the sister did send clothing, however, and later the older son went to board and work with his aunt.

In a surprising turn of affairs, Mr. Willis inherited another relative's property in rural Minnesota. Because Mrs. Willis and her lawyer had informed the court of the ex-husband's nonpayment of alimony, the inherited house was turned over to her, but this asset came with two years' back taxes and could not be sold in its current condition. The sheriff in the county where the house was located donated free paint; an upper-class lady on the agency's Relief and Service Committee paid the taxes, and thus the building was able to be sold for fifty-five dollars. Mrs. Willis reported that she used over half of this amount to pay her divorce lawyer. The record neglected to indicate if her debt for legal action reflected the fact that a lawyer had taken advantage of her, or that she herself had acted aggressively to find the "best" lawyer, assuming some way could be found later to cover the cost.

Wages from children's labor were a possible but temporary resource. As Mrs. Willis faced the reality of her own limited physical strength and temporary hospitalization, her family's economic survival depended more and more on the children. Her social worker assumed—as many charity workers did—that employment for children was preferable at times to employment for a mother. Thus the agent diligently looked for places where the adolescents might find jobs. When the case opened, a thirteen-year-old girl and a ten-year-old boy were the oldest children whose eventual employment—and unemployment—appeared irregularly throughout the record.

At sixteen Cecilia, the daughter, was initiated into her career in wage work dipping bonbons at the Paris Chocolate Company from 9:00 A.M. to 6:00 P.M. From the agency's point of view, such work was not suitable female labor. They made appointments for her teeth to be fixed at the University of Minnesota's Dental Department and encouraged her to consider a class at the YWCA in cooking or waitressing as domestic skills might bring her a "good position in [a] family." She objected and spoke of disliking positions of "servitude" where you ate in the kitchen. A millinery class was to be the compromise, but Cecilia never went; she lost a factory job after arguments with the forelady and drifted into domestic work. During a period when Mrs. Willis was very ill, Cecilia's five dollars a week as a nursemaid supported the entire family. This was heroic, but not easy. She and her mother began quarreling about work away from home and responsibility within the house. As a result Cecilia moved out, but the estrangement was temporary. When the young woman married a carpenter, she used her new financial security to assist her mother and the previous discord vanished. Mrs. Willis's conflict with the oldest son, however, led to blows and was not so easily ameliorated. The record reported that he "strikes family" and when he left, moving out West, his mother felt fortunate.

Descriptions of the character and experiences of the other Willis children is fragmented in the record. AC arranged for free railroad transportation to carry another unruly son to the country to work for rural relatives, and agents hunted city jobs for his siblings. A daughter said she hoped to become a nurse; a son aspired to mechanics or printing and even found a press to make cards at home, but menial jobs—and meager wages—came and went. When not at work, the boys began staying out too late while their sisters flirted outside the movie theater. An adolescent daughter refused to go to school because her clothes were inadequate, and Mrs. Willis, who had sewn the girl underclothes from flour sacks, called in a truant officer from juvenile court. The agency could and did find garments for the daughter, but repeatedly encouraged Mrs. Willis to hold her own in disciplining the young people's willfulness.

Although divorced, Mr. Willis seemed not to be far away during the early years of the case and contributed to confusion in the household headed by his ex-wife. She had custody of the children, but the sons on occasion would leave her after arguments and go stay with their father; he asked Cecilia to live with him but she refused. The case record is dotted with the man's failure to pay alimony and with Mrs. Willis pressing nonsupport charges against him. Yet she appeared ambivalent about separation; shortly after the divorce the agent learned that the ex-husband had come by asking to borrow ten dollars, and as poor as she was, Mrs. Willis found it and gave it to him. Three years later some of his belongings were noticed at her house. Whether she was washing his clothes or if he was staying there temporarily was not clear; however, Mrs. Willis said that she knew not to count on him. But she did not rule out relations with other men in arrangements that were expected to be economically supportive.

Opening one's home—or even a small apartment—to include a boarder had long been a common strategy among women needing to subsidize family income. Some of these boarders offered resources beyond the rent such as child care in an emergency and someone to talk to. Mrs. Willis's first boarder did all of this. But the agency began to suspect there was more to their relationship as illustrated by a social worker writing that there was "something wrong about this business." Mrs. Willis then announced that she and the boarder had a scheme underway. His father owned a restaurant in another part of the state; she could rent out her house in Minneapolis and go there to manage the café. The record made no mention of what was to become of the children, but Mrs. Willis believed she had "a good plan whereby she could be independent and take care of herself." The skeptical agent recommended that she "get a contract" before going. Mrs. Willis *did* disappear for a time, and rumors of marriage circulated; then she reappeared in the neighborhood, and the case continued.

Mrs. Willis was fortunate to have a guardian angel at AC in the person of Mrs. E. L. Carpenter, the wife of a wealthy man tied into the city's lumber and banking interests. For decades Mrs. Carpenter chaired the Friendly Visiting Committee, renamed the Relief and Service Committee, putting in hours as if in full-time employment. Most of her committee peers confined their participation to raising and supervising disbursement of relief funds and attending bimonthly meetings where speakers lectured on contemporary social issues. Mrs. Carpenter and a few others, however, provided a model of greater intervention by visiting certain families and giving financial support to others. Her personal funds had paid the taxes on the property Mrs. Willis inherited, and financed Cecilia's dental care. When the Willis house needed new shingles and a porch, she agreed to "pay what needs to be done." She, like the agent, believed Mrs. Willis and her children would be better off if the mother were at home more and employed less. Therefore, on at least two occasions Mrs. Carpenter financed a pension for her. At one point this amounted to $4 a week for a number of months; later it was $18 a month for an undetermined period. Over time she provided such assets for other women as well, but the records never made clear why one needy case and not another drew her attention.[6]

Mrs. Willis, as many others, had a story whose constant struggle was laced with repeated efforts to achieve self-sufficiency, but that did not make the woman saintly. Nor did the record generated about her family between 1907 and 1915 mean that the agency understood who she was. A case worker accused her—with no further explanation—of being "too fun-loving," and a grocer said Mrs. Willis spent so much time visiting people in the neighborhood that they had become tired of her. By the end of the case the reports were coming in that she "does not stay in nights. Leaves children alone, goes to places of amusement with men," and even "spent money on herself." When she left Minneapolis for the last recorded time, she was still a woman responsible for minor children, still engaging in relationships with men, and willing to take risks in pursuit of her well-being. Most of these activities she chose not to explain to agency staff.

When an agent discovered a For Sale sign in front of the Willis's empty house, the case was closed. According to neighbors she had left with the two youngest children for Deer River, Minnesota. A man had been involved; rumor said he was a lover from the past but that he already was married. Neighbors thought they also knew about the other children; Cecilia was living in south Minneapolis and her trouble-making brother seemed to have become a "tramp." The previously truant daughter was an unmarried mother who had found her way—or been placed by others—at the House of Good Shepherd. No follow-up was attempted to check out these stories.[7]

Case Three: Mrs. Pernet

Rather than asking for agency help, Mrs. Pernet turned to those who lived nearby when her husband, not yet fifty, lay dying of heart trouble at General Hospital. She had written a letter explaining her dilemma and carried it door-to-door. Those who showed concern were asked to list their names and the amount they were willing to donate, pledges to a personal charity to be collected as needed. One woman signed, offered to hire Mrs. Pernet to do the family laundry, and then called the agency to report what the woman was doing.

If charitable giving was to lessen poverty in Minneapolis, the board and staff at AC/FWA believed it had to be overseen by professionals who combined relief with thoughtful family work. Individually initiated "letters of begging"—such as the one by Mrs. Pernet were unacceptable to social workers who immediately went to her home to confront the woman with her action. At first Mrs. Pernet denied writing and circulating the letter; then she "bursts into tears and said everybody was against her because she was poor." Mrs. Pernet's initiative collided with expectations of propriety accepted by agency personnel. Such clashes characterized the irregular contact between these two parties from early 1910 to 1922.

A few months prior to the petition for charity, one of Mrs. Pernet's sisters had come to the office for her explaining that the husband was very ill and that the three young children needed care. A visiting nurse was stopping regularly at the home, and extended family had helped all they could, but matters now had reached a desperate state for both the Pernets and their kin. Wouldn't AC/FWA give help? The customary first home visit took place to open the new case and Mrs. Pernet immediately denied her relatives' involvement saying the family burden was on her shoulders alone. This led an agent to go out to ask neighbors further questions about the family.

The landlord dismissed the woman as a careless mother, a liar, and a thief; the husband was no good either—a dishonest "boozer"—and he wanted the family to vacate his property. Others were contacted who offered their own first- and secondhand experiences employing the same set of adjectives: "dishonest," and "given to drinking"; Mrs. Pernet furthermore showed "no motherly affection." Agency contact with the Pernets reinforced what others had charged. Mr. Pernet, a laborer and hack driver, was quarrelsome and had refused to go to the hospital at the same time he protested that he had lost "interest in his home" because his wife failed to prepare meals and neglected the children. When AC/FWA presented him the ultimatum of no material relief unless he consented to hospitalization for his heart ailment, he agreed. Meanwhile, further word came back to the agency supporting the complaints he made of his wife and home life. A visitor from a ladies' society reported hearing that Mrs. Pernet was trying to starve her baby. While the visitor herself had seen "some evidence to this effect" she "could not say whether it was intentionally done or thru ignorance." A few days later, however, the Humane Society called AC/FWA saying that Mrs. Pernet had given the infant away, a fact they had discovered through Mrs. Pernet herself who mistook their worker at the door for someone interested in getting a child. Many neighbors knew that when Mrs. Pernet was young—and perhaps unmarried—she had given her first child to relatives for adoption. Now she had tried a similar solution, but this baby was ill. In getting the infant into their custody, the Humane Society arranged for a medical examination that revealed the child had syphilis. Such putative evidence of parental immorality was added to the negatives already known in the case. Mr. Pernet was assumed to be at fault. Five days later, however, a minister called the agency to announce that the husband had died.

On the following Monday a caseworker set out looking for Mrs. Pernet to discuss her intentions now that she was on her own with two sons still in her care. It was the $40 funeral bill that concerned the new widow; she had paid $10 but owed on the rest and wondered if the Poor Department might pay the undertaker. The agent pushed the new widow to make some plans for the future and explain how she would feed her two sons if she insisted on keeping them. While not forgetting Mrs. Pernet's previous faults as a wife and mother, the worker now felt that discussing income was the imperative, and the two women clashed as to what was practical.

> Thinks she can get washing sent to the house. Agt. [Agent] argued with her that her washing, not being satisfactory, she would not be able to get much of it and it would be better for her to try and get a job at dish

washing. Also she should not try and keep a $15 flat and let rooms to men. This did not seem to please her particularly.

Male boarders had moved in prior to the husband's death; with a man already in the house such arrangements seemed proper. Now, however, the agent questioned their presence. Mrs. Pernet countered that the men were "all right" because they did not drink, but neighbors and a minister had stories to the contrary. Debate over the male boarders stretched through the summer. The men stayed on, but the laundry plans failed as Mrs. Pernet found doing washing for others "pretty hard." As an alternative she asked the staff at the agency's employment bureau to help her find a position as a janitress. They referred her to an office building in downtown Minneapolis.

The case record shows Mrs. Pernet in a series of short-term, low-wage jobs: day work, cleaning offices, dish washing (where work from 8:00 A.M. to 2:00 P.M. five days a week earned four dollars, meals included). At the Lutheran Hospital Mrs. Pernet's boss described her as a "good industrious woman," but other employers criticized her as not to be trusted. In one home where she did day work, the lady discovered doilies missing, accused her of theft, and called AC/FWA. Another employer found her bringing her own belongings to wash along with the assigned laundry. The social worker announced that with the reputation she was building, no more referrals for employment would be given her.

When the jobs ended that she herself had procured, Mrs. Pernet sought public relief from the city's Poor Department and from the county's Mothers'/Widows' Pension program. The Gospel Mission, the Swedish Tabernacle, the North East Relief Society, the Church of the Redeemer, the American Legion, Red Cross, and Veterans of Foreign Wars all had on file her name and need for material relief. Most of these places assessed her in negative terms—a bad mother and a beggar; yet her need was obvious, too, and at times resulted in the granting of assistance.

Other reports came in as well, that Mrs. Pernet had male visitors, that she was living with a man, and that she drank. In the summer of 1915 a caseworker stopped by unannounced to witness one of the sons carrying in a pail of what looked like beer. Mrs. Pernet claimed it was milk; the agent was skeptical as milk already was sitting on the counter and no creamery operated nearby. The worker called again in the evening and found Mrs. Pernet "neatly dressed in light col. [colored] cotton dress, beads and several articles of adornment. Her breath was strong with liquor."

The sons, Harold and Clifford, developed reputations as cloudy as their mother's. When they were only seven and eight years old, respectively, an agent had tried unsuccessfully to interest them in programs at Pillsbury House; as they became adolescents, caseworkers hunted for employment for them. One boy spoke of becoming a mechanic through schooling at the Dunwoody Institute, but menial jobs at the Minneapolis Park Board and at the Cannon Ball Alarm Company replaced such aspirations. For a time the boys gave Mrs. Pernet part of their wages, but she could not rely on them. They, too, were judged lazy and dishonest on the job, preferring to hang around on street corners and going to movies than working. Petty crime sent one to the Training School at Red Wing, Minnesota, and then he disappeared from the record for a time. When Mrs. Pernet's health deteriorated in 1920 and she contacted the agency after months of silence, the worker assumed the missing son was the appropriate resource and began to hunt for him. The mother disagreed with this.

> Mrs. Pernet showed visitor empty cupboard. Said she had only this one boy [who was living with her] and absolutely refused to admit that she had any other child when questioned. She had been ill lately and had been unable to do day work for nearly a month. Noticed a nice victrola and some records, and suggested that she try to borrow money on her furn. [furniture]. Gave her name of Equity Loan Co.

Mrs. Pernet kept the victrola in her possession, and the absent son came home, but the outcome was not what the agency imagined.

> BH [agent] visited. Found Harold at home playing the phonograph merrily to himself. . . . He said his mother was out working at present. Said he himself had been looking for a job all week. Advised him to get up early each morning and get out and follow up on the ads as it was undesirable for him to stay at home and play the phono while his mother went to work. Told him AC would be glad to help if necessary but hoped it would not be necessary with 2 strong boys in the family.

Harold, who once had expressed interest in mechanics, liked to draw and spent money on supplies, but the agent doubted he would turn this interest into a wage-producing job. At a case conference of personnel from AC/FWA, Big Brothers, Pillsbury House, and the Children's Protective Society, the staffs jointly devised a plan for rehabilitating the young Pernet men now 18 and 19 years old. The key was to find an employer who would agree to function also as a Big Brother and to teach good work habits along with social responsibility. The arrangement was made but lasted only a short time; the newly acquired Big Brother said that he gave up.

AC/FWA tried no more schemes; the closing entry in the record, however, did not appear until a year and a half later in 1923. A young man, either Harold or Clifford, came in to ask assistance in transporting Mrs. Pernet to Colorado. She had been admitted at Hopewell, the metropolitan TB sanitarium, and her son thought a change of climate would be desirable. When an agent called the attending physician at Hopewell, however, any plans for travel were vetoed by the advice that "change would be unwise." With this, the record ended.

For years members of the Pernet family seemed incorrigible to the agencies that knew them. Too many incidents suggested dishonesty, drinking, and child neglect, which were taken as proof of an immoral behavior that verged on the criminal. But overall, the Pernets' material insecurities and needs were not unlike those of the other families judged to be "cooperative" charity cases. Limited as a lower-class woman in a particular urban setting, Mrs. Pernet had to be the means to her own survival; she had her own vision of what was to be done, made her own decisions in as many ways as she could, and paid the consequences for what took place.[8] Periodically she brushed up against the network of charities, services, and institutions, which reached across Minneapolis and that were linked with those in other parts of the country.

The Charity, Services and Relief these Women Encountered

Gossip that circulated on the grapevine in poor neighborhoods included information about women's and men's experiences with services and benevolences in Minneapolis. While people usually *needed* the material assistance that others might extend, they often were leery of accepting help from strangers, particularly from programs run by public authorities. Hopewell TB Sanitarium, which Minneapolis civic leaders celebrated as a progressive achievement, was unpopular among the poor who entered as with Mrs. Pernet (Case Three). Similarly, admission to City/General Hospital was threatening to poor patients who feared doctors' decisions—a sentiment expressed by Mrs. Pernet's husband before he went there. The numerous private benevolent societies offering short-term aid were often a safer place to seek assistance.

Many private associations in the city had names that showed religious or ethnic affiliation, or suggested that they were run by people sympathetic to the plight of their less fortunate sisters. During a crisis Mrs. Pernet (Case Three) had asked help from the Gospel Mission, and Mrs. Willis (Case Two) had gratefully received a bag of groceries from the Ladies Auxiliary of the Switchmen's Wives. One of the Willis daughters—pregnant and unmarried—received temporary shelter in the House of Good Shepherd modeled after similar homes for wayward girls being opened elsewhere. For boys in the city, the Big Brothers offered role models of wholesome manhood—although the organization had given up on the possibility of reform with Clifford and Harold Pernet (Case Three). As with the Carlsons (Case One), parents and children alike were encouraged to join the diverse social, educational, health, and employment activities of neighborhood settlements such as Pillsbury House. Yet within the entire city, no one agency came to have as broad-based—and as intrusive—involvement with numbers of poor families as did the Associated Charities/Family Welfare Association.

When a caseworker first knocked on the Carlson's door (Case One), the family was confused as to who had sent the agent and why she had come. Although AC/FWA was initially *unknown* to the Carlsons, this organization had claimed a prominent position in Minneapolis social welfare since its origin when representatives from churches and women's benevolences met at the behest of George Brackett, a local businessman. He kept informed of social welfare experiments taking place elsewhere in the country and was pleased to make Minneapolis the first city west of Indianapolis to organize a Charity Organization Society in 1884. The first few years were unsteady, however, as participating organizations quarreled over autonomy and decision making. Financial and volunteer commitment proved to be insufficient until the agency undertook health reforms early in the twentieth century.[9] This new work attracted the well-meaning and donating public who could more easily perceive connections between illness and miserable living conditions than the ties between "organizing" family investigation and reducing the visibly poor population on urban streets.

Middle-class male citizens and community physicians joined board members in an Anti-Tuberculosis Committee, which educated the public about the prevention of the "white plague"; their successful political lobbying led to the construction of the Hopewell Sanatorium. Simultaneously, ladies in Minneapolis joined female board members in a committee to finance and supervise Visiting Nurses to carry simple health and sanitary measures into indigent households, including the Pernet home (Case Three). Law students, under supervision from the University of Minnesota Law School, began putting in shifts at AC to assist men and women with low incomes on the legalities of their wage or property disputes. And the agency's employment bureau kept busy matching the unemployed to menial positions available at businesses and private residences around the city.[10]

The Charity Organization societies that had sprung up in many other cities also engaged in campaigns to promote better sanitation and ventilated housing. Legal aid services, employment bureaus, and nursing programs frequently accompanied these agencies' involvement with individual families. To discuss and debate what worked best to remedy urban poverty, administrators and staff persons from COS nationwide met annually at conferences and used a publication entitled *Charities*, as their forum for exchanging information.[11] Mary Richmond, who had worked at the COS located in Baltimore, then one in Philadelphia, and then in New York City, guided this communication effort. In 1909, she was hired by the new Russell Sage Foundation in New York City to head a Charity Society Organization Department within their office. From this position Richmond worked first to standardize the operation of charity societies and then to encourage the evolution from charity into family casework as the dominant field in American social work. Partially in response to her urging, the director of the Minneapolis COS joined with other agency executives to initiate the National Association of Societies for Organizing Charity in 1911, known later as the American Association for Organizing Family Social Work.[12] This association, the fieldwork and writing sponsored by the foundation, and Richmond herself, linked relief and casework efforts across the country. While the population and economics of Minneapolis would never equal the dimensions of urban activity on the East Coast and in the industrial cities along the Great Lakes, the social welfare activities undertaken with families at this AC/FWA were mainstream at least and helped set casework standards at best.

The Minneapolis agency was well-known in social work circles. In 1931 when the National Conference of Social Work convened in Minneapolis, two hundred of the professionals in attendance scheduled a special reunion for themselves as all had been staff at the Minneapolis AC/FWA before fanning out to take on responsibilities in a variety of private and public social work agencies across the nation.[13] Years earlier, celebration of the agency's twenty-fifth anniversary in 1909 had been noted in the *Survey*, the national welfare and reform magazine that had replaced *Charities* with an extended circulation among socially conscious people in many professions. The administrative records at AC/FWA are dotted with consultative correspondence not only with Richmond and Francis McLean, who directed the Association for Organizing Family Social Work, but from persons like Edward Devine, director of the New York City COS, and Jane Addams from the settlement movement.[14] After Mary Richmond's death in 1928, Joanna Colcord, who had been directing the Minneapolis AC/FWA since 1925, was asked by the Russell Sage Foundation to assume leadership in its national work to further develop professional family casework.

Colcord and Frank Bruno, her predecessor at AC/FWA, 1914–25, had guided that agency's shift from organizing charity efforts citywide to focusing on family casework. Both were prolific writers whose articles appeared in diverse magazines, particularly in *The Family,* a journal created in 1920 to aid casework practitioners.[15] Bruno also initiated the social work training program at the University of Minnesota and authored one of the first histories of the profession, *Trends in Social Work* (1957); here he acknowledged shortcomings in the early efforts to shape practice.[16]

Casework, from the perspective of the staff at AC/FWA, began when someone claimed need or when others identified a family's problem—as when the teacher called AC/FWA about Annie Carlson (Case One). The assigned worker was to discover why a household had "failed to keep abreast of the current of life" and what might lead it "back to a position of independence and equality" in the community.[17] Most importantly, family work required a rational "plan" whose long-term result was to be economic self-sufficiency. In determining this, staff were to forego the unscientific approach of the nineteenth century with hasty judgmentalism and instead continue their home visits and intervention in family life in spite of disagreement or discouragement with family behavior. As a process, much of this "family work" occurred as discussion between middle-class female social workers and poor wives and mothers standing on back steps and at kitchen doors.

From the perspective of the recipients, the casework they received was an eclectic combination of advocacy and advice. In fits and starts family members received stiff lectures about proper household roles of provider, parent, and homemaker; inquiries about the past; and practical assistance. With little or no attention to the concept of confidentiality, agents spread word of a family's circumstance by contacting other individuals or organizations for verification of a household's character and to procure a layette, money for rent, a used bed, or some other item to augment resources in the needy home. When AC/FWA called a "case conference" to discuss the unruly Pernet boys (Case Three), the staff from the Humane Society/Children's Protective Society (HS/CPS) attended along with representatives from Pillsbury House and Big Brothers. A family might become a "case" at more than one agency or fall under a single agency's purview—through no choice of its own.

In seeking to supplement her household budget, a mother in Minneapolis could find herself in contact with the staff from AC/FWA although she had no intention of going there. One way this occurred was when a woman requested the Mothers'/Widows' Pension initiated by state legislation in 1913. The local juvenile court served as the administrative body; in turn, this court arranged with AC/FWA staff that they should investigate the home life of all pension applicants. Likewise, public school authorities called on AC/FWA when someone applied to them for a work permit that allowed a child to leave school. As follow-up, a caseworker would visit the home to determine if the family budget really *demanded* the addition of a youngster's wage.[18]

A household's need for casework attention as opposed to its need for cash relief was a persistent discussion among middle-class reformers and charity workers. At AC/FWA, donors and staff alike were assured that the "business" at hand was not to give dollars to the poor, but "skilled service." A ten-year summary report in 1927 explained that "relief is like a crutch—something very much needed at the time to prop up an injured member, but to be removed at the earliest possible moment lest it result in permanent impairment." "This thought has always persisted as one of the cornerstones of the family welfare movement." During this same time United Charities of St. Paul was repeating the admonition that the "really efficacious" agency made the "pittance of money or food" secondary to "the alms of good advice."[19] The COS in Boston, taken by many as the model of good charity work in the late nineteenth century, never had a general relief fund; agents solicited money for individual families as need be. While absence of a relief budget was common among many eastern agencies, at the New York City COS—as in most Midwestern cities—needy applicants might be helped from either an emergency or permanent fund. However *all* agencies emphasized that the *quality of casework—not the amount of relief*—ultimately rescued a household.[20]

In the process of casework at AC/FWA in Minneapolis, the agent could draw on an emergency fund for the purchase of little more than potatoes or bread to feed a family overnight. After an investigation was underway and the family circumstance better known, money from a special fund in the general budget might be given as direct cash—but more often went out in the form of a grocery or fuel order, payment for rent, hospital bills, or transportation. A small loan fund enabled people to make important investments—tools for a man to work or payment on property taxes, for example. After 1910, the Friendly Visiting/Relief and Service Committee of volunteers raised their own money so as to supply "pensions" for a limited number of sympathetic female-headed families—as they did for Mrs. Willis (Case Two).

Cash and material relief for the poor were not only available from AC/FWA and from certain smaller private benevolences, but also were distributed by the municipal Poor Department/Department of Public Welfare. This public agency made limited cash grants and could pay for transportation, groceries, fuel, or burial expenses—the latter being something Mrs. Pernet (Case Three) requested. Private organizations like AC/FWA assumed that their own relief funds, which were accompanied by a monitoring process and originated as voluntary donations, were automatically superior to public money gathered through taxes and dispersed by "untrained" public employees.[21]

Early budgets from the Minneapolis Poor Department are scant, but in 1907, the largest expense was $5,449 paid out for 2,166 grocery orders—at an average of a little more than $2.50 an order. That same year, 1,940 applicants for aid at AC/FWA received a total of $5,562 in relief. This is approximately $2.85 per case, hardly more than the assistance at the Poor Department, and little to boast about when compared to the expenses families encountered. In 1910 the Minnesota State Bureau of Labor reported that a family needed at least $2.50 *a day* to be at a "proper standard of life."[22]

Financial records for AC/FWA are unavailable for the entire 1900–1930 period, and the labeling of budget items changed, but existing materials suggest a notable increase in the total amount of relief given annually. From a little over $200 in 1901, the figure ballooned to $9,324 in 1910, and to $54,466 in 1920. By 1926, the last year with obtainable budget reports, relief totaled $83,072.[23] However, when changes in the number of recipient families and the cost of their daily needs are taken into account, the result again suggests inadequacy.

If the 4,179 families served in 1926 received equal portions of the budgeted relief funds, each got approximately $19.85; if only the 1,569 cases defined as "major" received relief, the average grant per family grew to about $52.30. The agency explained that a rise in the cost of living in Minneapolis forced the agency to allocate more relief; rooms that a family could have rented for $11 a month in 1917, cost $20 in 1926. Thus in the late 1920s, financial assistance from AC/FWA might have helped a household with a few months of rent but would still fall short of providing "an income." Realizing this, some social workers facilitated families' applications for additional relief from the Poor Department or from Widows'/Mothers' Pensions—neither of which provided much sustenance. In 1921, almost ten years after the pension program was enacted in Minnesota, a woman with one child received only $15 a month; a second child brought another $10.[24]

Whether from public or private social welfare programs, only a pittance in financial help was available to poor households and poverty itself was no guarantee of eligibility. Administrative documents from AC/FWA outlined standard situations that warranted relief, but case records were rife with exceptions that suggested that social workers made case by case decisions. Young women heading families with small children were most likely to receive extensive casework intervention, but this did not automatically mean access to financial relief. Half of the three hundred families in this study received at least one grocery order and a ton or half a ton of coal; some records showed more, but without mention of these items' dollar value or the total over time.

Unpredictability in the economics of social work largess reflected changes in agency resources along with variation and inconsistency in the approach and attitude of individual workers.[25] The fact, however, that most poor women so welcomed the material relief in spite of its inadequacy, testifies to the destitution families were experiencing. However, the preceding narratives from the cases of Mrs. Carlson, Mrs. Willis, and Mrs. Pernet show more clearly that agencies and formal relief were limited elements in women's struggle to make do.

The Ways These Women—And Many More—Struggled to Survive

An empty cupboard and coal bin were hallmarks of the urban poverty that Mrs. Carlson, Mrs. Willis, and Mrs. Pernet faced periodically. Millions of other women in the country found themselves in similar circumstances. For some households this was the usual state of existence; for others it followed a series of economic hardships that slowly drained away material possessions and hope. Still others had been confident of "opportunities" and then in a crisis suddenly saw their security dissolve. Certain poor families—like those of the three women described previously—shared another status of being "cases" and "recipients" at a private agency intent on "planting the seed of self respect" in them.[26]

All kinds of poor people became known at AC/FWA. If the staff there had measured women on a character scale using categories such as good or bad, honest or dishonest, cooperative or uncooperative, each would have scored somewhat differently. These assessments would also have been altered over time as client and agency got to know one another better, and as families confronted more problems and made choices independent of social workers' judgments. The following chapters illustrate that it was not personality as much as social and economic circumstance that were repeated in the lives of poor women.

Poverty meant coping with scarcity of the most basic material elements—not enough milk or bread for children, no coat for warmth, no underwear for respectability. Notes went to AC/FWA in the winter asking for half a ton of coal, and in the summer the request was for ice to prevent spoilage. For themselves men needed tools and transportation to work; women asked for false teeth and furniture. A social worker would note with concern that a family of five was sitting on only three chairs and sleeping in one bed. The serious question as to whether the cupboard held enough to "get by" was at times a problem to be negotiated daily.

Volatility was a second dynamic in homes; circumstances changed and demanded that women respond. They could and did scrimp on food; postponing rent payment was more difficult. Geographic mobility—indicated in the records by a series of crossed out addresses—reflected evictions for unpaid rent and the recurring search for cheaper housing and the better accommodation of changing household size.[27] A family would drag a cartload of belongings from an apartment on one block to another a few streets away. In turn, social workers hunted for missing case families by trying to follow directions given by neighbors. Owning a home, proof of better days that some families had known, allowed a family geographic stability. However, property often functioned not as an investment, but as a drain on resources. Repairing a roof—as Mrs. Willis (Case Two) had to do—and paying annual taxes could undermine tight budgets.

Flimsy housing and limited nutrition exacerbated poor health. In the early years of this century tuberculosis led as cause of death in the United States. Adults and children alike were victims with little prognosis of full recovery.[28] Social work agents thus registered particular alarm on discovering that a woman lived next to stagnant water breeding flies or had an unsanitary outhouse too close to the house. As a result, the City Health Department might mandate that she move her family out and it took no responsibility in seeing that substitute housing existed. Other diseases such as scarlet fever, measles, and diphtheria swept through homes with children and turned mothers into nurses who sometimes worked behind a closed door posted with a Quarantine sign. The records also show that mothers put children's health care before their own, and with little knowledge of or access to effective contraception, most appeared resigned to repeated births. Babies arrived indifferent to family income or maternal inclination but few women repeated the abandonment Mrs. Pernet had tried in Case Three. Some handled the mathematics of expanding family size by sending children to board with other relatives, particularly with kin living in the region's rural areas.

Regardless of the size of the existing family, shortage of furniture, or tightness of space, many women made physical and social household adjustments to include a stranger whose rent added to family income. But boarders could prove temporary owing to their own economic insecurity.[29] Irregular employment—the frequency of unemployment—

functioned as a most destructive and uncontrollable element creating and maintaining a poor class.

Fluctuation of the early twentieth-century business cycle had repercussions for every region of the country. In Minneapolis, economic success also was tied to the unpredictability of annual Midwestern agricultural production. Nonetheless, a stream of young people—such as the Carlsons in Case One—flowed steadily into the city.[30] The greatest percent of adults who became "cases" at AC/FWA fit occupationally within categories of "laborers" and "domestic workers" who often left home in the morning uncertain if the day would bring work and wage. The fact that a man was working steadily, however, did not guarantee that his wages could or did pay the rent. Publicly and privately, wives and mothers accused men of "nonsupport," and in many cases such charges were prelude to a man's desertion. Matrimony was transient and many women understood what it meant to become the head of a household.

Responsibility for the "household economy" meant a range of activities by Mrs. Carlson, Mrs. Willis, and Mrs. Pernet that showed the inadequacy of the prevailing definition of family life with women only in the kitchen and at the cradle. Poverty stretched women's roles back and forth across the imaginary line separating men's public world of business and employment from the private home where females labored out of duty and affection. In these case records women worked for wages, feeling little choice but to lay aside hesitations about searching and competing for jobs. And while individual employers may have felt special sympathy for the working mother with children at home and perhaps in poor health, in the scheme of the Minneapolis economy as elsewhere, each mother was simply one more unit of exchangeable unskilled labor: laundress, charwoman, waitress, industrial worker to be hired at the lowest wage. Lacking sufficient value in the job market, many mothers took on the additional work of negotiating for help in the multifaceted welfare network about them.

Neighbors made up one element of that structure. Within the apartment building or blocks identified as a "neighborhood," exchange of assistance and material assets served as insurance against everyday uncertainties. The woman who had enough of a certain item one week might need to borrow it the next; therefore, pragmatism—as much as generosity—encouraged patterns of aid among friends and neighbors.[31] This did not happen automatically, however, but usually occurred because women talked with one another across fences and at the corner grocery.

Women likewise maintained the oldest system of emergency relief available, asking help from or giving it to extended kin. In these records the luckiest women, like Mrs. Carlson (Case One) had relatives in the region who would "do for" one another, trading back and forth farm or garden produce, emergency housing, and child care. As mothers, grandmothers, aunts, and daughters, women helped one another make the best accommodations between need for room, food, and time. In this process children often were the "goods" moved around until a mother was better able to provide care. While the assistance of neighbors and kin fell short of providing fundamental remedies to women's needs, this aid had the advantage of coming on an informal basis. Women, regardless of men's presence in the home, were the ones likely to declare family impoverishment at the city's designated charity agencies. At such places females carried the relationships necessary to gain access to the middle-class resources and influence that existed beyond neighborhood boundaries. Yet help from outsiders usually came with controls and limitations, and the most independent means to income related to putting household members into the labor market.

Adolescents in these cases often held jobs; sometimes mothers solicited the initial work permit for them knowing the difference one more income could make. Very often women trod a precarious and exhausting balance between the demands of their own wage work and arrangements to care for and oversee youngsters' activity. Therefore, child rearing often was haphazard and children were left home on their own with unpredictable outcomes. Case records are dotted with adolescents such as Cecilia (Case Two) and Harold (Case Three) whose behavior worried mothers. Some turned "bad," appearing before juvenile court or leaving home with bitterness. But grown children's cooperation with mothers was obvious as well, and aged women frequently relied on assistance from these young adults. Filial bonds were one more basic element that developed under a woman's purview and were essential to supporting a family unit.

Not all reliances were traditional. Some women conceived and organized entrepreneurial schemes relying on their own skills. A few of these ideas were grand, like the possibility of running a café in rural Minnesota, which excited Mrs. Willis (Case Two). Other projects were small: sewing aprons or making doughnuts for sale door-to-door. Yet the hoped-for gains rarely materialized to improve their standard of living; plans of various sorts failed, and women lost heart. Many times in the records a mother would express willingness and eagerness to "work hard," but poor nutrition, little rest, and strenuous physical demands—particularly in charring—led to what was feared as temporary or permanent "breaking down." Other women's cases were open for too brief a time to provide full evidence as to the toll poverty took on their spirit and energy, but for many wives a husband's behavior was a central source of pain and anxiety interwoven with economic uncertainty.

Women's contact with men other than their husbands could ignite neighborhood rumors, and caseworkers often accepted such information as proof of female immorality. Seemingly impervious to this criticism, many women did seek and accept men's company, being silent about these relationships when they spoke with agents. But many women went on at length to discuss the behavior of husbands: drunkenness, brutality, and nonsupport. While a wife might feel that a cruel mate was better let go, she also realized the cost of losing his earning ability. And the status of being someone's wife gave social legitimacy to women who were doubly disadvantaged by their poverty and gender. Divorce as an alternative placed one seriously at odds with society's expectations, but many women made that choice. More of them became household heads through no preference and little choice of their own. But married or unmarried, women gave consideration to what role men should play in their lives and affirmed society's expectation that men were obliged to work toward family support. For themselves, however, they accepted far more complex roles.

Women's Independent Activity

The following Table 3 records multiple initiatives taken by the three hundred woman in a variety of settings. It is impossible to know with surety what advice friends and relatives might have given one another in making decisions. In the instances tallied here, however, the case narrative was closely studied to determine when women appeared to act *without* assistance from a spouse or the agent from AC/FWA.

Regardless of what poor women saw as necessary and perceived as options for themselves, the staff at AC/FWA made clear their own expectations for women's behavior. Caseworkers sometimes warned wives that leaving home for work would lull a man into laziness and jeopardize children's well-being. Consistent with this, some agents refused to give married women referrals from the organization's employment bureau, saying, "Send your husband instead," as it was men's proper place to labor for wages. Assuming traditional supportive roles for men and dependency for women, agents pressured wives to take nonsupporting husbands to court. The woman without a husband—present and able—was advised to go home to brothers or fathers who theoretically could offer her a more appropriate social and economic environment.[32] Often a woman rejected these options—or lacked them—and desperately

Melissa —

There are some bits here that resonate strongly with what you're doing — though I think you're far more sophisticated conceptually.

—Sally

(P.S. — return when you're finished with it, please.)

Table 3
Women's Independent Behavior in 300 Case Records

Women on their own	
found employment	151
asked for and received help from other private/public charities	102
arranged for health care	87
improved living conditions or moved to a different location	85
contacted relatives for help	77
initiated friendships with men	67
shared housing with friends and relatives	65
left Minneapolis	44

SOURCE: 300 Case Records, FCS Collection.

needed to find her own way alone or with other women in similar situations.

As heads of households, impoverished women pieced together budgets from multiple sources. While their efforts mattered little to those with power in the city, their actions mattered greatly to the lower class. In doing so these women defied and broadened the definition of the female role beyond that which operated in middle-class circles. The needs of minor children were foremost for many mothers; this responsibility in combination with a man's absence pushed young women to be the most assertive in making contacts and in attempting schemes to keep the home together. For the women as a whole, use of AC/FWA served as an indicator of "need" but not of "dependency." Families and the agency both envisioned self-sufficiency, but with various means of getting there.

The next few chapters combine the experiences of all three hundred wives and mothers to understand this female-directed urban survival. Chapter 2 illustrates how poor households served as the locus not only of homemaking and child rearing, but of income generation.

2

Women as Home-Making Mothers: "The Arch of Enjoyment Called Home"

American home life was "the highest and finest product of civilization . . . the greatest molding force of mind and character." And *mothers'* attention to children was its central aspect. So read the policy statements generated by the first White House Conference on Dependent Children in 1909.[1] The event had taken place as a result of pressure from social welfare advocates, and these affirming assumptions about family life were not new in social work circles. According to Edward Devine, longtime director of the New York City COS and an educator in the developing field of social welfare, it was the love women bestowed on others that gave meaning to "the arch of enjoyment that we call home."[2] Mary Richmond had outlined model familial roles early in her COS career, and these concepts continued to guide the direction she gave caseworkers as she organized family welfare agencies through her position at the Russell Sage Foundation.

It [the family] seems to me to consist of three elements:

1. The head of the family who gives, as his fractional part of the home unit, his loving, undivided service to secure the means of subsistence for the whole family.
2. His helpmate, who gives, as her fractional part of the home unit, her loving, undivided service to transmute this provided means into an adequate home environment for the whole family.
3. The children of this pair; and these must give, as their fractional part of the home unit, and as the only adequate return for the care lavished upon them, a teachable and obedient love to their parent.

> This bald and alphabetical statement about the home seems, in one sense, the dreariest platitude; but the refinements of the subject must be swept away, and the homes into which charitable relief enter must be considered in their fundamental aspects.[3]

While Richmond acknowledged that a woman's homemaking could be greatly constrained by the absence of a husband's income, wives and mothers were to be held accountable for the creation of a home environment. This was to be distinguished by tidy housekeeping, thrift in buying, organization of regular nutritious meals, and the moral development and control of well-mannered children. Regardless of a woman's class, society assigned her these tasks and measured her against these standards. Home life in poor neighborhoods, however, has to be evaluated in the context of the economic limitations women dealt with and the realization that they often were playing a broader role in family life than the one Richmond had defined for them.

The Means and Ability to Cook and Clean

Description of a family's life in the case record began routinely with physical details of residence at an apartment or house. Cold and overcrowded rented flats were common, but many in the working class squeezed household budgets to accommodate a mortgage. In Minneapolis access to cheap lumber made home-owning more common for all classes than in many cities, and over time owning increased for families throughout the country. Among the one hundred fifty households in the 1900–1910 sample used here, one in six families made mortgages rather than rental payments; among families in 1920–30, the figure changed to one in three.[4] In one unusual record "property" was a brick house with a $1,500 mortgage and $6 monthly payments ($3 on the principle, $2 for interest, and $1 for taxes). More commonly, however, a family owned "a shack down by the river" or a humble wooden structure of questionable condition. What mattered, was the woman who lived there and the energy and ability she expended in making this a "home."

According to social norms, all wives and mothers needed skills in cooking and cleaning; frequent information about these talents among poor women comes through caseworkers' willingness to judge. Most case records included comments about housekeeping, which together provide a spectrum from success to failure. In the home of the "bad" housekeeper, "the child. [children] were half dressed and what few clothes they did have on were black. . . . rooms dirty, smell in hall . . . toilet stopped up, using pail and emptying on ash pile," and "house full of flies, no screens; nothing particularly clean." In the latter case when the worker "called her attention to flies," the woman replied that "her flies would not harm anybody."[5]

Poor women often were ignorant of public health realities. For concerned social workers, however, dirty houses carried a second danger beyond that of health—poor housekeeping was assumed to loosen marital bonds and thus could threaten a family's self-sufficiency. A husband was faithful and supportive only if his wife did her part. At times therefore AC/FWA tried in-home education and hired a part-time—then full-time, visiting housekeeper in 1909, an older married woman encouraged to "ingratiate herself" with the selected "pupils" so that they would be receptive to the teaching.[6] An agency publication in 1917 used the following hypothetical conversation to affirm that a family's long-term interests were served better when wives' home management skills improved. In the scenario a husband comes into the AC/FWA office and seeks out a worker.

> You see, Miss, I've got a good wife but she doesn't know how to manage. She always worked in factories before we married and the house work seems so hard for her. The best year we had ever had was when your Society used to send us what you called your visiting housekeeper. My wife needs her so, now, to show her how to do things and encourage her. Can't you send her again?[7]

Men's own involvement in domestic work appears slight in the records; responsibilities fell to women, and the services of a visiting homemaker could mean regular in-home sessions of a few hours monthly. Rather than clarifying homemaking essentials or questions from the viewpoint of a poor woman, notes from these encounters primarily suggest what outsiders identified as absent in both women's knowledge and their material resources.

> "Discussed necessity for cleanliness, economy in home dressmaking, health and care of children"; "Discussed necessity of having cooked food for the children and providing better care for them when she goes out washing"; "Discussed washing lace curtains, preserving and canning"; "Baisted hem in table cloth."[8]

Not all women welcomed the resources or direction from this visitor; some accepted parts of the education offered but maintained emotional distance. Occasionally the visiting housekeeper became a female confidant as in the following case of a mother with a baby and other young children who coped with her husband's desertion and her own tuberculosis during the eighteen months she was visited. The chronological notes from these visits reveal a mix of observation and discussion as it took place between the two women. Health and housing, marriage relations, and child welfare were integrated into the matter of homemaking. The listing suggests how building skills competed with the other needs this poor woman named "Ella" faced in a difficult and changing family situation.

> [Woman] Taking all care to build up health of self and baby.
>
> Oppty. [Opportunity] to talk on T.B. precautions. A marked improvement in house keeping, better care of the baby than she ever gave Roy or Thomas [older children].
>
> She asked for cake receipts. Uses 2 lbs. of shortening a week. Would like to know how not to use so much. Uses suet receipt.
>
> Opened up account book and bills of fare. Ella [woman] homesick for Roy [at his grandmother's in the country]. Took an 11 year old boy to board. [Boarding children was not an uncommon means to earn money among families known to the agency.]
>
> 
>
> Certify accts. and discuss bills of fare and nutritious article in diet.
>
> [Ella's husband returned.] They moved to a very good neighborhood.
>
> Boards 3 children. She manages by baking bread to keep her grocery bill under $10.
>
> She can't go to U. [University Dental Clinic] to get her teeth fixed or to Pills Ho. [House] with baby as #1 is jealously suspicious of her.
>
> Asked about cooking venison. Chas. [husband] assists a taxidermist who is a friend of his who gives him deer and moose.
>
> [Her husband would not give her any money to buy Christmas presents.] Is tired and discouraged—so concluded to take rest by visiting cousin in the country.
>
> Made starch for her one morning as hers always stuck, and starched clothes. She concluded hers wasnt boiled enough. Will be obliged to move next month.
>
> Started keeping accounts for her own satisfaction. . . . The attitude of the man is so changed it's hard to realize he's the same man. Since she has been sick he has become very careful of her.

> Have cooked greens. Plan to make the work easier in every way as she is going downhill rapidly.
>
> Ella at Hopewell [tuberculosis sanatorium] pronounced by MD to be improved.
>
> We baked biscuits, made pie crust and apple pie. Meanwhile talking over the food questions from point of economy.
>
> #2 supplied with small sum for Xmas gifts. Could not do shopping herself so planned gifts and I did the same for her. Very weak. #1 not working regularly. Had a nice Christmas.
>
> The old friend [Ella] dying of T.B. is still visited regularly and there is always something to do.
>
> #2 passed away. Family breakup. [The children went to live with their grandmother; no word as to their father.][9]

If a woman knew security in health, marriage, and income—as Ella did not—developing or implementing proficiency in "homemaking" was easier. Poverty more than will was the barrier against satisfying many domestic standards, but amid impoverishment, women managed their home life with serious responsibility. One of their tasks was to enlist children's assistance in the work to be done.[10]

Occasionally sons and frequently daughters, played messenger and applicant for aid by handing the grocer a note asking for bread and credit, or delivering oral and written messages to AC/FWA saying the cupboard was bare, the heat gone, or the new baby delivered. Mothers, however, maintained traditional gender expectations when they sent sons to hunt fuel and daughters to watch the younger ones. Boys routinely scouted for scrap wood and dead tree branches to burn for heat. If a family was lucky enough to have a child's wagon, this was the conveyance, but a bicycle or a baby carriage could also be put into hauling service. Daughters were kept home to cook and care for younger siblings and to take part in the heavy work of washing when the mother was ill or had to work outside the home. But mothers were not exempt from any of the jobs they delegated to others.

Women, too, searched the river for scrap wood and the railroad tracks for coals. They dug rags out of garbage cans and saved them for multiple uses—"sold old rags that morn. [morning] for $.20 which was enough to buy meat for dinner." Old newspapers could line shoes when soles wore thin, and in the absence of much heat, a new baby could be laid in or on the cook stove to keep warm. Ironically, "budget-saving"

measures—canning fruits and vegetables—often were beyond women's abilities because they lacked jars, sugar, and fuel for heating water to boil. Some city homes lacked running water and sanitary facilities as late as the 1920s, which meant that women had to carry pails up and down stairs themselves.[11] Yet 48 of the 300 women in this study were described at some point in the record with the phrase, "good housekeeper," with only half as many judged "bad." Many were referred to as "hard workers" who took pleasure in their accomplishments, the kind of women who white-washed dirty walls and tried to cover cracks.

Some families had had more prosperous times in the past—the evidence being comfortable furnishings purchased prior to a plummet from financial security. These wives struggled to maintain the sense of propriety they had known. "Mrs. G. showed considerable pride in her little home and that the bed and most of the furniture were things which she had bought when they were first married. On the sideboard were a few cut glass dishes." The historian Arthur Calhoun, in his study of families of all classes, wrote in a 1919 publication that "wives of poverty could give many a lesson in economics and character to women of the upper world that aspire to elevate them."[12]

Responsibility for budget management and decision making was complicated by minimal financial resources; the daily tasks of child care and food preparation became more trying with the discouragement and ill health that often accompanied poverty. Thus even the "good" homemakers failed at times and felt that things were beyond their control. The following series of case excerpts suggests how a woman's home could simultaneously bear witness to her deprivation and her conscientiousness:

> When questioned about their food supply, Mrs. B. said that they had a few potatoes, some butter, coffee and a little sugar. She had used $8 or $10 a week [for groceries] when her husband had work, but now if she had the means she thot she could get along on $5 a week.[13]

> The boys were eating lunch on one side of the room and Mrs. M. was washing clothes. The clothes were strung across the room drying. . . . The room was clean but very much crowded.[14]

> Mrs. R. had just prepared lunch for the 2 boys of mac. [macaroni] prep. [prepared] in chicken broth. They eat mac and rice often for they found it was cheap and nourishing.[15]

> She said that she knew how to save; that she had been making their food and coal go just as far as possible. . . . The room smelled foul and Mrs. Z. herself was very dirty.[16]

One mother's "rooms were disorderly," and she and her children were "dirty," but in talking about her situation the woman "was quite pleased with her workmanship and spent much time pointing out to [the] visitor the method she used in making quilts." This environment and the joking sign on the wall that said, Don't Swear Here, It Sounds Like Hell, bore witness to the fact that within constraints, women still made individual choices as to what was important to them at home.[17] But these choices also could put them at odds with social workers' priorities as when a woman had to justify having planted flowers in a yard where the worker felt "several [more practical] tomatoes might be."

When budgets slipped, money for rent, food, and burial insurance took priority over clothing as a household expenditure. Social workers heartily supported women who saved money by sewing for their families as this domestic activity combined personal skill with frugal watchfulness in responding to children and husband. The role of charity recipient also came into play as women often relied on hand-me-downs for fabric to rip apart and reconstruct. To request or receive old clothes from relatives, neighbors, or benefactors lacked much of the stigma that accompanied a request for money.[18]

According to the reformer Katharine Anthony, who investigated the homes of working mothers in New York City in 1911, women there not only made frequent requests for used clothing, but a high number had sewing machines. In Minneapolis, too, many lower-class homemakers owned, borrowed, or were buying a machine.[19]

> [A mother, Mrs. W.] showed visitor with a great deal of pride some little things which she had been making for the children from Mr. W.'s underwear and of pieces which Mrs. T. [landlady] had given her. She said the LL [landlady] was a wonderfully good woman. She [Mrs. W. herself] had been advised not to use the sewing machine [after an appendectomy] but she got so restless she had to do it anyway. It was the only way she had to keep her busy. She was as dirty as usual and even more hard of hearing, due perhaps to her cold.
>
> [Two weeks later the agent returned] Mrs. W. was standing up sewing at the machine. She showed visitor with great pride some mittens which she was sewing from the tail of her husband's military overcoat [he was a World War 1 veteran]. The bottom had been cut off and she was using this part to make the mittens because if Mr. W. went to work he would need these. She realized they were not a great success.[20]

A Slovakian immigrant lacked confidence that she could make suits for her sons with the material offered, but knew she could succeed with other sewing.

> Took material for blouses for the 2 boys and for Easter dress for Pearl. Pearl [11 years old] was very much pleased and cried when she saw the material. Said she was tired of having only dark dresses and was happy because she could have a light dress for Sunday.
>
> [Two weeks later] Pearl brought out the little dress her mother had made her from the material given by visitor. Pearl was very happy over it. There was enough material also to make a dress for the baby.[21]

Some women were versatile seamstresses happy to show off what they had done; for others, homemade items were make-do at best and provided only basic covering. Whatever their level of skill, most women were limited in fabric by what they had been given; drabness could stifle creativity and the pleasure of something "new." The sensibility of outsiders who advocated growing tomatoes rather than flowers was repeated in clothing donations by do-gooders who often believed the poor would do better with things sturdy and practical than colorful or light.

Accepting Motherhood

The realities of class and gender worked to deny and complicate the choices women wanted to make. To have children was almost an inevitability, and youngsters generated both the daily pressures and long-term purpose that underlie much of the female activity recorded in the agency's case records.

Pregnancy initiated the demands of motherhood. Twenty-five women were expecting to give birth when they first became known at AC/FWA, and almost twice that number delivered babies while in contact with the agency. Oftentimes women were slow to admit their condition although the worker already had speculated within the record on the pregnancy. In discussions that did follow, most women spoke as if resigned to the financial strain of another dependent, the dangers of delivery, and their own uncertain health. "Female problems," often a prolapsed uterus, was included in many records as a description of a woman's condition. However, expecting mothers turned to agents not for themselves, but for immediate material help. Many requested layettes with "nappies" (diapers) and linen or rags for the birthing bed if delivery at home was intended.[22] Reliance on midwives at birth had lost much of its legitimacy, except among poor and rural populations, while male physicians were asserting their roles in hospital deliveries. Studies at the time associated home births with infant mortality, and social workers urged pregnant women to use the prenatal care offered by nurses at some of the settlement houses and then to go for "confinement" to City/General Hospital.[23]

Not all women could accept the future as ordained by biology; some lamented that they had "been careful" and their husbands withdrew, but pregnancy occurred nonetheless. A few were admitted to the hospital after induced abortions brought serious infections. The telling medical reports found their way to case records at AC/FWA, but agents neither wrote down their reactions nor did the women explain their own actions. Abortion was not a strategy to be discussed with middle class outsiders who held authority, but rather an attempt to control one's own life that working-class women might share with one another. The number of women in this study who had successful abortions without serious complications is unknown.[24]

In the case records conversation about contraception was almost as scarce as references to abortion. Some of this silence reflected women's own ignorance as well as discomfort in talking about such matters to a social worker. In the early 1920s the Women's Cooperative Alliance in Minneapolis undertook a sex education project and a survey of residents with the ultimate intent of uplifting the community's "moral integrity." The status of respondents is unclear, but the project appeared to have focused on the lower class. Ninety percent of 322 women questioned agreed that mothers needed to talk to daughters about reproduction, but two-thirds had not learned from their own mothers, and one-third felt young children should be told that babies came "from God."[25] A visiting nurse from AC/FWA encouraged an expecting mother to explain the "matter of birth" to her twelve-year-old daughter, but the woman declined saying that Mary had "probably heard about childbirth from other children." Regardless of what Mary knew, the mother felt "too nervous to under take such a thing" and described her own adolescent unawareness of sex and reproduction:

> When she [the mother] was 16 and wanted to go to dances and have a good time, her father forebade her for the reason that her oldest sister had had an illegitimate child. . . . She compared the present generation with her own and said she was entirely ignorant of such matters until she married and she had never wanted to hear about these things.[26]

Just as some women "never wanted to hear about these things," most social workers appeared to agree—a conspiracy of silence for which poor women paid. An agent might write sympathetically that a woman with many children was pregnant again, but legal statutes and social mores prevented that observation from being translated into a provision of contraceptive information. The few times that women asked direct questions about what might limit their fertility, the standard response was referral to a nurse or doctor. No case record indicated that those professionals proved helpful or their advice preventive to any of these women.[27]

Women were not only to bear, but to raise children. In this study 19 of the 300 women rejected the latter mandate and gave away or left an infant permanently with others. A very few of these abandoned the family, leaving both husband and children, but the majority of the 19 had given birth outside of marriage. In these cases relatives' gossip might lend details, or the woman herself made vague comments about the past and where the child might be. Often kin or friends had expediently stepped into the role of parent, and the woman went on to marry later, give birth to and raise other children. Within the entire sample, social workers rarely heard mothers railing against the obligations of parenthood. The following excerpt from the case of a divorced woman was the fullest expression of resentment over motherly obligation:

> Mrs. C. didn't care at all for children. She said some women probably do, but they were a matter of indifference to her and she would really rather get rid of them. It provoked her very much to think she had any at all. She was very grateful to her sister for taking her daughter, but she had to buy clothing for Henry [who lived with his grandmother].[28]

Indifference to children was unlike the dilemma that faced 43 mothers—almost a sixth of the total—who concluded at some point that regardless of affection they were unable to continue caring for a youngster. For them, the absence of sound health, of income, or of adequate arrangements for child care led to the decision. While many mothers turned to kin for emergency placement of youngsters, this smaller group of 43 seemingly lacked that option and asked the staff at AC/FWA to locate some private home, farm, or institution where a child could go temporarily. While not officially orphans, these youngsters filled up foster placements and likely were used—or abused—as free child labor in some of the places. Parents usually paid a small price, and a case record might include dispute over the amount owed. However, many records were too short or incomplete to account for how children fared, when, and if they returned home.[29]

The rhetoric of family ethos emphasized the importance of women's tender influence. Across the nation growing attention to children's character formation reinforced preference for a mother's guidance rather than institutional discipline.[30] Agency social workers wrote respectfully about scenes such as the following where domestic tranquillity with maternal, and even paternal, affection could survive in spite of poverty's blemish:

> Their home was four rooms, neatly kept. All the children were running around barefoot. Mrs. T. did not have any shoes for the younger children. She had purchased shoes for Bernadette and Delores 2 wks. ago. Bernadette's were $2.45 and Delores's were $1.67. The children were clean and attractive. Mr. T. came in to talk with visitor. The moment he came into the room three children climbed into his lap. He was patient and held all three.[31]

In these case records, description of a loving father seen at home was rare; proud and caring mothers were more apparent. Joanna Colcord, who directed AC/FWA, 1925–29, also had worked with poor families in New York City, and she outlined social workers' observations in an article titled, "Strengths of Family Life. "In simple justice to the mass of our clients," she began, she wanted the public to understand that there were "examples of wise parenthood among the humble folk known to us." Colcord pointed to affection between family members and listed strengths that occurred in spite of the material deprivation children often knew. These included "a sense of security," "sharing of pleasures and successes," "unselfish attitudes," "hopeful and unified aims," "fortitude," and the "utilization of opportunities."[32] Notes in case records show mothers' willingness to indulge children though they had slim resources with which to do it. On July 5, 1921, an agent recorded that Michigan relatives of a particular young mother had sent her $1.00 in the mail and she "let the kids spend $.50—firecrackers, all day suckers and rest on oil for baby."[33] Another woman organized a going away party for a beloved daughter about to leave for the tuberculosis sanitarium; well-wishing neighbors came in for coffee and cake. "Mrs. C. had not worked all week. She had been trying to get Ilse's clothes all ready . . . she had had to buy her underwear and stockings and a bathrobe." When Ilse visited briefly at home a few months later, her mother bought bed springs and a mattress (presumably on credit), more stockings, and underwear. The daughter reported that she liked the institution with its bead work and weaving activities, and she "was treated as well as any of the paying patients. " But her lungs failed to improve, and in a few months the doctors sent her home where she quickly died.[34] From the physicians' point of view, this was logical as the period of contagion was past, and Ilse as a "nonpaying" patient was using up room that could profit another. Her mother, however, was left frantically seeking cures and then an easement to the death, wondering what might have been different had she had more resources to offer her daughter.

Mothers often felt they were struggling uphill to provide for children's futures and to be a conscientious parent did not guarantee the outcome. When young, the sons of a deserted woman were applauded in the case record for they helped out by locating abandoned wood for fuel, and they attended catechism classes at a settlement house. "She always tried to make her children proud of the way they looked when they went to Church," she said, "and that she had always made them go to Church very faithfully and regularly because she believed it was good for them." This woman had lost four children, one at birth, two in illness, one owing to an accident. Then one of her remaining sons was arrested for theft and the other involved with a neighbor man in what the records referred to only as "abnormal sex." The "mother very much upset when Charles had been caught with Mr. . . . but she had talked with him about it and was watching him closely."[35]

The case records are not complete enough to clarify all the child-rearing norms motivating mothers to act, nor were the writers open about what was identified only as sexual impropriety or immorality—the aforementioned comments were unusual. However, every case with minors had examples of the mother worrying. Women were concerned about food, health, and warm clothes, anxious about safe places to play and companions of good influence. Many expressed the simple hope that children "turn out fine," and that included finding a way to escape poverty. In the records, however, daily responsibility for children was mundane.

Children's ill health plagued a third of the homes to the degree that the agent made note. Bad teeth and poor eyes were common reports from school officials; poor nutrition led to rickets and anemia; pinkeye and scabies passed among children in the classroom and playground. Communicable diseases were as yet uncontrolled by regular vaccinations, and diphtheria, whooping cough, and scarlet and typhoid fever spread throughout neighborhoods. Children as well as parents succumbed to TB. Visiting nurses brought milk and eggs so the afflicted could be strengthened by better diets.[36] In addition to nurses who came by, most neighborhoods had at least one doctor willing to extend credit to poor but honest patients, and City/General Hospital took charity cases. The first line of defense, however, was a mother using camphor rubs, catnip tea, and patent medicines that were exorbitantly costly and that had questionable promise. Mothers did what they knew to do, often with limited access to heat, water, and cleanliness.

Health problems and misery seemed to mount unjustly in certain households with a string of misfortunes that toppled a precarious security.[37] In the same family where Bernadette and Delores were treated to new shoes, the youngest tipped over boiling laundry water on herself and died of burns a few months after the visit described earlier. The social worker arrived to find kin mourning in the front room and Mrs. T. combing children's hair in the kitchen.

> When visitor came in, she burst into tears. . . . Visitor told her it was probably much better [that the child had died] as she would doubtless have been a cripple all her life and had been so marked. She [mother] said she realized this and her life [the daughter's] held so little for her anyway, that it would have been cruel to have made her go thru a life of poverty without the use of her limbs. She asked visitor if she would not go to the Quist [Funeral] Parlor where the body was and look at her as she was so sweet.[38]

Among the 300 women in the study, 46 in addition to Mrs. T. had lost a child; 8 had experienced multiple children's deaths. In the investigation of working women in New York City at this same time, Katharine Anthony interviewed mothers who believed death was preferable to being poor and sick. She found them "apathetic" about their children's demise.[39] While the poor mothers in this study acknowledged death as "release," they routinely reacted like Mrs. T. in wanting a respectable funeral for which insurance never existed and economic sacrifices were made.

On a daily basis even the "best" mothers were inconsistent in reacting to youngsters' needs. Emotional strength necessary for parenthood was exhausted by other responsibilities. The social worker who dropped by unannounced saw a range of care. The following scene occurred in the home of a grandmother who frequently spoke about the grandson who lived with her, a young boy almost blind and perhaps disabled in his development or traumatized in some way. While the agency recommended placing such children in one of the state's specialized institutions, parents and grandparents usually resisted sending young ones whose behavior was "not quite right" to strange places. From a mother's viewpoint, institutionalization resembled the "child snatching" that was feared as the possible imposition of social workers or the state.[40] To keep such a youngster at home, however, meant further demands on a parent's energy. Bobbie, the boy in this case, had successfully gotten up on the stage for a school program and "did credibly," to the delight of his extended family in the audience. The grandmother, Mrs. D., was "thrilled about the performance," but taking care of him exasperated her.

> Bobbie had been giving [her] a good bit of trouble . . . it was hard to manage him as he had been having whooping cough . . . he had gone back to his old tricks of beginning to yell at the approach of anyone. . . . When called to by the visitor he got up and ran like a scared rabbit into the corner under the kitchen shelves, crying that he did not want anybody to come near him.
>
> Mrs. D. walked over and slapped him and told him to cut it out. Visitor said if he was let alone as long as he was not well there was no need of aggravating him. Mrs. D. was rather disgusted to think he had gone back to his old tricks for during the time he had attended school he was quite friendly with everyone.

This woman's knowledge of child psychology and human biology—as well as her patience—had limits. However, when Bobbie needed to go back to University Hospital she went door-to-door in the neighborhood trying to raise money for the bill because she understood quite well that charity cases received "different" treatment.[41] If possible, youngsters were to be protected from discrimination though mothers could not often provide for that. As with housekeeping, women had ideas about bringing up children that in practice fell short at times.

In an initial visit to a young widow, the agent favorably noted how the woman was soothing ointment on her baby's sores and carefully bandaging them. But a few weeks later when the caseworker stopped by things were different; the same mother came to the door "in a sullen manner . . . house was dirty and she carried the very dirty and smelly baby." Yet she was generally a caring and efficient person, and in another two months the agent asked her to help another client family by caring for their children every evening while the parents, Mr. and Mrs. F., were both at work. By doing this the widow could earn a bit of income for herself from the agency's relief budget.

> She said that she would try it for a week. She always made her own children take a bath before they went to bed at night, without shoes and stocking, their feet were always dirty anyway and she thought a bath made them sleep better. It would be a good idea if she could get the F. children to so the same thing.
>
> [Three days later] Called and found Mrs. L. doing her washing in the midst of a very much cluttered up house. She apologized for the way it looked and said it was impossible for her to do her own work and try to help Mrs. F. as well.[42]

The agency's plan failed as poverty and motherhood were already pushing this woman against her own limits. Both her own standards for child care and the opportunity to earn money had to be put aside.

The Vexation of Adolescents

As youngsters matured, the independence shown by some created new conflicts with mothers. These parents described themselves as losing control over how adolescents spent time and with whom. Young people who passed hours on their own in the city or with peers became aware of the poverty that their home represented and felt the shame of their lower-class status. In response mothers felt guilty they had not been able to provide more.

School attendance was a controversial issue. In emergencies mothers purposefully kept older children home to help care for those younger, but sons and daughters also chose not to attend, thus making truancy the most common of youthful "vices." When confronted by officials, juveniles often explained their behavior saying they had no suitable clothing. Mariam was fourteen years old, the daughter of Russian immigrants who came to the agency's attention when Mr. K. temporarily deserted his non-English-speaking wife. Eventually Mariam stopped attending school, and the teacher called AC/FWA; an agent visited to find out what had happened. Mrs. K. needed to work but could leave home only if Mariam stayed with younger siblings, but the girl stated another reason for why this arrangement suited her.

> Mariam says her shoes are all worn out. Agent asks where the last pair is that she gave her. Mariam says they were too large, brings them down . . . says she will not wear them because does not like the shape and they were too big for her and the heels were too high. Agent tells her to take them to the cobblers and have the heels cut off and the buttons set over. . . . Mariam says she won't wear them and will not go to school until she gets some new shoes. Agent tells her she had better go to school or she will have to go to the truant school. Mrs. K. says those shoes are all right for Mariam to wear.[43]

Adolescent girls were sometimes at home when the agent came by, and thus many cases described the interaction observed between mothers and daughters, but sons rarely were to be seen. Social workers therefore recorded what parents and others said with little firsthand knowledge. Sometimes it was the neighbor who reported "bad" boys standing in the alley smoking stolen cigarettes, or a grocer might suspect one of lifting items from his store. Mothers reported sons' stubbornness, foul language, late hours with an unruly crowd, and disrespect at home. They saw negative behavior developing but felt uncertain how to change it; some asked social workers for advice. Mrs. A. had four sons closely spaced in age and reputed by neighbors to be insolent, if not vandals and thieves. The mother regretted that she had "no control" and "could not understand why she could not manage the children as well as Mr. A." He was home irregularly, but was a cruel man who "would simply have to look at the boys and they would hurry to do as he ordered."[44]

The "worst" of such young men stole cars or broke into businesses at night; in these instances news stories offered a more detailed account than agent's own case notes. Young women committed another set of "crimes" and were subject to a sharper dichotomy than were their brothers in being judged "good" or "bad." While girls, too, could be sighted on street corners late at night, the issue more clearly was one of morality; suspicious loitering was the first step in the "fall" of a young female.

In the case with Mariam and her immigrant parents, Mr. K. returned home and soon was complaining to the agent that his daughter expended too much time in the company of young men. "He also finds her spending more money [from part-time work] for her clothing than she ought to . . . he finds her very impudent and he can't have her going out nights when he does not know where she goes." Mr. K.'s concern sounded disingenuous; Mariam had repeatedly confided to the agent about her father's violence and his demand that she give him money for liquor. When she worked temporarily in domestic service her money had gone for clothing, but for her brothers as well as for herself.[45] However, the attraction of increased personal material consumption, the lure of commercial entertainment at movie houses and dance pavilions, and the potential of sexual experimentation were realities for adolescents and perhaps more so for those wishing to escape disagreeable situations at home. Mothers as well as social reformers saw this and were troubled.[46]

Mariam, growing up in the very early twentieth century, believed she needed decently fitting fashionable shoes in order to fit in; by the 1920s advertising told young women that hair color and mascara made them up-to-date. Glamour enabled one to catch and keep a man and working-class girls tried to exercise this option at dance halls where success for the evening could mean being treated by a male. Many young women perceived marriage as the means out of their current poverty.[47] In one particular case a neighbor woman contacted the agency to report a thirteen-year-old who appeared "too old for her age." The worker responded by signing the girl up for swimming lessons, taking out membership for her in the Ureka Girls Club, and monitoring her attendance there over the next few months. A year later, however, another neighbor called saying the same girl was soliciting, flirted with married men, and rumors existed that an abortion had taken place.[48]

Throughout the whole 1900–1930 period, sex outside of marriage, venereal disease, and prostitution were considered by the public to be "social hygiene" concerns endangering society and necessitating remedy. Girls were held responsible for *sexual delinquency*—a term that failed to distinguish between incest, sexual abuse, and developing attraction to potential mates. What growing sons did was much more their own business, but unmarried pregnancy made female sexuality a threat to social well-being. However, the most notorious young women, as seen in the records, were guilty not simply of immorality, but that in combination with bravado. One assertive mother had her daughter arrested for vagrancy, for "she will not work, uses bad language, goes to wild parties and sells moonshine with her brother." Both were put on probation.[49] Table 4 shows how gender affected the experiences of families with adolescents. A mother could be at her wits' end with children, and from feelings of powerlessness contact the law but then *resist* a legal decision that sent the child to a detention home or the Training School at Red Wing. While a few parents were relieved when "mean" sons were taken away, in the records more mothers wondered what had gone wrong and questioned whether an institution would cure it.

Psychology, as it was unfolding at the time, emphasized the malleability of youth, deemphasized youngsters' own responsibility, and focused instead on adults' role in shaping their development. The juvenile court, as a new urban institution, reflected this outlook and in many cities became the locus of broad authority to deal with adolescents.[50]

Table 4
Adolescent Behavior by Gender of Youth in 300 Case Records

	With Sons Involved	With Daughters Involved
Families with		
children truant from school	37	31
mother accusing child of incorrigible behavior	30	5
mother's admission of no control over child	21	16
children charged with criminal behavior involving sex	7	26
children charged with criminal behavior—nonsexual	37	10
children institutionalized for criminal behavior	31	10

SOURCE: 300 Case Records, FCS Collection.

Mothers who came there for help ran the risk of finding themselves indicted as failures in child rearing, particularly regarding their daughters' moral development, which reinforced public opinions that the lower class had loose morals.

This kind of criticism appeared in the case of Millie, an adolescent with a "painted face" who hung around dance halls and the bath house at the swimming pool. On such occasions she could simultaneously meet boys and escape from home where her father drank too much moonshine. He deserted the family, and then her older brothers—reputed to be "lazy"—did likewise, leaving Millie with a mother now forced to find employment. In the course of an appendectomy on Millie, doctors determined she was not a virgin and reported her to juvenile court for further dealings. While the agent wrote little in the record about her or the extenuating family difficulties, the hardworking mother was accused of being "flippant" with "irresponsible attitude and lack of training ability."[51] Regardless of what mothers may have taught young women—or failed to teach them—about sex and appropriate behavior, in adulthood many daughters came to share with their mothers the experience of being deserted by men and the pain of physical abuse. These tragedies brought females in a family together across age lines in ways that excluded sons and fathers.

Relations with Adult Children

One mother grieved, "They get 21 and die or go bad."[52] This was an exaggeration, but the fact that children were grown meant no exemption from worry. Some sons left home for the West never to be heard of again, and daughters took off with the wrong men. Women wondered aloud if they ever again would hear from these youngsters. The agency itself could be aggressive in trying to locate absent adult children, often in hopes of getting a regular pension for a mother or to establish housing for her.

When grown children were available to discuss a mother's poverty, daughters—but rarely sons—were called on to justify any reluctance to bring a parent to live with them. A few young women resented both agency intervention and parental needs, and they spoke of old grievances. Three sisters felt they had been "dropped" as children to be raised by an aunt whom they loved more than their mother. The record noted that they bitterly "refused to do anything for #2."[53] Another set of daughters accused both parents of being "beggars" who asked for charity when jars of preserved fruit and vegetables sat spoiling on their kitchen shelves.

With their spouses, grown sons and daughters argued back and forth about whose responsibility it was to care for a bedridden mother. A daughter-in-law complained, "#2 groans and cries all nights and keeps her [the daughter-in-law] awake and worries her . . . #2 has a very disagreeable odor because of which she [the daughter-in-law] has to keep the house fumigated." And in this particular case the doctor agreed that "#2 was a great trial."[54] An old woman living on her own lamented that when the children visited they "sat on the edge of the chair and seemed anxious to get away." The infirmities of aging could generate conflict, but they also brought forward people's willingness to care for one another, and that sense of obligation was the stronger theme that ran through these case records. "Mrs. B. was in her son-in-law's house as they [she and her aged husband] had no coal whatsoever. . . . Mrs. B. was piecing quilts [and] had been able to fix up all the bedding for the two families."[55]

Most frequently grown children who lived apart from parents but in the geographic vicinity, felt the obligation of family ties, may have sympathetically understood the constraints on parents, and sent home small amounts of money for emergency medical bills, burial insurance, or rent. Younger siblings received school money, surprise Christmas presents, and sometimes a place to live. Housing was often reciprocal. A mother opened the front door when a child's marriage dissolved or when a job ended.

The pattern of relationships with adult children varied by gender. Young men were more likely to disappear without word and then reappear, being suddenly attentive to the needs of an aged or widowed mother, and express great commitment to providing her a living.

> He is very anxious to have a job and support his mother so that she will not go in a home, because he feels that while she took care of him when he was not able to work, he ought to return the favor. . . . He says his whole attitude toward life has changed since his father's death.[56]

Mothers' relationships with grown daughters appeared to be more consistent. When the women lived in the same city contact between the two routinely included household tasks and intimate personal tasks designated as "women's work." That is, daughters far more often than sons came by to cook and clean, and bathe and nurse parents. Sometimes two generations of women lived together as refugees from failed marriages with drinking and abusive men.

In the following case a mother and her married daughter had just moved out of the latter's home and into a flat for the two of them. The husband had beaten both when the three lived together; one clash had come over the question of whether or not the mother should be sent to the St. Stephen's Ladies Home. The daughter had consulted a divorce lawyer who advised her to continue living with the man and to ask her mother to leave instead. The daughter refused.

> Agt. visited #18. [the new apartment]
> House looked very neat as did also #2 [the older mother]. #2 and #31 [married daughter] had been to St. Paul the Friday before and not getting home in time to have Mr. #31's [the son-in-law's] supper ready when he came home from work he was furious and accused wife of being immoral and not fit to live with. He went to look for his revolver which #31 had hidden . . . so when he had gone she and #2 with aid of friends carried all the furniture which belonged to her from her first marriage and part of the groceries to #18. . . . #2 and #31 now live in #18 where they have things fixed up very comfortably. They intend to do sewing [to support themselves].[57]

Another mother and daughter mutually encouraged one another to resolve their violent marriages by divorce. For a time they sought their fortunes together and with a baby grandchild moved into the home of a brother/uncle in Wisconsin, cooked for threshers in North Dakota, opened a boardinghouse in Minneapolis (it failed), and finally shared a job, each doing laundry on alternate days at the National Hotel for twenty-seven dollars a week. When neighbors gossiped that the daughter accepted gifts from men, the mother defended her saying that without clothes, a woman in the city could not get work.[58]

And daughters defended mothers, not simply in being available to nurse or house them, but in accepting women's personal choices about men and marriage. In 1920 someone reported to AC/FWA that an old woman was begging at the state fair. An agency staff member investigated and recognized the person as a "case" from years earlier. Divorced, remarried, and then widowed, the woman was now living in a tar paper shack with an old widower whom she said she would marry "someday." "Visitor asked if her 'man' was not good for coal and such. She replied, 'oh, yes, he did his part, all right,' but she must also do her part." Her youngest daughter was building a house next door and discounted the agent's concern over the immorality of the situation by saying it was "nicer for #2 to live with a man than to live with her children."[59]

Caring for One's Family in the Midst of a Community

Adult children could be valuable resources for older mothers, but neighbors and extended kin often provided the crucial support for younger women on their own. A family might first come to agency notice because a neighbor drew attention to impoverishment after having already given as much assistance as possible. This was the "face-to-face" charity that Helen and Robert Lynd found when they examined social and economic conditions in Muncie, Indiana, with their results published as *Middletown* in 1929. Members of the working class passed the hat for one another because they were aware of their own insecurity and potential want. In 72 cases among the 300, neighbors' assistance was evident, and sometimes organized. People took turns in bringing food to a home where someone lay sick, or they raised money to help cover funeral costs.[60] For some families residential mobility reduced the number of acquaintances they could call on, and marital status somewhat altered the help for which a household seemed eligible. Married couples, widows, and women with absent spouses were all likely to benefit from neighbors' material support, but aid in the form of house repairs, carrying, and lifting, were jobs men did for women without husbands.

When questioned by agents, neighbors did not *always* have kind words for one another. Women criticized other women on female-centered grounds—poor housekeeping and neglectful parenting, or suspicions of immorality. But in living together on the same street or in an apartment building, most women shared similar exigencies and understood how the combination of little money and young children complicated good intentions. They visited and commiserated, tended one another in confinement, fixed lunch for youngsters when the parents were at work, and lent a coat for a winter walk to the AC/FWA office.

A family "friend" was a designation distinct from "neighbor" in the records. There were only one in every eleven cases—and they were always women. Compared to neighbors, friends rarely spoke critically of one another, were usually more supportive with material goods, and were less likely to live next-door. The youngest wives and mothers enjoyed the greatest number of these relationships. Friends not only gave moral support and attention in health crises, but lent money and provided housing as well. Among the 27 women whose friends appeared in their case records, 25 went to reside temporarily in that person's home. Children came along on these moves, but not husbands, as a man's departure—in death, desertion, or divorce—was usually the cause of falling back on a friend. Payment for such hospitality was never discussed in the case record; instead a barter system was more visible. Women traded child care, shared housework, and sometimes even shared one job and its wages.[61]

More than friends, kin from the family of origin provided insurance when economic or emotional stability collapsed within a nuclear family. Relatives' names and addresses appeared in the records of 280 families;

186 had kin living within Minneapolis or St. Paul. Therefore case narratives came to include descriptions of the situation, assistance, and attitudes of these people indicated on Table 5 who functioned importantly as links in survival networks. While the role of kin in material assistance could be broad and continuing, these people also were usually living on limited means.[62]

Pooling and dividing resources was the basic strategy that kin employed. Here it is expressed in the report of a letter from a widow in Ohio who was answering the agency's request that she help out her grown son's family in Minneapolis. Doing four washings a day she could provide necessities for her children who still lived at home, but nothing was left to send elsewhere. She wrote, however, "If they were here she would be glad to 'divide' with them whatever groc and food stuff she has. She has never seen Mr. Phillips' wife or children."[63] When families lived in the same city, a bushel of potatoes or two loaves of bread could show up in a kitchen without explanation. Money came as well for rent, transportation, and doctors' bills and although women worked out schemes of reciprocity with one another, want could foster discord.

Geographic and financial intimacy among kin meant awareness of one another's daily lives wherein the ups and downs of housekeeping, child rearing, marriage relations, money management, and morals could be wearing. When agents went hunting for information they sometimes found relatives annoyed and disgusted with one another, an attitude described in the records as being "fed up." Occasionally relatives were bitter and had stories to tell that went beyond the impressions that neighbors offered or agents perceived.

> Visited Mrs. A [the mother of the woman in the case] and Mrs. P. [the sister of the woman], say they don't think children should stay in the house any longer as they are taught to lie and steal while they are there. Woman seems to have sunken to man's own level. He has forced her to drink beer and now she does it willingly. While sister was down there a few weeks ago she had only codfish and potatoes for the children. Later, about nine o'clock when the children had gone to bed, man got out 2 or 3 cans of oysters and clams which were hidden under the back steps where the children could not find them and started to make a fine supper . . . man and woman drank a quart of beer between them. Man goes under various names and gets work that way.[64]

This sister and mother condemned both partners in the marriage and showed little sympathy with the husband's resolution to unemployment, but usually kin were partisan in finding fault. As with neighbors, the behavioral standards they used were framed by expectations that men

Table 5
Evidence of Relatives by Gender in 300 Case Records

	In Wife's Extended Family	In Husband's Extended Family
Families with evidence		
of sisters as kin	155	76
of brothers as kin	147	82
of parents as kin	84	58

SOURCE: 300 Case Records, FCS Collection.

be providers and women be homemakers. In taking sides with a wife or an ex-wife, her kin typically complained of the need to "get rid of #1" who never kept a job. In turn, a man's relatives criticized the wife who left food standing on the table, "meals never ready and no acct. of household made. Didn't make breakfast so he has coffee at moms."[65] These same critics would assert that they could not—or would not—provide further aid.

Table 6 shows how often women's relatives asserted a final limit to their assistance as they talked about family problems to a social worker. But the second column illustrates that *in spite of* such declarations, these same individuals—usually female—came forward again and again. Kin

Table 6
Conflict in Relatives' Words and Actions by Gender in 300 Case Records

	Say or Imply that They Cannot, Will Not Help	Do Help In spite of Indicating the Opposite*
Families in which women's relatives take negative stand:		
female relatives	43	43
male relatives	38	26
Families in which man's relatives take negative stand:		
female relatives	22	11
male relatives	30	6

SOURCE: 300 Case Records, FCS Collection.

*This is *not* the sum total of relatives who helped, but only a counting of the number of cases in which assistance followed a declaration to the contrary.

helped one another, but the aid occurred as part of twisting and turning relationships that social workers only slightly perceived. Women were not always surrounded by *loving* relatives, but many of them had kin they could rely on instrumentally.

Solidarity of Sisterhood

Stories that interweave kinship, charity, and want in AC/FWA records are primarily in those cases where women were without husbands. If a marriage had ended in desertion or divorce, the wife was unlikely to expect the man's relatives to offer aid for her and the children. The male spouse in many of the three hundred households was long dead or absent when the case opened, and in these instances an agent was unlikely to seek out his relatives as potential support or sources of information for the record. Therefore the quantified account of relatives in both Tables 5 and 6 is skewed toward a woman's family, but within that, kin relations took on a very female-centered character with women and their sisters at the core.[66]

Among relatives listed in the cases as living in Minneapolis, sisters were in greatest number. This might have represented a conscious choice to be close to one another, or perhaps information about sisters' whereabouts was given most freely to social workers because women felt confident about the quality of these relationships. Records suggest that women received outright grants of money—some very small—from sisters as often as from brothers, but sisters also pitched in scrubbing the floor, washing clothes, and rocking babies during illness or pregnancy. If the woman was alone with a house full of very small children, the likelihood of getting help from a sister increased, as it also did from friends and neighbors who realized the demands of young dependents.

After a visit from her sister, a woman would explain that she "felt better." The possibility of moral support, but also of cramped quarters occurred when sisters lived with one another as many did. Among the 300 women, 1 in 7 moved in temporarily with relatives; 1 in 10 packed up her children and went to a sister's, and for 1 in 15 a turnabout took place with the sister coming back to live with her for a time. As shown in these examples, living together symbolized broad cooperation among sisters.

> #2 divorced from #1 who lives in Council Bluffs Iowa. . . . #3 [oldest child] staying with #28 [woman's brother] during the summer but . . . she wants to get him back for school. . . . #28–#29 [brother and wife] very poor and she does not desire to add to their already

> heavy burden. . . . #31 [woman's sister] who works in a hotel in Arlington is also deserted by her husband. #2 wants her to come up here so that two can room together.[67]

> Mrs. Brown of Unity House [settlement house] telephoned. Mrs. W.'s sister had come to Unity House and tried to make arrangements for Mrs. W. to leave the children at the nursery. . . . [Ten days later] Mrs. W. had received notice that she had to move by the first of May. . . . She and her sister would spend the next two days in hunting for a house for Mrs. W. . . . . Visitor looked in the vicinity of Unity House, found a house but with outside toilet.[68]

> Her sister's husband and their two children, Mrs. P. [woman in the case] and her two children were all in one large room with a curtain hung through the middle. Mrs. P. was paying $8 a week to her sister for board and lodging for the three of them. She was making $25 a week and had sent her mother $18 . . . was trying hard to save something for future use.

In the last case crowded quarters made bathing a difficulty; the answer was sending the sister's husband out for the evening so the women and children could share a tub of water. "They had all laughed a great deal over the arrangements."[69]

The frugal world sisters could create for themselves was a world with youngsters in it. When the cost of urban living and the stress of wage earning became too great, a woman was fortunate to have a sister—or mother—living on a farm where she could send her children. One in ten women practiced this strategy, most commonly in the summer when extra youngsters could be out-of-doors, and the mother who stayed to work in Minneapolis could cut her costs. By renting one small room, eating little, and saving up wages, she then could be "ready" in the fall when children returned for school and the coal bill crept up. Mothers negotiated this with relatives they trusted; desperate women without help from available kin were those forced to enlist AC/FWA in finding temporary placements. At times the only way to be a responsible parent was to break up the home and farm out children. In other settings preserving the home was possible only if adolescents joined the labor force.

Child Labor on Behalf of the Family

Kin might provide housing, child care, and moral support, but most urban women still had the need for cash. Within the household economy, potential resources included the wage labor of children as well as adults.

Early century labor statistics showed that far fewer young people in Minneapolis families were employed than was true in other cities of like size. In 1908 5.6 percent of the girls and 8 percent of the boys between 10 and 15 years old earned wages, figures only half the size of those in Milwaukee, Chicago, and Indianapolis.[70] By 1909 no one under 16 could be in a workplace during school hours. To guarantee compliance, state inspectors made spot-checks at work sites, and truant officers patrolled the street.[71] And as child labor figures dropped throughout the country owing to its opposition, Minneapolis consistently had the lowest or next to lowest youthful work rate among all urban areas in the United States.

When the Bureau of Census began to include the work records of sixteen- and seventeen-year-olds in labor statistics, the impact of young persons' economic responsibility appeared greater than it had earlier. And in addition to the young workers who were formally counted, many adolescents were employed irregularly or after school, on weekends, or in defiance of regulations.[72] From the perspective of parents in individual households and of youths themselves—males and females alike—"child" labor mattered greatly in some Minneapolis homes.

Sons and daughters held different kinds of jobs. But both worked, and rarely did either males or females choose their first position out of particular interest or aptitude. Knowledge of openings came to young people usually by word of mouth. Helen and Robert Lynd described working-class youths in Muncie, Indiana, as "stumbling into occupations."[73] Employment might last only weeks or months and then a lull might occur before the next low-wage job came along. Given this pattern and the gaps in case records, the preferences and disappointments of youths as workers are hard to determine, with the exception of attitudes about domestic work. Owing to the low status and social isolation of that job, girls regularly rejected it, but eventually many repeated the experience of their mothers and went into someone's kitchen and back hall. This employment demanded "no special skill," but more than many other jobs made females aware of class differences.

> [Harriette] was very anxious to get work. She preferred not to take home work [domestic service] but would take it if she could not find anything else. She would be interested in the work in tea rooms. . . . Mrs. D. [the grandmother with whom she lived] had kept her out of school this year as she did not have clothes. . . . Mrs. D. wished she [Harriette] could find work . . . said she was a good housekeeper and a good cook . . . said the bed bugs were very thick in their rooms and if

Harriette got work she would have to have all her clothes fumigated. She would not want to take bed bugs into anybody's house.[74]

Beyond kitchen work Minneapolis did not have many options for girls and young women. Commercial laundries and department stores employed a limited number in their workrooms, and by the 1920s a few of the most presentable young women found employment in business offices training as stenographers and telephone operators. In almost equal number daughters and sons went into factories. Females worked most often on some stage of food processing—candy, cereals, or pickles—or ran the sewing machines that turned out flour bags, winter underwear, and woolen blankets. A few sons went out West with fathers or brothers to harvest in wheat fields. Many more brought home wages from unspecified jobs at city factories and plants, sold newspapers, or delivered messages between the downtown corporate firms. The tally of employment certificates distributed in Minneapolis in 1920 described the majority of boys as "errand runners, office boys and factory workers or helpers." Because domestic work lacked formal arrangement and work certification, girls and young women showed up in this same count as primarily factory workers and clerks.[75]

As the historian Arthur Calhoun surveyed families across class lines in the 1910s, he observed that the poor consciously considered children to be economic assets.[76] In these case records mothers spoke of youngsters as *additional* wage earners more often than as *exchangeable* workers with themselves and sought work permits for both sons and daughters, a practice that lessened in the 1920s when sentiment and regulations against child labor had mounted. While mothers expressed concern about their children's strength for work and wanted to keep frail ones at home, they never spoke as if females were automatically exempt from the labor force. Mothers in fact could be directive and occasionally shrewd about employment options for daughters as well as sons. A widow complained that domestic science courses at her daughter's school were supposed to teach "practical knowledge of tea room and restaurant methods," but in truth, "all the teachers ever wanted them to do was to stay in the kitchen and wash dishes." Thus her Colleen remained at home when the class was "demonstrating things." The mother of a fifteen-year-old Western Union messenger encouraged her son to quit as she saw the job as "dead end"; "he needed to learn a trade or business because twenty two cents an hour in 1920 just was not enough."[77]

From some mothers' perspective, child labor offered a discipline for unruly or lazy behavior. It was not unusual, therefore, to find mothers actively seeking employment for adolescents and young adults whose actions were troubling to them.

> #2 [the mother] further says that Elmer has been giving her a great deal of trouble this summer; has been drinking and going to resorts. At one time he left home, was gone several nights. #2 went to see City Atty., but they could do nothing about it. She then saw James Brothers Auto Co. [former] employers of Elmer who agreed to send for him and put him to work as soon as he got back. Also to have an oversight over him.[78]

To an anxious mother "oversight" of a working child could be an inestimable contribution to her peace of mind, but it was the *wages* of work that mattered in most families.

Details from the AC/FWA records, however, provide no pattern in the application of sons' or daughters' earnings to household needs. Most records lacked specific budget calculations unless the mother was among the few receiving a special monthly pension from AC/FWA, and budgets also changed month by month as resources dried up or expanded. The following alternative economic arrangements were possible however: youths might use their earnings for "pin money" as they pleased, and mothers were found to support their right to buy clothing—a purchase long delayed in many homes. Children might also pay a regular share of household food and shelter costs with the rest of their income at their own disposal, or they could turn all their wages over to a parent.[79]

Years prior to the following case excerpt, the same mother had been quite demanding that a daughter find work to help finance the household, but when the youngest became employed, this parent's attitude about the disposition of wages had changed along with lessened family need. Mary earned $13 a week at a candy factory—$4 went in payment on a new coat, $5 to her mother, and the amount left became spending money. "Mary gives part of her salary to her mother but the maj. [majority] she needs for her own use. Mrs. T. feels that Mary is right in this." Her mother explained, "She needed clothes the same as any other young girl."[80] Another immigrant widow reported her sense of the rights and duties of working children.

> So far Mrs. D. has been getting earnings from Helga and Hans buying their clothes for them and giving them from a dollar to a $1.50 a week spending money. She feels that she should no longer do this as they are getting old enough to need the training of spending their own money.

She preferred that they should begin paying her board and room now and buy their own clothes.[81]

Certain labor research at the time found design or conformity in the arrangements for young people's wages, but in the cases here, it is only possible to assert that this money had an impact, for mothers so clearly expressed the *need* that children work. Among the families with adolescent members when the case opened, half of them relied on youthful wages to help maintain the budget. This was as true in families of two parents as well as those where women alone were in charge. In at least 18 of the 300 families, earnings of sons and daughters appeared to be the only means of livelihood for a series of months. As an example in 1905, a 14-year-old boy supported his deserted mother and four younger siblings in a miserable existence by working every day from 7:30 P.M. to 5:30 P.M. as a stock boy.[82] Table 7 shows how lower-class families' needs for additional wage earning obliterated the importance of gender as a factor in some of young peoples' labor experiences.

Table 7
Adolescent Work Experience by Gender of Youth in 300 Case Records

	Adolescent Sons	Adolescent Daughters
Families where		
youths were known to work*		
before case opens	9	8
during case	64	65
in a factory	23	18
work permit sought through AC/FWA		
by youth	7	7
by parent	26	31
by agent	9	14
family income known to be provided		
by adolescent alone	8	10
by adolescent in part	38	42
by young adult in part	41	41

SOURCE: 300 Case Records, FCS Collection.

*In reading these figures bear in mind that only 180 of the 300 families had adolescents or young adults when the record keeping began.

When a mother needed assistance, the ages of her children greatly influenced her options. While older ones could bring monetary resources *into* a household, the demanding dependency of younger children pushed women to create reciprocal supports and exchanges with neighbors and kin. By taking in boarders and laundry, a woman could simultaneously earn essential cash while being at home with youngsters.

Keeping Boarders

Shared living had practical social and economic benefits that made it common among households of all classes in the nineteenth century when economic and geographic expansion pulled young men into new localities. By the twentieth century, however, boarding came to lose its respectability; reformers objected to the practice on both environmental and moral terms. Adding strangers—usually men—to overcrowded slum dwellings meant too many people breathing the same germ-laden air. Strangers threatened the ideal of the well-ordered private home, increasing chances that children would see, hear, and experience too much about life.[83] The lower class, and particularly immigrant families, continued to use boarding as a strategy for survival, and in this study outsiders frequently joined families to bolster income. The nature of these agreements varied greatly; some persons paid for bed and board; others rented half a bare house or apartment living independently with their own possessions but side by side with the case family. Many labels were applied: renter, subletter, roomer, lodger, boarder; here the latter term is used inclusively.

A boarder's rent could mean bread on the table. Ninety-five of the three hundred women in this study took in one or more boarders during their association with AC/FWA, and a few did so on a regular basis. Although the practice decreased nationally in these years, poor families whose cases opened in the 1920s were only slightly less likely to take in strangers than those from 1900 to 1910. Widows opened their doors twice as frequently as married women, and three-fourths of all landladies in this study had small children. Therefore, it was the most vulnerable women who took on responsibility with boarders, an arrangement that not only could tax their patience and management skills, but initially put pressure on household finances.[84]

> #2 has put what furniture she can spare into the big front room and thinks she can make more on this room than on smaller back room. She needs table and bureau. Has gas stove chairs and bedding enough; will get an airtight heater in 2nd hand store as soon as she can . . . says

> she has spent $1.50 for bug poison etc. Bugs still pretty numerous . . . . Agent secures bureau and table for #2.[85]

Women asked for help with furnishings and even for finding boarders, and cooperating agents put up notices and searched the AC/FWA caseload for individuals who might double up in housing for mutual savings. Simply because a woman readied her home, however, carried no guarantee a boarder would move in or stay. Boarders lost jobs and thus the means to pay rent just as husbands, wives, and children did. They could leave when the furniture was repossessed or when the coal ran out; they could disappear in the night with the last bite of food in the cupboard. Old women hesitated to demand rent from burly men, and even burly men moved out when contagious disease put the home in quarantine.

Some women viewed female boarders as the safest solution, a "middle aged maiden lady" who would be proper and might assist in overseeing youngsters' activities. And many women *were* accustomed to shared lodging with sisters and friends, but too often the unknown female boarders came with preconceived notions of cleanliness and cooking and meddled in family affairs. Male boarders, however, could threaten family well-being in other ways, and sexuality complicated boarding as an income strategy. A widow who had just fixed up her front room complained to an agent.

> Several men looked at it but all asked if she objected to having women brot. there, and she would not stand for that, whereas they had not rented the room. Mrs. N. spoke at length of the immorality of many men. She said with her girls growing to be the size they were it was one thing she had to guard against.[86]

Mothers attempted to be watchful on the behalf of maturing daughters, but as for themselves, some welcomed the adult company that male boarders could provide. The records suggest that in 23 of the 95 homes with boarders, relationships with a boarder included sex, marriage, or pregnancy (with and without matrimony). The female involved was almost always the mother in the house though occasionally an adolescent daughter. However, further case information on these relationships is limited to bits of gossip by neighbors, and social workers never tried to distinguish between consent and rape or sexual molestation.[87] In the records the lines between loneliness, lust, affection, and exploitation are fuzzy. Relationships that began as mutually satisfactory could go awry. To the news reporter who wrote the following story, the fact that the victim was a "pretty woman" but poor and with a house full of children played a part in the dynamics. On October 24, 1904, the *Minneapolis Times* carried the headline, "Jealous Lover Shoots Woman and Kills Self," and the article explained that a Mrs. Nagler, separated from her husband and the mother of six, lay wounded at City Hospital. The story continued:

> A year ago she became acquainted with [the boarder who] asked her to permit him to board with her. The board which he paid would just cover her rent and she accepted the proposition thankfully. Soon after his installation as a member of the household he began to pay her attention which culminated shortly in a proposal of marriage. She told him to wait . . . his attention became insistent until at last, five weeks ago, she ordered him from the house . . . Mrs. Nagler is about 38 years of age and is a pretty woman.[88]

In talking to social workers, women emphasized the economic benefits of boarding and denied that the men in their homes drank, but they usually were silent about what these men meant to them personally. Like much else in daily life, however, boarders' income was a very temporary defense against need that carried its own set of risks. But it generated funds without taking women away from the house or separating them from a traditional domestic role.

Household Entrepreneurs

In a limited number of cases enterprising and desperate women pushed possibilities further and created household businesses based on food and handcrafts.[89] Gardens yielded produce for sale; chickens were raised for eggs; and fried doughnuts could be sold door-to-door. Mothers took children and picked berries at Lake Minnetonka to sell for $1 a bucket or to be hawked as a summer treat to park goers. Standing outside movie theaters, poor women sold popcorn. Youngsters on the sidewalk peddled raffle tickets for a homemade quilt or original painting.

Some women exhibited valuable learned skills. "Sews very neat dresses & bloomers—wanted $5.00 for each for small children, prefers to go door to door than sell at stores, more money"; "knits for Powers, [a department store] .50 to .75 daily before Christmas." A few immigrant women knew how to weave, "got the warp with trading stamps," and caseworkers wrote letters to friends of the agency soliciting them to buy. "We have an interesting little woman, a widow with two children, who is doing some good work in rug weaving and will certainly appreciate any work that can be given to her. I believe that her charges are 30 cents a yard."[90] A widow with grown children wanted "to give lessons in music, painting and wax flowers"; instead she invested money in paper for an art show but "only made $5—has trunk full of paper left." By selling paper dolls at church bazaars she used up the materials but never recouped the investment nor her artistic confidence.[91] Every seller needed a buyer, and buyers—like boarders—were not available on demand, particularly not to poor woman who aspired to use themselves doing "finer things. " Many businesses could fail in poor neighborhoods, but there was precedence and sometimes "success" in taking outsiders' laundry into one's home.

Bent over Washtubs

Washing for other families was a common strategy but hard work. Case records of forty-three women described them bending over washtubs with red hands and sweating faces and then hanging clothes and linen on cord strung wall to wall in humid rooms. In 1910 doing a week's worth of laundry for a customer family usually consumed the day and could earn a Minneapolis woman only a dollar.[92] A few very efficient women, however, pushed this drudgery into a career. One was the wife of a man who had been institutionalized for years. The caseworker was favorably impressed with her ability to manage. During a home visit the woman led the agent into both kitchen and woodshed to see laundry in tubs, some articles drying on a line, and others ironed. The agent wrote that all looked "*very nice*" but added that the woman was nearly out of flour and wood. The laundry business continued, and five years later

> she has started to build a room to serve for hand laundry in connection with her house on the first floor. . . . She thinks she could make good thing of it as her boy 14 could go for the clothing. . . . [The next month] #2 phones she had moved downstairs. Is going to re-rent second floor furnished. Would like us to send her roomers. Girls if possible . . . would like washing machine agent spoke to her about.

The possibility of a machine promised increased productivity, and according to customers, the woman did "splendid" work. She asked the agent to arrange for her to get dirty laundry from hotels. Then she brought price lists for hand laundry, and the caseworker agreed to post these notices at student residences at the university. Two years later the agent began sending her own washing to the laundress who had as much work as she could handle. She relied, however, on her son's help. As he grew older, she knew the time would come when he left home. What she feared happened, and her laundering income slumped; working on her own she could not earn enough.[93]

Laundry additions, washing machines, and price lists were far more sophisticated than most women's efforts. Nor did everyone turn out good work in the midst of settings that were less than clean and convenient. Many women complained of exhaustion from carrying water in and out, up and down stairs. Scrubbing and wringing wet clothes hurt the back and fostered hernias.[94] Laundry was understood generally to be such a drudgery that even poor women—if in bad enough health—sent their belongings to the woman next door or out to a commercial laundry with the approval of budget-minded agents who deplored spending on what they considered to be nonessentials.

Like taking in boarders, doing wash at home called for an investment. Heating water demanded a supply of wood (which was scarce for poor urban families) or coal (which was costly). And the laundress needed matches to strike the fire, soap and blueing for a clean white wash, and starch if she was to iron—small costs that could add up to prohibiting figures. With an eye to economics, therefore, women were better off going to wash in middle-class homes where supplies were already at hand, but this alternative had its disadvantages.[95] In this study women who took in wash were often the same ones seeking boarders, for they were predominantly mothers of young children with little freedom to leave home to earn an income elsewhere. When they did become part of the recognized labor force as the next chapter explores, the combined responsibilities of parent, homemaker, and laborer weighed heavily.

Conclusion

Across class lines in Minneapolis the most basic elements of home life were repeated. Wives and mothers maintained private households and raised children—"women's work"—which society assumed was in exchange for economic dependence on a supporting male. In reality most of the three hundred women in this study could not count on marriage or the economy to deliver a secure and structured life; in the absence of this, homemaking tasks expanded. Poor women coped with problems that middle-class women did not, and in necessity they created additional ways, means, and reciprocities for survival.

Owing to lack of money and education, homemakers often fell short of maintaining the standards others set as constituting a clean room and a wholesome meal. Homemaking often appeared erratic. Women had to create and make do with what they could hunt out, while the demands of children, husbands, and poverty nibbled away at their energy. Yet some of these poor homemakers impressed social workers with their skill and pride, and many articulated personal priorities about what had to be done. To act entailed making difficult but necessary choices. Should a bit of unexpected cash be used to whitewash the walls or to treat youngsters who had grown accustomed to a drab existence? Should a household go into debt over burial expenses? Should relatives be asked for help one more time? Were children with ragged clothing better kept at home or sent to school where others judged them critically?

At times choice was absent. Motherhood occurred and recurred almost as an inevitable part of being an adult female. Women in turn were anxious over little ones' vulnerability; poor nutrition, sanitation, and housing fostered illnesses that cut into general well-being and sometimes were fatal. Worrying over young children's safety could be replaced with trying to discipline willful adolescents. The same older daughters called on to function at home as their siblings' substitute mother could get into trouble with neighbors and juvenile court by demonstrating too much independence and claiming sexuality. "Bad" boys and girls troubled their mothers, but more adolescents played a role integral to family life by joining the work force and earning wages—if only at low rates and inconsistently. As mothers themselves accepted the hard labor of keeping a home together, they called on youths to help. Many young people participated with a mutuality that extended into adulthood.

People with marginal resources aided one another in survival by exchanging goods and services at crucial times. These helping networks existed not only within nuclear families, but more broadly among neighbors and sometimes included grocers and landlords. Most of all, however, extended kin had to be the rainy day insurance. Help did not guarantee harmony between people; individuals might disagree and enumerate another's weaknesses—usually based on traditional standards of domestic propriety for females. But the dominant pattern was of women supporting one another in myriad forms. And in this study *young* mothers of little ones who lacked the support of a present and able husband most often sought and received available aid. Their steadiest allies were other females whose own situations were often insecure; working together they bartered child care and housing.

The home itself could be put to economic use and the space squeezed to include a boarder. Washtubs regularly used once a week could be kept busy doing others' laundry daily. Both schemes comprised risks: a boarder could turn out to be exploitive, and lifting tubs and wringing laundry encouraged the onset of back trouble and varicose veins. Rarely did these efforts, which were so common among poor women, generate the amount of money needed. The issue, however, was not simply creating income but being able to juggle that with the tasks of raising children. The challenge to do this was heightened when women left home and joined the insecurity of the wider work force, the issue to be examined in chapter 3. As opposed to the intimate view of women's household efforts in chapter 2, the next section opens with a description of economic conditions that dealt impersonally with all involved. To understand the work experiences of wives and mothers calls initially for a description of the labor market that defeated men's abilities to support their families.

3

Women as Wage Earners: "Willing to Do Anything in the Way of Work"

If a family could handle the "vicissitudes of life" *without* relying on either charity or the wage work of a woman, it had an "adequate" income, according to Edward Devine who taught a course for social workers titled "Standard of Living" at the New York School of Social Philanthropy and later at Columbia University in the early part of the century. His perception of *inadequacy* in family life developed from observing poor households who made use of charity at the city's COS. He sensed that children from these homes would never know health and prosperity unless they had access to further resources in growing up. Devine outlined what he believed were minimals: sufficient food served regularly; light, airy, and safe homes with at least three rooms for every five persons; pure water; clean streets; care for eyes and teeth; seasonal clothing; and a decent burial. When he reviewed this issue in the 1920s, he added another element to the list of essentials—the "right to life with meaning." However, if a wife and mother was to be able to preside over such a household, Devine calculated that her husband needed the wages of steady work at sixty hours a week throughout the year.[1]

Without using the language of "Family Wage," Devine was affirming that a man should—and should be able—to earn enough that his dependents might enjoy both health and satisfaction. For many households, however, this was only hypothetical. Women's employment outside the realm of family was the crucial addition to many households' meager budgets.

Public spokespersons and male workers themselves argued against females in the labor market, but discussions focused primarily on the growing numbers of single women within factories who were expected eventually to marry and replace wage work with the care of home and children. Less public recognition—except on the part of social reformers and those in charities and casework—focused on the economic roles of married and once-married women. For decades these homemakers had earned funds by bringing strangers, or the soiled laundry of strangers, into their homes. But many of them also regularly left their own kitchens to labor in the residences, businesses, and factories of others. The necessity of this female labor served for some onlookers as evidence not only that homes were in peril, but that wages and employment were amiss.

At the turn of the century, researchers from many private organizations and public agencies launched a variety of wage and budget studies focusing on the jobs and homes of the urban working poor. The purpose of some studies was simply to examine patterns in industrial expansion, but other investigations were meant to illustrate that poverty was inherent in an industrialized market economy and did not arise from individual fault or moral degeneration. Reformers sought new documentation to support lobbying efforts for social insurances, minimum wages, and protective legislation for women. Definition of an American living standard and the size of a model family varied among these studies, but results constantly showed that in many working-class families, *women's wages were essential* in the struggle for health and decency.[2]

Statistically, the country's income had been on a steady upward climb from approximately $9 billion in 1875 to almost $30 billion at the turn of the century, with that doubling again in the 1920s. Immigration provided the labor to run industrial machinery and created a market for goods. But into the twentieth century growth slowed, and while the figures said per capita income was increasing, urban living and technology were forcing up the daily cost of living. Although innovation and new products pushed elements of the economy forward, the various studies contributed to a body of statistics proving that even in the absence of a recession, national income was inadequate to provide even subsistence for all families. In this climate, low-income workers faced a fluctuating demand for their ill-paid labor and found self-sufficiency precarious and survival not to be taken for granted.[3]

Labor Surplus in the Gateway to the Northwest

Regardless of findings from research, many early century entrepreneurs were fully optimistic about opportunities for success in Minneapolis. Public relations write-ups touted the area as the "Gateway to the Northwest." Situated on the Mississippi River, the city had access to both transportation and waterfalls that provided hydropower to turn gears first in lumber and then in grain mills. Engineers discovered ways to redesign the milling process to roll grain rather than grind it, which lessened waste from the outer kernel and drastically increased salable flour per bushel. As a result, Minneapolis captured the world flour market before the turn of the century. Giant elevators dominated the early skyline.

Six railroads converged in Minneapolis and St. Paul carrying grain from the fields of immigrant farmers in the Dakotas, Canada, and Montana. On the return run cars brought farm implements, parts, seeds, and consumer goods. Flour that once had gone downstream in barrels made of Minnesota north woods lumber, began crossing the country by rail in bags or as boxes of crackers, macaroni, and breakfast cereals processed in factories lining the river's banks. Wool from Montana sheep was woven into blankets and winter underwear; factories pressed linseed oil from North Dakota flax. Around the Great Lakes expanding urban populations moved into structures flung up with Minnesota timber, doors, and sashes. The flow of money encouraged linkages between Minneapolis banking houses and rural communities throughout a multistate region and legitimated the city as a center for Federal Reserve activities.[4]

Families amassing the first fortunes combined their economic success with promotion of civic assets, including a state university, an art institute, and an orchestra with national status. Branches of the public library opened throughout the city and pleasantly navigable canals linked two miles of parks and lakes.[5] This was the Minneapolis that William D. Washburn, Jr., apparently had in mind when he stepped up to the podium at a session of the National Conference on Charities and Correction, which convened in Minneapolis in 1907. The wealthy son of a pioneer milling entrepreneur, Washburn declared, "Notwithstanding the various failings in our social condition, one may say that the average type of life in the Mississippi Valley is the highest the world has yet produced in any such large section or community upon the world's surface." He characterized the state's labor environment as offering higher wages and lower hours than elsewhere. "Where laboring men and women who can draw wages, fall into poverty and crime it is due largely to moral and mental degeneration which apparently follow our great prosperity."[6]

Minneapolis functioned as a place of convergence, which included a *surplus* gathering of labor. From throughout the rural prairie, native-born young men and women flocked to the opportunity and excitement they imagined awaited them in the city. Dozens of employment agents set up makeshift offices between the taverns on Washington Avenue, the street that ran parallel to the river and railroad tracks. These agencies redirected men to the iron ore mines and forests in northern Minnesota, Michigan, and Wisconsin. The Federal Bureau of Labor licensed agents to fill farm labor orders for the "seasonal exigencies of the agricultural cycle" in the grain fields on the Plains.[7] As business prospered within the city itself, new jobs were primarily in wholesale and distribution rather than in industry, which meant that the skills of many rural youths were only minimally salable.[8] Common laborers were in oversupply and continuing innovation in milling reduced the human labor necessary in this most prominent enterprise.[9] When no jobs existed for men—even those with specific skills or crafts—they sat on the curb and waited. If these men were married, their own unemployment sent wives seeking work.

> Mr. M. was getting very discouraged [he had gone to work in the North Dakota harvest and came home broke but still owing money to the employment agent who sent him there]. . . . He had filled out an application blank in every factory and foundry in Mpls. He was willing to take any kind of work.
>
> [Six years later little had changed for Mr. M.] He had been working for 37 cents an hour since fall and had not put in one full week . . . . as an iron moulder he should be getting 85–90 cents an hour.[10]

Information about male employment was available for 182 husbands among the 300 families studied here, but only 106 actually held jobs while the family was known to the agency. The greatest number—51—called themselves laborers; others worked as teamsters, carpenters, railroad, or streetcar men. A few were farmers, salesmen, or cooks. For many men, practicing one's trade was a habit or opportunity of the past. "Work History," as written into a case record, showed a fragmented series of jobs in the secondary labor force with skilled and unskilled efforts interspersed following industrial layoffs and seasonal contractions.[11] The following list and comments regarding one husband's chronological employment—not atypical—is given just as it appeared in a family record opened in the early 1920s:

> 1915 enervating fats for soap
> fireman in Chicago
> shoots horses Chicago (Fats)—he didn't mind but she wouldn't let him cont. after marriage
> Ice Cream Com. cares for their team
> Pure Oil comp.
> Anderson Construction-contractor
> selling furniture
> William Bennett Construction
> 1931 Cedar Lake Ice Company
> McKirk Company—they build elevators
> Howells Greenhouse[12]

"Some people are never wanting a situation but the great mass of working men and women do not have permanent work." This was the observation of the general secretary from the Minneapolis AC/FWA to the Minnesota Conference of Charities and Correction in 1895. He went on to explain: "They are always looking for a job. The work that occupied them to-day is finished tomorrow, and a thousand others could have done it just as well anyway. They are unskilled . . . often uncapable."[13] From the vantage point of the largest charity in Minneapolis, the staff at AC/FWA held prime positions for observing the relationship between poverty and employment. Agency annual reports often discussed local economics as the context behind requests for family assissistance and as the motivation for program expansion.

Very early in its history AC/FWA opened a room where needy but unemployed women could earn a grocery order by picking apart old clothes the agency would sell as rags. An alternate employment opportunity existed for men—a wood yard where chopping and stacking yielded similar remuneration. Other COSs repeated these work options, but many agencies preferred running an employment bureau. When AC/FWA opened theirs in the 1890s, optimistic personnel imagined this to be temporary until their own work with family problems was more effective. Private businesses or households wanting laborers on a short-term basis and often for just a day contacted the bureau to find an employee from the list of registered and worthy applicants. Seemingly everyone benefited from the arrangement; poor women and men received income as well as the dignity of labor; the community's civic order and prosperity were enhanced by the industrious work efforts of more citizens, and the agency reenforced its local value by functioning as a conduit for cheap labor.

Regardless of the agency's approach and the economic security enjoyed by many in the city's middle and upper classes, the numbers of job hungry people coming in to the bureau showed no contraction. The 1902 *Annual Report* complained that employment requests from a daily average of thirty desperate men and women jammed phone lines and disrupted other agency business.[14] In 1907 when the state opened a *public* employment bureau next to the AC/FWA office in City Hall, the agency gladly sent men there so as to focus the agency's own work on job opportunities for the "handicapped" and those who "could not compete,"—a category covering women with children to support.[15] In the harsh winter of 1911–12 a local ice company intended to put on extra men to chop ice for the next summer and asked AC/FWA to screen candidates in order to guarantee that jobs went only to "family men." Five hundred unemployed men appeared at the office when the notice went out. The agency's executive director spoke to groups around the city, discussing the employment crisis and saying that twenty thousand more men on the streets could probably have joined these applicants.[16]

Again and again agency documents noted unemployment and low wages: "Industrial Disabilities" were the "outer crust " obscuring the rest of family behavior.[17] A depression in the Midwest accompanied the opening of the great war in Europe, and in 1916 the agency reported, "Unemployment was so great, and the need resultant upon it was so complete, and it entered so inextricably into every instance of dependence that no other question could be considered."[18]

When the United States itself mobilized for war, the demand for grain brought peak prices, and jobs in the city increased—a temporary respite lasting until 1922 when the agricultural economy clearly began to slide. In response, the Minnesota industrial commissioner lobbied in Washington, D.C., for highway construction monies so as to put laborers on a payroll.[19] It was the government's responsibility—or that of business—to increase jobs; at least this was Mary Richmond's response after representing charity organizations at a 1921 White House Conference on Unemployment. She felt that the labor situation was a problem beyond the control of caseworkers who nonetheless had to deal with the repercussions of unemployment through increased caseloads of needy families.[20]

At the end of 1922 when applicants for aid at AC/FWA greatly exceeded the number from the previous year, volunteers were enlisted to fill gaps left by overworked staff.[21] By 1927 the entire employment operation had been closed in favor of sending people to the public bureau, but a special employment agent went out to survey opportunities for the "better sort" of client and to weigh the impact of the recession on family life. When husbands lost jobs or left the home, women and children had always tried to pick up work, but the agent discovered such action was becoming less and less possible. Relatives who had helped poor kin were now unemployed themselves. Older working children were losing jobs to married family men, and those capable only of light work were replaced as employers had their pick from a sizable labor pool. Men once accused of being shiftless and lazy now had authentic cause for sitting at home. When the special agent circulated a list of 96 unemployed household heads to area businesses, only 1 job materialized—housekeeping for a woman. That position appeared, the agent said, only after 147 calls and visits.[22]

Six months before the stock market crash Joanna Colcord, then director at AC/FWA, wrote to the local Council of Social Agencies documenting her sense that local families were in grave economic trouble. Her letter began, "Is our population poorer?"

> In spite of the rosy picture of conditions in Minneapolis painted by our newspapers, our workers know that ever since the fall of 1927, conditions for our clients have been bad. Unemployment, while never reaching epidemic proportions, has been endemic a good part of the time. Economic conditions in the rural parts of this state and other neighboring states have brought many former tenant farmers and farm laborers to the city to seek for work, and we are struggling with an increasing burden of nonresident need. . . . An employee of the gas company told one of our staff that never in their history had they had as many delinquent gas bills as at the present. Another firm selling on the installment plan received a telegram from its home office recently inquiring "What was the matter in Minneapolis? They had more bad accounts there in proportion to population that anywhere in the U.S." These things are all significant of a population forced to go on a lower scale of living, and with resources depleted.[23]

Six months after the stock market crash in October, the staff from AC/FWA began meeting with a committee of clergymen, labor leaders, and employers to see what measures might be taken cooperatively as remedy. Jobless men defined their own solutions, however, and many in the city were shocked when individuals milling around employment offices in the Gateway district broke into a riot and looted nearby stores.[24] The Great Depression of the 1930s forced families that had felt relatively secure to reconsider how little they could get along on, who in the family should work, and where jobs could be found. For the poorest urban workers, however, these were the usual questions from decades of employment insecurity.

The Poverty of Local Wages and Compensation

In their 1910 biennial report officials in the State Bureau of Labor explained that while Minnesota wages had risen between 1900 and 1910 as much as 10 and 25 percent, "wages [had] not increased equally with rents and prices." These necessities had climbed an average of 25 and 30 percent. The report continued:

> Two and a half dollars a day seems to be the minimum wage that permits a family to enjoy those necessities and comforts that insure efficiency and constitute a proper standard of life in Duluth or

> Minneapolis—probably in all of Minnesota. . . . 72.68 percent of all male wage earners are paid less than $2.50 a day. . . . It is true that many of these men do not have families dependent upon them. It is equally true that many more of them do have families.[25]

And in Minneapolis no union activities mitigated this discouraging economic reality for in 1903–4 a strike for the eight-hour day at the largest flour mill had collapsed when bosses planted informants in workshops and hired scabs to keep the machines running. From then until the 1930s the city was recognized nationally as being "open shop," strongly anti-union, and crowded with laborers.[26]

Unemployment and underemployment insidiously wore away at a man—or woman's—wage-earning capacity. Industrial accidents, however, could quickly deprive a household of wage earners owing to businesses' willingness to sacrifice workers' well-being for profit.[27] Ironically the railroad, a primary carrier of wealth into and out of the state, was the primary site for male labor fatalities and mishaps. The Labor Bureau emphasized in the 1909–10 report that accidents meant irreparable loss. While it was "commonly asserted that employers' liability works better in Minnesota than elsewhere because the Minnesota Courts put a more liberal construction upon the legal rules," workers were cautioned to beware. A bureau study of three hundred accidents showed that after loss of the male breadwinner, 50 percent of the female-headed families received no compensation. When payment was made, "the average price paid for a human life by the industries of Minnesota was $536 and funeral expenses."[28] Six years after the state's Workman's Compensation Law was passed in 1913, the labor commissioner asserted, "It appears that the injured workman and his family are still left to bear, without any possibility of shifting the burden to the industry or to the ultimate consumer, a major part of the financial loss arising from industrial accidents.[29]

A decade later in 1921–22 when AC/FWA staff compared the wages and needs of case families to a minimal household budget developed by the Home Economics Department at the University of Minnesota, over 40 percent of the men had been earning *less* than the minimal standards *before* added difficulties drove their families to seek charity.[30] The inadequate working-class wages criticized years earlier by the Minnesota Bureau of Labor had continued to hold true, worsened, and then dropped precipitously in 1929.[31] From the beginning of the century, underemployment and minimal wages had made a mockery of the concept that men—or women—in the working class earned a "family wage."

"Will Do Anything in the Way of Work"

Long-held popular perceptions assigned men to the workplace, but Census Bureau figures told another story. From 1900 to 1930 between 20 and 25 percent of the total female population over fourteen years of age were collecting wages as someone's employee. This number remained stable over time as shown in the bottom row of Table 8, and there was consistency as to which women were likely to find themselves counted here. Matrimony removed many females from paid employment; being single, widowed, or divorced pushed them into the labor force. The

Table 8
Number and Percentage of Women over 14 Years of Age in Female Labor Force in United States by Marital Status, 1900–1930

	1900	1910	1920	1930
Married	13,810,057	17,684,687	21,318,933	26,170,756
In labor force	769,477 (6%)	1,890,661 (11%)	1,920,281 (9%)	3,071,302 (12%)
Widowed or Divorced	2,832,362	3,361,296	*	5,307,355
In labor force	920,441 (33%)	1,147,065 (34%)	*	1,826,100 (34%)
Single and Unknown Status	8,381,996	9,913,490	14,871,550	12,534,937
In labor force	3,424,543 (41%)	4,751,100 (48%)	6,509,426 (44%)	5,781,646 (46%)
Total	25,024,415	30,959,473	36,190,483	44,013,048
In labor force	5,114,461 (20%)	7,788,826 (25%)	8,429,707 (23%)	10,679,048 (24%)

SOURCE: This is a compilation of material gathered by Women's Bureau, Janet Hooks, *Women's Occupations through Seven Decades*, #218 (Washington, D.C.: U.S. Department of Labor, 1947), 39. Percents are rounded to the nearest hundredth here and in subsequent tables.

*In the 1920 census the single, divorced, and widowed women were grouped together.

image created is skewed, however, for census takers ignored women's work at home both with boarders and doing laundry.[32] More importantly, the census was an ingathering of female experiences from *all* classes. The high work rate of *poor* women and the recognition that class alters peoples' lives, gets lost in the total percentages.

Over half of the three hundred women in this study worked for wages during the time they were known at AC/FWA. Consistent with national figures, married women were least likely to do so, but it was more specifically those married women with grown children who lacked the economic and maternal impetus of hungry babies and the physical stamina that many jobs demanded.[33] Children and husbands altered the need and resources each woman could draw on, but if a husband fell victim to unemployment, illness, or the simple fact of low wages, his wife had little choice but to offer herself in the labor market. Deserted, divorced, and separated women caring for young children and adolescents dominated the group numerically. A young deserted woman in 1900 was not alone in saying, "Will do anything in [the] way of work to keep her children from starving."[34] Katharine Anthony described this as "obeisance" to "the most primitive maternal instinct."[35]

Most of the working women counted in Table 9 resembled Mrs. P., who assumed that employment was a female experience.[36] Before mar-

Table 9
Women's Work Experiences
in 300 Case Records

Women's experiences with wage work*	
discussed in record	218
work prior to marriage	44
work prior to case opening (often this was prior to a particular crisis of desertion or widowhood)	65
work during the case	170
work with husband in household	91
work with husband absent	151

SOURCE: 300 Case Records, FCS Collection.

*These figures are overlapping; one case may be counted in more than one category. Female labor for the care of boarders was not counted for household arrangements varied greatly; women did not speak of it as a job nor talk of the money; doing laundry at home *was* included, however, as women referred to this specifically as "getting work" and discussed their wages.

riage she had cleaned rooms in hotels and described her behavior there as "very independent" and was able to "ward off dangers" (sexual harassment). After marriage she worked intermittently until her husband took charge of a newspaper stand in the lower section of the downtown business district. Although the caseworker judged him "very capable," he deserted Mrs. P. and their children in 1921; she then assumed that she would find work. The agent encouraged this by referring her to the employment bureau at the North East Neighborhood House.

> Mrs. P. said she was sure she could make a living after she got her light housekeeping rooms rented out and got to work herself. She thought perhaps the boys could make more than a dollar a day . . . said she worked out for awhile during the war, but had never done any day work. She would be willing to do anything now in order to get along. [Two weeks later] Mrs. P. phoned asking for work. Said she would rather get work than ask for help. [Another two weeks later] . . . she had a promise of a job at a laundry and so thought she could manage from now on.

She wanted to do "hotel or restaurant work" and did so. In a few years she was waitressing for twelve dollars a week, but staying on her feet was exhausting, and she began to insist that when the oldest son and daughter reached sixteen they should leave school "to help her as soon as possible."[37]

Like many wives and mothers in this study Mrs. P. consciously sought ways to earn cash income and had a variety of jobs in female-dominated fields. Her employment was irregular, physically strenuous, monotonous, for little pay, and never promised mobility. She had narrow job aspirations and met disappointments. Her husband left and matrimony ended, but wage labor continued, though inconsistently.[38] Women from the case records opened in 1920–30 were more likely to have worked prior to marriage, had a bit more diversity in their employment, and relied on themselves more for finding jobs. However, other elements of female wage earning described on the following pages were constants for poor women in Minneapolis throughout the 1900–1930 period.

"Always an Army of Charwomen Available"

In contrast with the prevalence of employment as a female experience in these records, scant detail was offered to suggest anything but routine in the jobs held. Twenty-eight women found clerical or shop work, 27 were seamstresses, and 26 labored in industry summarized by terse comments such as:

clerk at Powers Mercantile $6.00 weekly
sews flour sacks at Bemis Brothers [and got blood poisoning from an accident there]
Tailoress—10–12 vests a week at $1.50 per vest
$7 a week at Sunshine Biscuit
Has been running the nine needle machine at Munsingwear, she knew people at Munsingwear who were earning $35 a week on the nine needle machine. She expected to keep on and secure the same salary.

This latter career expectation showed rare optimism, most lower-class women known by the staff at AC/FWA worked within a narrow range of employment possibilities that changed minimally over time and paid little.[39] In 1926 when agency workers read through cases opened ten years before, they noted "no significant change in the number of women who leave their own homes to earn." And over that time the majority continued to be involved in domestic work.[40] While a few women clerked, sewed, and ran machines, many more of them cleaned, scoured, and scrubbed.

Of the 218 women known to have been employed, 67 did or had done domestic day work in private homes; 50 of them cleaned offices, theaters, hotels, and hospitals; another 50 had been housekeepers or worked in boardinghouses. Thirty washed dishes in restaurant kitchens, and 19 cooked there, 14 handled linen at commercial laundries where steam and heat made conditions particularly unhealthy, and 10 did practical nursing—not only for neighbors but for strangers elsewhere in the city. Brief, matter-of-fact comments again described this world of wage work.

washes dishes with husband 7 pm to 7 am Elgin Luncheon
scrubs Yeates Building 11:30–5 am $1.75 a day
Red Top Taxi washes windows with mother-in-law
washes B and S laundry, not home till late in evening
has 2 or 3 steady places weekly where worked for many years
shampoos grain bags at home for Miller Milling Co.

In the country as a whole, domestic service dominated as the largest employer of female labor in each national decennial census from 1870 to 1940. The absolute and proportional number of such employees began falling back, however, owing first to increased opportunities for women in factory labor and then to the impetus of the great war and expansion of retail shops and business offices between 1910 and 1930.[41] Case records from the 1920s showed a handful of both mothers and daughters speaking of the possibilities of being a telephone operator, a multigrapher, or secretary. It was primarily young single women, however, who left "service"; wives and widowed and divorced women continued as the work corps with fewest alternatives.[42]

Table 10 shows the same trend in Minneapolis. Although the number of working women in the city tripled from 19,719 in 1900 to 64,393 in 1930, over time those in domestic service became a smaller proportion of the labor force but one dominated by those women most likely to have responsibility for children.

To the public, jobs classified by the census as "domestic and service work" meant "unskilled." Women simply were doing what sup-

Table 10
Marital Status of Women Engaged in Domestic and Personal Service in Minneapolis, 1900–1930

1900	Married	Widowed and Divorced	Single	Total
Females in labor force over 10 years of age	1,450 (100%)	2,051* (100%)	16,218 (100%)	19,719 (100%)
Females over 10 years in domestic and personal service	590 (41%)	1,067 (52%)	7,024 (43%)	8,681 (44%)
1930				
Females in labor force over 15 years of age†	14,682 (100%)	8,315 (100%)	41,396 (100%)	64,393 (100%)
Females over 15 years in domestic and personal service	4,710 (32%)	3,922 (47%)	9,489 (23%)	18,121 (28%)

SOURCE: U.S. Bureau of the Census, *12th Census of the United States, 1900,* Special Report, Occupation, 614, and *15th Census of the United States, 1930,* Vol. 3, Population, 853,854.

*In 1900 widowed and divorced women were counted separately but combined here for improved readability of the graph.

†In 1930 changes in state child labor laws led the Census Bureau to count the work force as those aged 15 and older rather than 10 years and older.

posedly they already knew—scrubbing, serving, and cooking—acting as servants, housekeepers, office cleaners, laundresses, and waitresses and thus needing little remuneration.[43] One reformer observed this unregulated employment saying:

> Many women combine this work with taking in washing, and nearly every untrained woman who has fallen upon evil times turns to one or both of these occupations if she is unable to go to the factory and is within reach of people who can employ such help. . . . If there are few good servants, there is always an army of charwomen available.[44]

In 1909 the Minnesota legislature acted ahead of many others by creating a Department of Women and Children within the Bureau of Labor. Its first report illustrated the dominance of day work offerings at public employment bureaus with charts and narratives pointing to the extremely low wages available.[45] But nothing changed; in 1910 a quarter of all women working in Minneapolis earned less than $1 a day while those in domestic work averaged even less, as little as $3 a week and rarely over $6.[46] Although the state passed minimum wage legislation in 1913, sections applying to women and minors were subsequently declared unconstitutional and the matter lay unresolved until 1917 when minimums of $8 and $9 dollars a week—too little to live on—were affixed to various female occupations—excluding domestic service which was beyond the reach of regulation.[47]

In 1918 a variety of ladies' organizations in the city collaborated with the state's Department of Labor to survey the plight of working women. With information on more than 50,000 females employed around Minneapolis, the study concluded that most were "in service" and underpaid. One-third were earning less than $10 a week, a sum considered to be "below minimum subsistence." Another one-third made between $10 and $14 weekly judged to provide merely "minimum subsistence." Almost 20 percent were married, and half of these had two or more children.[48]

Women served, but often unwillingly. They said such things as, "Will not do day work . . . would rather beg . . . prefers laundry or restaurant work to housekeeping." Employment in private homes offered secondary status at best, task repetition with little lasting accomplishment, and isolation without any buffer between the woman herself and her female employer. In the absence of adequate wages, proponents argued publicly that when lower-class women were brought into the kitchens of their betters, they learned valuable lessons in cleanliness, thrift, and efficiency. Service reinforced female roles and aptitudes and encouraged immigrant women's assimilation into American ways.[49] A few women in this study supported the contention that they had profited from kitchen employment; a young deserted Norwegian mother explained that her first American job was for $3 and then $5 a week as she learned to speak English. "People would tell her to bring certain meats from the ice box and foods so that she picked up many words in this way."[50] Some domestic employees brought their own personal standards for cleanliness and management with them, and employers sent back words of praise to the agency, but contrary reports came as well.[51] Employers accused a few women of theft, of leaving before the work was done, or of allowing some garment to get torn in the wash. Women with years of caring for their own homes could be reluctant to follow instructions set out by others.

In 1924 an agent came by the back door of a big house hoping to catch her client—the cleaning woman—for words about the woman's poor health. Instead, she was called in to moderate a debate over housekeeping standards.

> Mrs. Klein [employer] said she was going to appeal to ML [agent] to what ML thot [thought] about this. She said she had told Mrs. Minor [cleaning woman] to take the rugs [room size carpets] out at least twice a month and beat them, or leave them out for a man to do. Mrs. Minor had told Mrs. Klein that she was foolish, rugs were put down in the fall and were never taken off the floor until spring. Mrs. Klein said . . . sometimes she had girls who took them out every Wednesday or Thursday when they did the general sweeping. . . . Mrs. Minor also appealed to ML [who] told Mrs. Minor that people in Minneapolis usually took their rugs out oftener [to "keep down germs"]. . . . Mrs. Minor seemed to be quite disappointed at this and seemed to become quite sullen. However she brightened up and became quite pleasant again when ML told Mrs. Klein that it was a pretty hard job for a woman of Mrs. Minor's build to lug out all three or four big rugs twice a month. . . . Mrs. Minor said she did not like this working all day long and never sitting down. ML then told Mrs. Klein that in any house a good house work girl usually arranged her work so that she could have her afternoons except on ironing day.

Mrs. Klein continued with comparisons about the "girls" she had previously hired, and the agent excused herself to make a call in the next room—a ploy to have a minute alone with Mrs. Minor. Hurriedly the agent expressed concern about a growth on the woman's neck and told of an appointment she had arranged for her at General Hospital. Synchronizing an employer's demands with the servant's own sense of work to be done was one possible source of friction; correlating the stamina necessary for a job with the level of the employee's health was another.[52]

"In Need of Rest" But "Could Not Take One"

Case records spoke repeatedly about the problems women dealt with as mothers, but difficulties on the job were not something that agents often observed or that women talked about. Some labor disputes, however, were resolved quickly; the employee was fired or moved on in spite of the difficulty in finding new positions.[53] When AC/FWA opened its Legal Aid Bureau in 1913 more than half of the first year's thousand applications were grievances against employers. The majority were wage claims brought by both men and women.[54] Legal Aid advertised its services and success with this notice:

LEGAL AID BUREAU

CASE NO. 1
GIRL 19 YEARS OLD
Worked 12 hours—7 p.m. to 7 a.m.
7 Nights Every Week
$6.00 a Week
$0.86 for 12 Hours—Each Night as
Cashier in a Downtown Restaurant
Found Day Work—Quit
Had 3 Nights Pay Due—$2.57
Refused Payment
Accused of Theft

Nothing to it!
Got the Money in a Jiffy![55]

Here a young woman "escaped" an all-night job to go into domestic work in a private home. Not only did she earn little as a waitress, but being downtown during the evening she might well have contended with sexual harassment. But domestic work—whether she realized it or not—promised little guarantee that the same problems would not recur. In any event, this particular young woman was assertive, got legal assistance, and the employer paid the wages due.

When women spoke out against domestic work or other employment, most often it was the physical demands of the job they dreaded. The customary requirements of doing housework for others demanded a toll paid in loss of health, a dilemma without simple remedy. "She hated to do the housework but wanted to find work of some sort. She found day work too hard for her." After years of consecutive child bearing and poor care at birthings, inadequate nutrition, ill-fitting shoes, and heavy service work, women looked older than they were—with painful feet, bandaged legs, and hernias protected by secondhand corsets. "She did laundry work instead of cleaning lately because her feet had bothered her so much that it was impossible for her to kneel as much as was necessary for scrubbing."[56]

One hundred twenty-seven of the 300 women were identified by agents as having chronic health problems. Young, middle-aged and older women were all susceptible to the diagnosis that went no further than "weak and nervous," "bad eyes," or "bad teeth." Twenty-three had medical care related to cancer; 21 were treated for "female problems," 18 for heart trouble, and 15 for tuberculosis. Many records showed physical deterioration in the course of the case; sometimes this was simply exhaustion—known at the time as "breaking down"—which also happened to men in heavy industry.

For one in every ten women from the study, friends, relatives, an agent, or a doctor recommended that she was seriously "in need of rest." However, care and convalescence were mismatched with the other responsibilities women accepted. In the following note a physician attempted to establish his patient's "worthiness" to receive assistance from AC/FWA. While he recognized the woman's need for relief from juggling multiple demands, he was unrealistic about the ease of putting down that burden.

> To Whom It May Concern: This is to certify that undersigned has this day examined Mrs. Hulda Mackley for her physical health and finds her to be unfit for any hard work or nervous strain, worry or excitement for the following reasons: She has heart murmur (endocarditis) and is in climactoric [menopause] very nervous and easily upset. Mrs. Mackley has undergone too much work in the last few years and has always had a family of many children to care for, which has helped to bring on such a condition and failing health.
>
> I therefore, advise her not to go out to work and to stay home quietly attending to her own health, doing only light work in her own house and taking life as quietly as possible.[57]

In another case a woman with both diabetes and heart trouble needed medical attention. While her husband was willing to work extra hours so as to buy medicine for her, hospitalization was out of the question.

> Mr. H. came in and when visitor mentioned the subject of the hospital he became quite excited and said that he would not consider letting his wife go at all. . . . He was more than willing to have her go over to the

> disp. [dispensary] for treatments but he would not let her go away from home. He thought she could get just as much rest at home. . . . The boys could do most of the housework and there was no need to overwork at all . . . he did not realize that she was in bad condition at all. . . . Mr. H. said the reason he would not let his wife go to the hospital was because there would be no one at home to do the bossing then.[58]

Many wives and mothers knew that "resting" at home was a contradiction in terms. If the husband were present, he might be stubbornly committed to a division of domestic responsibility and "bossing" that required her activity; young children, too, could be insensitive to a mother's need to care for herself. The pressure to earn income, however, served as the major prohibition from resting. Thus it was with great reluctance that almost a fourth of the three hundred women quit a job at some point owing to ill health . Any such accommodation, however, had to be slight in both time and money.[59]

> #2 doing [work] 4 or 5 days a week. Becomes so exhausted. Can do little at all. Thinks her abdom. organs have sagged out of place due to standing. Refuses to see the doctor for fear he will refuse to allow her to work now when she feels she must [her husband had recently died of tuberculosis]. . . . Visitor explains to #2 concerning County Aid [Minnesota's Widows'/Mothers' Pension program]. #2 does not wish to apply until can no longer work herself. . . . In June Hazel will grad. from 8th grade and so can work.
>
> [A few weeks later the agent reported the woman was more run down and in need of rest.] She felt she could not take one [a rest] because her wages were needed.[60]

In hopes of improved health a woman might make minor adjustments in work, giving up one home where she weekly did laundry or half a day of labor elsewhere. But anxiety accompanied any decision affecting money coming in, and women felt compelled to resume activity as quickly as possible without waiting to get "well."

Patching Together Income

Economic strategies within a household were neither simple nor constant, but pragmatic, hopeful, and tainted by the threat of ill health. The following budget comes from a record in 1907 and suggests how the mother of a crippled adolescent daughter planned to survive after her ill husband regained enough of his health to desert her and leave the city.

Over time she was a janitress in an office building, cleaned in a few homes, and had an assortment of customers who brought laundry to her. She had two boarders and received minimal aid from the Poor Department. In whatever ways she could, she garnered income, and the agency recorded these multiple sources in the following format:

> [Daughter] says #2 was blue because had lost her place as a domestic and could not meet her rent. However, things are dif [different] now. Yesterday rented front room to a man by name of Kelly for $4

Rent 2nd floor	8.00	
" 1 floor	4.00	
	12.00	Now has only $3.00 rent to pay
[Works] 7:30 am to 2 pm as domestic across town	7.00	
	3.00	City Poor Dept, (one load of wood a mo. and 2.50 groceries)
Washing for indiv.	.60	
" " Visiting Nurse	.80	
" " priv. fam.	.62	once every two weeks

> On this income #3 says they get along fine.

This mother was optimistic about supporting her family, and for a time she succeeded. Three years later, however, a doctor advised her to do only a "little light work, but no washings, needs nourishing food." A visiting housekeeper stopped by with a health tonic, and the caseworker located an alternate job to the one she held. On her own, however, the woman had resolved the course of action to take and wrote to AC/FWA that she would continue as before doing "one or two washings a week." Her current position was too good to give up as it provided "my dinner and good lunch and $1.50 per day."[61] Another mother, deserted and then widowed, voiced a similar commitment to doing whatever labor she saw fit, saying, "It would make no difference to her what the doctor said as she worked just as much as she possibly could anyway."[62]

Regardless of the will to work, the number of women in service—married or alone, young or old—exceeded the demand in Minneapolis. While national figures on female employment fluctuated with the availability of jobs for husbands and children as alternate family workers, these case records make clear that wage-earning responsibility might fall on a woman who could find no job. Men stood idle waiting to be called at factory gates, and women were turned down at the employment bureaus where ladies called in their requests for "girls."

"As Yet Had Found No Work for Tomorrow"

"Days" measured domestic labor; two days usually meant two "places," two houses to be cleaned weekly. In the records, "Four days a week reg. for two years" was the clearest example of a woman's full and permanent employment; "Works Sat 1/2 day for $2" was alternatively slight employment but with high remuneration. Laundry, day work, and even the jobs available to janitresses often had a weekly and a seasonal rhythm that functioned to women's disadvantages. In many homes and offices, cleaning was not daily but inherently part-time with the demand at Christmas and spring followed by slack time. Families who provided "places" in the winter, went on vacation in the summer. In Minneapolis many of the middle class spent summers at a lake. Pregnant or sickly mothers of the middle class might hire a domestic worker temporarily who later would be told she was "no longer needed." Katharine Anthony's study revealed the same impermanence in work among poor women in New York City at this time. She wrote that to be laid off without warning was feared more than the "direst sickness."[63] The language of a "family wage" and "occupation," which characterized discussions about male labor force, were far removed from the experience of domestic workers. "Places" easily disappeared necessitating search for another. One of every 4 women in this study used the AC/FWA employment bureau at least once; 1 in 6 also tried to find work through a bureau located elsewhere in the city—usually at a settlement house.

Mrs. R. was one job seeker who "laughed when she said she could not possibly tell the visitor her age but could tell the visitor that she came to this country in 1901 and had worked as a laundress and cleaning woman ever since." She began at fourteen as a housemaid for board and room and continued finding jobs during her years of marriage and after being divorced. With four children to support, Mrs. R. had more need than ever for funds and was eager to work. She called herself a "trained waitress—waits tables in private home," but also was familiar with cleaning private residences, hotels, and the Lee Clothing Company. During the summer, flower sales from her garden brought in a bit more money, but all these efforts combined fell short of creating an adequate living. Between March and May in 1926 Mrs. R. had the following series of experiences hunting for work:

> She had no definite places promised her where she was to work but was certain she could find something at the Public Employment Bureau.
>
> Had only one day's work last week. . . . AC doesn't have . . . anything. . . . She was very much disgusted to think there was nothing for her and said it was the way it always was when she asked for work.

She had had only 2 days work since last week and as yet had found no work for tomorrow. She planned to go to PSH [Pillsbury Settlement House] in the morning and if she was able to obtain work thru them would phone visitor, otherwise she would like a visit [from the social worker].

She earned only $6 during the week.

She had done only 2 days work this week but had the same places for next week and expected to find more besides.

Mrs. R. phones that she had worked every day this week and would not be able to see visitor.

Mrs. R. had been working quite reg. and had managed to pay her taxes. . . . She was planning to put in her applic. at several places for a steady job so she would not have to worry next winter.

Mrs. R. was not fortunate in finding work. There seemed to be nothing to do and each week she had several days free.[64]

Just as Mrs. R. became accustomed to uncertainties and disappointments accompanying her efforts to earn, other women did also and lived with the pain of being unneeded workers regardless of their desire to work.

Mrs. B. wondered why people would not give her sewing . . . she was so anxious to work . . . she had written some friends for recommendations which she hoped to use to procure more work here.[65]

#2 was working nights at the present time, in the Physicians and Surgeons Bldg. She was to get $50 a month. She was just taking another woman's place, however, and did not know how long she would be there.[66]

Mrs. H. had tried to find work. She wanted restaurant work. She had had a position until last Oct. which she realized now she should have kept. She hoped to go to work as soon as she could find something.[67]

One half of the women in this study found jobs without any apparent assistance by agents, but looking for work required a boldness and willingness to compete with others that for some came only with desperation. A caseworker found Mrs. W. about to go out to an employment bureau. The woman was "neatly dressed in a blue serge dress with pongee collar and cuffs." She already had filed numerous applications and would gratefully accept any offer, but she knew "her timidity was against her," that a "more aggressive person" might have fared better. The solution, which the agent recorded as coming from Mrs. W., was to "cultivate an air of greater assurance."[68]

Certain aspects of women's confidence—or lack of it—related to personal appearance, and poverty was forceful in deteriorating its victims. Mrs. S. "tried to appear clean and attractive as she could, being limited by not having good clothing and stated good naturedly that she knew the values of appearing clean before the public."[69] In the 1920s the entire nation's attention to hair, dress, and teeth was heightened by the accent on youthfulness and the claims of cosmetic and personal hygiene advertisements. Just as adolescent daughters talked more then of makeup and bobbed hair, records from that decade show an increase in women's concerns about their own appearance. The disfigurement of bad teeth created particular self-consciousness. Some women asked for help in getting them fixed and the agency obliged. A Swedish immigrant doing domestic work was judged by her employer as "unusually brilliant considering the few opportunities she has had." This woman, however, needed to find other work that would ease the pressure on her varicose veins, but she feared any job bringing public exposure. "She had two or three wax teeth in her mouth at the present time, which she tied to her own teeth in order to fill up the front of her mouth. She could not bear to go out on the street with her teeth gone and was extremely sensitive about them."[70]

Wage work confronted women with the fact that others judged them as a surplus with limited value. Minneapolis was a sellers' market where a poor woman had to wonder if she would find a vacant position, and if so, would others see her as suitable? Was she strong enough to do the work? And would it last beyond the week? The employed mother also wondered what her children would do while she was away.

Combining Wage Work with Motherhood

In poor neighborhoods the working woman who came home to children often had limited energy—and time—for attending to them as she wanted to. Absence of a mother during the day or night could mean no breast milk for babies, irregular opportunities for children to eat, and limited watchfulness for their physical safety. Sociological studies, some of them insensitive to the multiple demands on these women, documented the negative repercussions of female employment pointing to infant mortality, school absenteeism, child neglect, illness, and delinquency. For mothers who saw the choice as staying at home with a bare cupboard or finding employment, survival was the priority—not neglect of children. But many struggled over ways to combine these roles of wage earner and mother.[71]

In 82 of the 300 families, women confessed to social workers that the absence of child care complicated their intent for employment. Forty-one mothers in the study gave up a job during the course of their case because no immediate solution could be found to the problem. Unemployed fathers could help—unless they were too ill, out hunting for work by the day, or simply out. The records had little specific evidence of men in this role or how they fared in homemaking tasks, but occasionally a wife or an agent was impressed by a man's aptitude at keeping children clean and happy. Men, if they commented about caring for children, expressed frustration. The needs of a nursing baby were a particular dilemma. A few women tried to bring young children along on domestic jobs, but employers complained about one more mouth to feed and interruptions to activities in the women's scheduled work. Hiring out as a live-in housekeeper appeared to allow for both roles of mother and earner, but even then children could be a disadvantage. One deserted woman with both an adolescent daughter and an infant held a new housekeeping job for only a week, as she found that her "feebleminded" daughter was "not wanted."

Long-term placement of children with kin in the country was practical although the distance and separation could upset both children and mothers. The most fortunate woman had parents or siblings nearby with whom children could be left during the day. Sometimes out of kindness but often in bartered exchanges, or for a fee, neighbors and friends helped out. At such times two women could clash over standards of cleanliness and meals. In 1921 a mother reported:

> She had been leaving them with a neighbor who charged her $4 a week for the two. The neighbor woman had them from 7:45 to 5:15 pm but Mrs. F. furnished the milk and lunches for them. This lady however had 5 children of her own and wasn't at all clean. Mrs. F. claimed she did not change Ellen's diaper from morning til night.[72]

Mothers' most common solution was simply to leave children on their own, an early version of "latch-key children" who were in charge of one another (often under the oldest daughter's purview), and vulnerable to the "influence of the streets."[73]

If youngsters were to be home alone for long, a woman had to arrange some way for them to eat. One mother regularly tacked a sack on the back door of a house, labeled, "Lunch for Billy, will be home around 6." Another mother "cooks Cream of Wheat in morning in double boiler, leaves," and when the boys woke up it was still warm. They got their own lunch, and in the evening when she could get time away from her job, this mother would rush home to cook an egg or soup. She "admitted they were not getting as much as they need."[74]

Critics argued that working mothers squandered wages, making unwise purchases of time-saving but expensive crackers, bread, and pastries with which to stuff their children. Others judged careless cooking by the working mother as a "most effective home wrecker." In her study of working mothers in New York City, however, Katharine Anthony found no evidence of such neglect; instead, women bought foods that were cheapest, rather than what was most easily prepared. Most women also relied on traditional cooking and eating habits that were hard to change regardless of the time and resources available. Therefore, while women's earnings made more money available for food, it usually was evident in the quantity, not the quality in what was eaten.[75]

Anxiety about children drove some mothers to take whatever job was geographically closest to home so that they could steal time to hurry back and survey how things were getting on. A few had jobs where a window allowed them a glimpse of their children coming home from school or playing in the street. Another option was to work at night when buildings downtown needed charwomen and children were sleeping. News exposés of the period pointed to the trick of cheap narcotics to keep babies slumbering while the mother was out at work.[76] But leaving youngsters alone made many women uneasy about their well-being. It also left the parent susceptible to accusations of child neglect. The following excerpt shows one mother's consideration of what it meant to keep a night job:

> They could have given her a night job, but she said she wouldn't think of going off on a night job and leaving the children alone. . . . One family who lives next door is composed of a widow and several children. The one on the other side has an old man, who would not be able to help the children out at all, if anyone should come into them and try to harm them. It wouldn't be so bad if Joe [oldest son] stayed home with them all the time, every evening, but occasionally he liked to go out for awhile himself. While he usually gets in at 9:30 or ten, she could not leave Frances alone [an adolescent who was talking of bobbing her hair], because she wants to know what Frances is doing.[77]

Being home was a concern for mothers of adolescents as well as for those with small ones. The real or anticipated behavior of adolescent girls on their own, more so than of sons, concerned working parents as well as social workers. Here Mrs. L. made a decision within tight constraints—weighing family economics with the questions of "morality" raised by the social worker.

> HMG [caseworker] discussed with Mrs. L. the danger of working at night, and leaving the girls alone at home . . . she knew it meant as they grew older they would have company and would not be chaperoned. She preferred to work in the daytime, but had not been able to turn down this job as she needed the money."[78]

Working mothers felt torn by their responsibilities and some reformers were empathetic and tried to improve the work environment for women in industry by lobbying for "protective legislation.[79] Other critics attacked wage-earning women as shirking their natural duties; homemaking—even among the poorest—could not wisely be relegated to second place.[80] According to them, a woman who walked out the door to labor elsewhere jeopardized not only her children's well-being, but the respect and affection of both youngsters and husband. And if she grew slack in household duties, then rebelling children and a deserting, drinking spouse were only following suit in setting awry the natural order of family life.

Domestic Survival, Not Independence from Men

In 1909, when the employment bureaus at social agencies and at the public and private ones downtown were all doing a brisk business, the personnel at AC/FWA worried about how self-sufficiency meshed with family roles. The agency director queried:

> The important question for all the agencies that are attempting to provide work for women is whether such women really need to work. Are they widows with small children who are left to shift for themselves each day while the mothers go out to earn? Are the husbands idling away their time since the wives are too willing to assume the part of wage-earners?[81]

In this study of case records, women were *very* likely to worry about ways of combining wage work with care for children. They were much less prone, however, to express concern about the conflict of responsibility in being both an employee and a wife. While the majority who sought employment and worked were disproportionately those heading their own households, some married women with husbands at home established their own understanding about who could or should be earning. Over time this could shift as unemployment and hard work took their toll on consensus.

A particular woman had been a domestic before marrying and then continued to seek employment as her husband seemed not to keep his jobs. He worked as a "fry cook and counter man" he said, but in the summer he wanted to be out-of-doors; sometimes he did carpentry and sometimes drove cabs. Months passed during which he deserted, returned home, found part-time labor, and then deserted again. She charged him with nonsupport and cared for the children with her own wages from waitressing and packaging writing supplies part-time in a factory. The man then reappeared and settled back into the home, but with incongruity he said to the caseworker that "he did not like to have her working because he felt that it was better for her to be at home and [any] way 'he wasn't much of a nurse'." One day the agent "knocked several times on the door and could hear the children inside calling 'daddy' but there was no answer and visitor finally left." Midmorning a few weeks later the visiting agent came by again:

> Could hear the children calling Daddy and after an interval of several minutes Mr. Cox stuck his frowsy head out of the door. He said his wife was working and if visitor would wait a few minutes he would dress, which she did. . . . He produced a cigaret and settled down for a comfortable talk. Said that his wife was still working. . . . Asked if his wife were working to buy him cigarets and he grinned and said he thought that was fair. He talked at length about the rich oppressing the poor and how willing he was to work if he just had a chance. Pointed out that he was not likely to find a job when he stayed in bed until 10 in the morning. He said it was no use wearing out shoe leather trotting around all over the town and looking in vain for work. . . . Mentioned the fact that the children had not had much milk to drink lately and visitor suggested that his cigaret money might well go to buy milk.

Although this man's behavior annoyed the social worker, his wife was reported to be "perfectly satisfied with the way things were going." Mrs. Cox believed that her husband had put in all the employment applications he could, and his help at home included doing the family's wash. She agreed, however, that she would be glad when it was possible to exchange work roles with him. Six weeks later she appeared at AC/FWA vowing "not to put up with her husband's action any longer." According to Mrs. Cox, her husband assumed she would "take care of him all the rest of his life." She said she had no such intention. Not only did she charge him with nonsupport again, but accused him of physical abuse. Living then on her own, she enrolled the children at a settlement house day nursery and continued to work.[82]

This story includes elements common to many of the family records. As outsiders, caseworkers often and openly criticized the distribution of employment, time, and money in a family and questioned the earnestness of a search for work. Men *did* wear out shoe leather hunting unsuccessfully for jobs, and many held a series of positions—seemingly unrelated—except that all were low skill and poorly paid. And men deserted and abused their families, whether driven to violence by the demoralization of their own situations, by inclination of character, or by the "rights" of men in a male-dominated society.[83] Women pitched in to cope with situations as they arose and kept *re*-determining what was acceptable and what had to change.

Wage work carried no shame, but when exhausted, women's willingness to push onward came from commitment to children more than to husbands. Pressing charges against a man rarely released a woman from the labor market but illustrated that women set boundaries as to what could be endured for how long. To be a wage earner gave a woman a greater sense of her right to demand that a husband "do his part," but the inadequate wages available to these women belied the possibility of true "independence" for them.[84]

A small group spoke clearly of the liberty they felt in wage earning. Mrs. T. moved from Pipestone, Minnesota, to Minneapolis after being deserted. The staff at AC/FWA contacted the Pipestone Red Cross for further information and learned that "Mr. James T. [the woman's brother-in-law still in Pipestone] says the trouble arose between Caroline and her husband because he was lazy and she was a hustler." She had not wanted to stay there with a child and live with relatives; instead "she wanted to support herself if possible and be independent." Having become an urban working woman in the city, Caroline complained to an agent about her cleaning wages. "She thought she should be paid more, as the men who were doing the work [scrubbing walls in an institution] were getting $8 to $10 a day."[85]

Particularly for immigrant women the potential of self-assertion through paid work seemed to come as a new discovery. One explained:

> The condition of women had been different in the old country. There they were expected to do all the chores, black their husbands shoes, and do absolutely as he demanded. When she came to this country Mrs. D.'s sister told her she should not do these things any longer, but should insist upon her rights as her husband's equal. This Mrs. D. had done with the result that her husband had apparently turned against her and there was constant friction. . . . She thought she would take the 2 children and go off by herself and earn her living. . . . She had put an ad in the paper [asking for a housekeeping position] and had had many responses to it, most of the men, however, . . . wanted a housekeeper with the idea that they would marry later. Mrs. D. said that she had told them she wanted a job, not a man.[86]

Consciously and with great delight a few women identified themselves not only as wage earners, but as women whose work would enable them to get along without men. These declarations about economic self-reliance apart from marriage, however, were rare, with the strongest such statements coming from women in cases opened in the latter period 1920–30. As shown in Table 11, the majority of women in cases suggested that they were working to *compensate* for a man's irregular employment or for his absence from home rather than striking off on their own.

Most working women did not step out of the context of family; they continued to be related to men and—by choice and in necessity—their roles as parents were prominent. When the records offered details of women's relationships with coworkers at hotels, laundries, or factories, their comments and actions centered around their family. A woman might have made clear to co-workers that she worried about her children

Table 11
Circumstances Surrounding Women's Work Experiences*
in 300 Case Records

Women working	
while husband absent owing to	
death	61
temporary absence from home	56
desertion	48
divorce	25
husband present though	
ill	34
underemployed/unemployed	34
nonsupporting	23

SOURCE: 300 Case Records, FCS Collection.

*One woman's work experience could be represented in more than one figure; for example, a woman might first work because her husband was ill and then after his death continue to do so; thus the case would be represented twice. These figures, therefore, do not show the total number of working women (for this see table 9), but indicate the frequency of various situations as identified and reported in the records.

and wanted more time for them, or a surprise baby shower was planned, or money collected for a crisis at home. Paid work also increased women's reliance on female friends and relatives who occasionally shared jobs by going to work together or on alternate days. More often, women used one another for child care. Regardless of their time spent working and hunting for employment, women identified themselves primarily as being wives and mothers, not laborers. Necessity—not independence—motivated their temporary and permanent efforts as supporting heads of household.[87]

Conclusion

Commercial and industrial expansion in the early twentieth century promised national prosperity but produced instead an upward spiral in the cost of living that was dollars ahead of working-class wages. Minneapolis was no exception, and regional development created an ongoing labor surplus that converged in the city and left a shortage of jobs for skilled as well as unskilled workers. Across the thirty years of this study, lower-class men who faced unemployment and inadequate wages were in a sorry state to support dependents. When they left their families through death, divorce, desertion, or nonsupport, wives had little choice but to step into the wage-earning role. National statistics showed a minority of women in the labor force, but among lower-class women, wage work was well-known. Even its meager earnings had the potential of keeping a family together.

Finding employment enabled women to carry through on basic responsibility to children and home, but women assumed dual roles at sacrifice to their own health. The jobs that kept them on their feet, lifting and bending, literally wore women out, and rest was often an unattainable luxury complicated by the need for maintaining child care. Yet to outsiders willing to criticize, overworked women appeared to jeopardize both children and marriages by behavior that violated female roles.

Caseworkers at AC/FWA knew the dire poverty existing in certain households and because the agency was unprepared to substitute continuing or adequate relief as remedy, an employment bureau had been created and was much used by women. But social workers themselves reinforced the proposition that women's employment was of secondary importance. The first page in each case record allowed equal space for specification of female and male occupations; this was filled in briefly for only 79 of the women although 170 of them earned wages during involvement with AC/FWA. They noted a woman's use of the employment bureau which was taken as a good sign of her initiative, but paid minimal attention to defining and describing where she worked or under what conditions. The long hours a woman put in cleaning, washing, and waiting on others, go almost unmentioned in the case records. It is also true, however, that the work experience of most females had little to commend attention.

The skills most women drew on were those used daily at home without pay. All over the country domestic and personal service positions were similar—being done at the employer's whim for wages scarcely allowing minimal living. Yet regardless of many women's desire to avoid such day work, little evidence suggested they turned down these jobs or challenged their wages as many females assumed it was natural to receive less remuneration than men. None of the jobs described in the records paid enough to provide a woman margin for the self-conscious pleasure of power over a budget.[88]

When women spoke of employment, "necessity" was the context and within that two laments—that too few jobs were available, and that work was hard and that their strength was limited. Employment of wives and mothers could be primary to a family's economic survival, but it was *not* the arena in which many of these women appeared to assert their rights or to reflect on alternatives.[89] This latter behavior was much more evident in relationships with men and with the institution of marriage. Chapter 4 details the complexity of matrimony with the issue of *male* earning as a point of substantial conflict between husband and wife.

4

Women as Wives: "Only a Face in the Wedding Picture"

"Here some woman is trying to do the work of 2, trying to be both father and mother to the children and too often being unable to do either adequately."[1] This concern in the agency's 1910 *Annual Report* focused on widows whose status as single parents and household heads resulted from circumstances beyond their own control. Regardless, however, of what caused a woman to become a single parent, her ability to *defy* middle-class mores of female dependency in marriage meant survival for her children. Yet the necessity of going to work quickly translated into exhaustion with little relief from hard times. Many women affirmed the practical alternative of remarriage.[2] In announcing plans for her future, a widow "coquettishly laughed and said that she was [getting married]. She said that she had a 'good man' who had a steady job and who worked seven days out of every week."[3] While lower-class women equated a "man's place" with support of wife and children, experience had also taught many of them another reality, that security via a man was temporary and illusive, that matrimony was fluid and filled with problems.

Many marriages began and continued under stress. During a social worker's first visit, a woman explained to her that five years earlier she had gotten pregnant by her employer in a housekeeping position. They had married and "her life since had not been very happy." She explained that she had "been obliged" to work much of the time; the agent noted that she seemed "a rather nervous woman, yet tried to have patience with the children."[4] Other couples' marriages moved toward dangerous crescendos. "She said he was very cruel to her, that the other day when she had been sick and lying upon the lounge, he came in and told her to get up or else go to her mother's, and threatened that if she did not do one of these things he would kill her even if he had to go to Stillwater [Minnesota state prison] for the rest of his life for it."[5]

On the first page of most records an inscription indicated whether the applicant was or was not in an intact marriage, but this labeling was deceptive as the status of a woman and household shifted. In conversation a fifth of all women spoke longingly of times in the past when a husband had been alive or well, had had regular work and his own set of tools, or had brought his wages home rather than spending them on liquor. A mysterious resilience held some couples together through years of penury, discouragement, and bad faith, while other marriages halted temporarily in desertion or separation, or permanently with death or divorce, and new spouses appeared. Structurally and emotionally, marital standing changed, frequently causing women to invest their energy in the shifting relationships. And the women in many cases implied that they deserved better.

The Bending and Breaking of Marriage Bonds

Death and divorce permanently altered women's marital statuses, but in addition to desertion, a husband in prison or a state asylum, searching for a job, or working away from the city could set conjugal relations awry.[6] Table 12 illustrates volatility in women's lives by comparing marital status at the opening and closing of each record.

When cases are divided by time of opening, 1900 through 1910 and 1920 through 1930, as shown in Table 13, the ending of marriages reflects broad American social trends. Chronic illness, tuberculosis, pneumonia, and childbirth, as well as fatal industrial accidents, all had disproportionately claimed the poor at the turn of the century, but lessened in frequency by the "modern" 1920s.[7] In Minneapolis—as across the country—improved health translated into a decrease of marital unions ending with demise of a spouse; in this study that number fell from 57 among the first case families, to 36 among the later ones. Simultaneously, however, the number of marriages closed through divorce increased; in Hennepin County, which was dominated by the city of Minneapolis, the 1890 divorce rate of 78 per 100,000 almost quadrupled by 1920. Divorce in this study occurred among 15 of the cases opened in 1900–1910, a rate of 1 in 10. Among the cases opened in 1920–30, 26 divorces happened, involving almost 1 woman in 6. Desertion—rarely so final as death or divorce—recurred steadily among households through these decades and sent a constant flow of anxious women to the attention of AC/FWA.[8]

Changes in the opportunity and dangers of twentieth-century society altered *why* a woman's marriage might end. Timing *internal* to families—the age of children and what that suggested about parents' age

Table 12
Change in Women's Marital Status from Time of Case Opening to Time of Case Closing in 300 Case Records

	Women Who Began Case with Status	Women Who Shifted from Status during Case	Women Who Ended Case with Status
Married, by civil and common law	120	73	91
Divorced*	19	NA	41
Deserted	64	NA	38
Separated by man's institutionalization and other misc. reasons	37	NA	33
Widowed	60	49	73
Women deceased during case	0	0	20
Women institutionalized and status unclear	0	0	4
Total	300	122	300

SOURCE: 300 Case Records, FCS Collection.

*In searching the records initially for a sample of female-headed households where events other than death caused a spouse's absence, divorce, desertion, and separation were all options; in column 1 the exact number of each was a function of the varying frequency with which these situations appeared within the case records established at AC/FWA. For more about the system of selecting records for examination here see the Introduction.

and length of marriage—also affected household dynamics. The case records indicate that the youthfulness of both youngsters and parents worked against stability; children's material and emotional dependency could too easily upset marital equilibrium. In half the households with young ones and in almost that many homes with adolescents, the mother was the constant figure and a father was present only irregularly. However, within older marriages—as indicated by the presence of grown children—only a quarter of the husbands moved into and out of the family while the case record was open. Additional years worked as a sieve; the demands of children were lessened, and the difficulties of living together had been resolved or accepted. Increased age not only

Table 13
Change in Women's Marital Status by Time of Case Opening in 300 Case Records

	All Case Openings	Case Opening 1900–1910	Case Closing 1900–1910	Case Opening 1920–1930	Case Closing 1920–1930
Married by civil or common law	120	60	40	60	51
Divorced	19	5	15	14	26
Deserted	64	34	19	30	19
Separated					
by man's institutionalization	12	8	6	4	6
by man's work search	4	3	2	1	1
by misc. reasons	21	10	9	11	9
Widowed	60	30	44	30	29
Woman deceased during case	0	0	13	0	7
Woman institutionalized during case	0	0	2	0	2
Total	300	150	150	150	150

SOURCE: 300 Case Records, FCS Collection.

reduced the inclination to part company but limited the number of alternative marital partners that women encountered. Young women, however, actively responded to broken nuptial bonds by remarriage.

Women reentered the marriage market subject to various public perceptions. The poor but honest widow was a favorite heroine in Romantic literature, in contrast to a woman's gaining independence through divorce and perceived as "adulterous" or "selfish" and seeking freedom for sexuality.[9] But both women faced disadvantages in attempting to survive on their own, and to seek or accept a husband was a primary and obvious strategy. Over a tenth of the 300 women were *already* in a second marriage when a social worker at AC/FWA first opened a case record on them. Another 18 remarried while known to the agency, making a total of almost one-fifth of the women who married twice. A few did so three and four times. National statistics from the first decades show approximately three-fifths of the divorced and widowed population remarried, and the majority—like these women—did so within a few years.[10]

Only fragments of the courtship process can be found in the records. It is likely that not all the claimed marriages had been authorized by civil law—a condition that troubled social workers. In this study, however, classification of people as "married" relies on what they said, although agents were less accepting. By the 1920s, casework at AC/FWA demanded systematic verification of marriage licenses at the courthouse. On being confronted or nagged about legal bonds and past relationships with men, a woman commonly would snub the worker's inquiries and inferences about sexuality. An agent recorded, "Called Mrs. V.'s attention to the fact that Agnes was 12 years, and she told visitor that her husband had died 16 years ago. Mrs. V. then said, 'A woman can have more than one husband can't she?'"

Women spoke defensively about their right to join with a man by civil or common law. However, the affection or romance with which some described a first decision to marry was often brushed aside as women attempted a second time to weigh the merits of a future spouse. Too frequently the marital problems that first had plagued a wife reappeared, or new troubles replaced the old. The same Mrs. V. who asserted that women could marry twice was quoted in the record that she had "whipped" Agnes's father years before, and he took off leaving no word behind.[11] Another widow, Mrs. C., explained her marriage to a man she did not love, declaring, "He made all sorts of promises."

> He was in good health and had always been able to make good wages and so was amply able to take care of her and her children . . . saying he would educate the children and see that she would never want for anything. . . . Soon after they were married he gave up his job there [working in a lunchroom] and had never had a steady job afterwards. Mrs. C. had had to work and support him and her own family. . . . The last of April he left the house saying that he . . . was going to church and had never been seen or heard from since.

Like many deserting husbands, Mr. C. eventually contacted his wife, sending her a card from California saying, "Hello, Kiddo, hope you are well old girl." He offered to send her money for the trip out West but made no mention of her children. She responded by telling the agent that he was "worthless" and she intended to forget both him and his note.[12] Another widowed mother admitted: "She knew very well that looks weren't everything. She had taken her first husband because he was good looking and then found out afterward that he drank very badly.

He used to make quite a fuss at home." After bouts of beating her, he died a violent drunken death, and she disappeared until eight years later when the case reopened. She was then cleaning an office building six hours a day for $1.25 a week and spoke of a second husband who "did not drink nor have any particularly bad habits but she considered he was not capable in handling money for he did not have much initiative in doing anything and was satisfied with the wages he got."[13]

Regardless of personal satisfaction or discontent with their own marriages, women of all ages in these records agreed implicitly or explicitly on men's economic role and obligations. A husband or father's commitment to working was taken as basic verification of decency and good faith. In expecting an industrious husband, poor women in Minneapolis unknowingly aligned themselves with the middle class, which also defined economic support as central to men's role. When the sociologists Helen and Robert Lynd listened to working-class families in Muncie for their 1920s study titled *Middletown,* they too found the nineteenth-century consensus about gender roles holding strong with "emphasis on the function of man as good provider and woman as homemaker and child rearer." In most states, marriage laws enforced the requirement of male financial responsibility. Many legal codes also expected husband and wife to live together in sexual exclusivity, being sober, moral, and with a "consideration" precluding "cruel treatment."[14] But instead of wedded happiness as defined by custom or the law, the violation of marriage expectations spotted the three hundred records.

When the Household Head Fails to Support

Part of the cause for marital problems lay in the environment; the historian Arthur Calhoun wrote in 1919 that the "ideal family" had probably never existed, but the "capitalist system" with low wages and unpredictable employment was a "menace" to current family survival.[15] Not only were resources for housekeeping strained when a husband earned insufficiently, but living with an unemployed man usually meant that a woman had to cope with his discouragement and potential anger.[16] A middle-aged railroad man sitting at home bleakly explained his own sense of obsolescence that made a job search pointless and family life tense.

> They [the railroad companies] did not have the necessity for car repairing that they had formerly had as the cars were so much better built . . . consequently there was no hope he would ever be re-employed in that dept. . . . He said that the Marquette Emp. [Employ-

> ment] Agency was a regular riot. The men were lined up for 2 blocks outside of it.[17]

In one-sixth of the families the husband passed long periods of time at home owing to just such a dismal employment picture, his condition often exacerbated by ill health. While these conditions brought gloom into a household, difficult times could also be the framework in which wives showed loyalty and sacrifice for mates. The case records carried little evidence that women spoke of affection within their marriages—except in past tense—nor did they expect the "companionate marriage" touted by a youthful middle class.[18] But some wives, with their own physical strength waning from overwork, sat up nights with men too sick to sleep and tried to buy medicine and comply with prescribed diets. A very young woman whose husband was succumbing to TB believed his collapse related to working "too hard" in the cold without proper clothing, and she worked to guarantee that his last days and burial were better.

> When she realized that there was no hope for him she felt she would like to do all she could for him and then had spent the money that she had on little delicacies of food and other things which he asked for. She had wanted him to be nicely dressed when he was buried and she had bot [bought] a few little things and some underclothes.[19]

Other women begged agents for a man's coat or added hours on their own jobs in order to buy shoes for a husband's job hunt or a used suit—because worn overalls were all that he had. A few men likewise expressed concern over a wife's health fearing that she would "break down" with detriment not only to herself, but to the neglect of family income and child care. No comments in these cases, however, reflected a husband's reciprocal attention to his wife's need for clothing nor to the demands small children made on her, though by the 1920s a few men insisted to an agent that the wife needed false teeth or that her "broken plate" be repaired.

Only when men were at home during the day did social workers have the opportunity to glimpse the interaction of husbands and wives. Among the few men observed, some seemed to have receded in decision making, at least in regard to dealing with an agent from the local charity. Women answered inquiries about family credit and debts and listed places the man had worked and for how long. But social work's commitment to traditional gender roles made agents impatient with the competent wife who seemed protective of an unemployed husband. "Mrs. S.

seemed very naturally to assume the burden of support and was quite anxious to shield her husband."

Family dynamics could and did change. A wife who took any job available would initially commiserate with her husband who did not want to accept menial work. As time passed, however, the wife might join an agent in distrusting the cause of male unemployment. Wives vacillated between believing their spouses earnestly sought jobs and questioning their complete willingness to work.[20] Certain discouraged men *did* stop treading from factory gate to employment bureau; others lost the desire to maintain jobs offering small return and sought the solace of a bottle or male company at the corner saloon.[21] Some husbands, without telling their wives, found work but spent their wages on other women while wives at home worried about rent. These men were the "nonsupporters" that Mary Richmond wrote about as "married vagabonds," worse than tramps, for they violated sacred principles intrinsic in marriage and created "sham homes."[22]

At some point in married life, almost a quarter of the three hundred women faced the insecurity brought on by a husband judged to be "nonsupporting," a behavior that took many forms. One husband would be "too slow" finding work after an illness; another would willfully refuse to share income with his family.[23] The wife who complained about a man who could—but would not—seek wages and use them for his family, was backed up not only by social mores, but by state laws in many parts of the country.

Minnesota courts did not consider nonsupport illegal or immoral enough to be grounds for divorce, but this behavior *did* constitute a breach of family ideals that threatened the public good. In 1901 a man's willful failure to feed, clothe, and shelter his family was adjudged a felony carrying up to three years' imprisonment, but this strong law had weaknesses. Convictions were few, and in the next few years the legal definition of punishable behavior was reduced to a misdemeanor. While poor wives suffered the consequences of men's actions, lawmakers and reformers debated whether nonsupport of one's family was a civil or criminal matter. Should the court attempt foremost to guarantee family support or to punish the man? After what length of time did nonsupport become desertion, which *was* a felony subject to being tried in district court? And how should a wife's own testimony figure in the legal actions—was it one piece of evidence or the only means by which criminal procedures could begin?[24]

Wives as well as judges and social workers realized that a man locked up in the workhouse continued to deprive his family of income, further straining the limited resources of both families and charities. As alternative strategy in 1913, the judge of the Minneapolis municipal court sentenced men brought to trial for nonsupport but recommended probation when they promised to do better. The court claimed to have "reconciled" 75 percent of guilty husbands who went on to correct their own errors but rehabilitation was complicated if the man not only failed to provide support, but spent his days and nights in a local saloon.[25]

"He Was All Right When He Didn't Drink, Otherwise He Was Cruel and Abusive"

Taverns functioned as neighborhood institutions offering working-class men food and drink as well as companionship and information about jobs. During a discussion at an AC/FWA board meeting in 1916, members acknowledged that the saloon was a source of "relief and recreation from the deadly monotony of the unskilled labor's task." But those present noted, too, that drunkenness existed at times of both employment and unemployment with deleterious effects on home and family.[26] Drinking was often the violent side of nonsupport; many wives who faced one problem dealt with the other as well.[27] A woman explained, "Her husband drank heavily every Saturday usually spending about $4.00 but [she] preferred to stay with him for the sake of the children." Two months later in early January she was "found washing. Said her husband got paid December 24 and had been drunk all day Christmas."[28] One-fifth of all three hundred wives told similar stories. Employers verified reports of men too drunk to work, or too often absent from the job. "He used to work for the Flour City Transfer where he was fired on account of getting drunk. . . . He tells that he has been drinking since he was a mere child." Neighbors offered details of drunken behavior, and some reported more detailed stories, that husband and wife together had created the pile of empty beer bottles in the alley. Most wives, however, appeared to be onlookers, feeling impotent to change men's habits and reestablish access to his wages. The following exchanges took place in one record over a period of two years:

> Agent asks her about #1's drinking [a teamster who had lost his job because of drunkenness]. She said it was second nature to him as he had done it from a child up. Told that he got two cans of beer Saturday brought them home. Not in the habit of drinking in saloons. #2 is pregnant again.
>
> #2 says that #1 has done better this summer than he has for years. Is drinking very little.

> She comes for baby clothes, says #1 has been kind, "does not now drink."
>
> Man said he had been out of work now about two weeks. . . . Visitor asked if he had been drunk and this had been the cause. He looked rather shifty and said, no, it was not the cause on this occasion, said he had not been drinking much lately, seemed willing to talk about this.
>
> Said she had never known anything about drink til she married her husband.[29]

A few wives speculated aloud as to why a husband drank; had it been learned in childhood—as this woman thought—or was it the influence of "bad friends?" Most women spoke only in comparative terms, that he was drinking "more"—perhaps after the birth of another baby or after the loss of a job, or he was drinking "less"—after chastisement from the priest. Women wanted and needed men to stop; they would look hopefully for signs that the husband was changing and would implore a brother, employer, or the social worker to "scare him into not drinking."

While many problems facing poor women were theirs alone, the issue of alcohol and the frantic hope for some solution put them in a hundred years' of company not only with other wives but with male and female social reformers. Intemperance was a national problem, and from the early nineteenth century people had organized voluntarily—and with little success—to separate men from the bottle and in doing so to save wives and children from drunkards' cruelty.[30] Social work professionals recognized the heavy repercussions of alcohol on family life and documented drinking, seemingly more concerned that it dimmed possibilities of economic self-sufficiency than that it put family members in danger of abuse.[31] At the municipal court the same judge who placed nonsupporters on probation called on men to make vows of abstinence and frequently demanded that the wages of a drinking husband be turned automatically over to a probation officer or wife.[32] However, "No one thing can be laid down as the cause or cure of inebriety," concluded the AC/FWA director in 1907. "We must treat him as a composite man, because he is influenced by so many different things on the outside."[33]

No one truly understood why some men imbibed to drunkenness and what would save them, but Prohibition seemed to promise a halt to liquor traffic. Statistics showed that police arrests for drunkenness in Minneapolis fell following ratification of the Eighteenth Amendment in 1919, and one of the state's new "inebriate hospitals" closed.[34] In AC/FWA case records, the number of wives complaining of drunken husbands was only half as great in 1920–30 as it had been in 1900–

1910—prior to Prohibition. Agents applauded the decline, but were skeptical that men were truly so malleable and immune to the lure of moonshine. In an anecdote titled "Optimist"on page 1 of a 1920 agency newsletter, the widow of an Irishman who died with delirium tremens bemoaned to the staff at AC/FWA, "If me poor Jim had lived 'til pro'bition came he moight 'uv reformed before he died."[35] In spite of the legal prohibition, drinking continued. Saloons located next to employment bureaus along the river and railroad tracks reopened as soft drink parlors featuring moonshine in the back room. In St. Paul the liquor syndicate became a regional conduit for Cuban rum and Canadian whiskey.[36]

Distilling moonshine carried lucrative entrepreneurial possibilities, not only for the rich but the poor as well. A few women saw this opportunity and turned kitchens into distilleries and bar rooms; during a home visit an agent would determine that the "house had odor of mash," an ingredient in liquor. When police investigated they too would catch the odor but find "no evidence of moonshine." Such disregard for the law threatened the community, but city reformers also feared "the moral conditions which result from such arrangements often cause serious domestic trouble."[37] A few men and women spent time in jail for liquor enterprising, but those imbibing the products of makeshift stills also suffered repercussions. Homemade liquor exacerbated the weakness or illness already afflicting certain men, and their wives found little solace in the new laws.

> He has been drinking moonshine lately. Before Prohibition was always a heavy drinker, but she finds the moonshine makes him almost crazy at times. She has pleaded with him many time to quit this and support his family rt. [right], and not to be a bad example to them but it never did any good. It resulted in his getting very angry and she thinks this is prob. [probably] why he left.

Six months later this deserted woman spoke again about her marriage, saying "she looked better and felt better now than before her husband left her, because when he was home he scared them all the time."[38]

Not all nonsupporters drank, and not all drunkards abused their wives. In these records, however, unemployment, job insecurity, and the meager contents of a wage envelope translated into a shortage of material resources that alcohol could fuel into quarrels between a man and woman. Within a society that assumed and applauded male domination, domestic arguments about how to allocate slim resources were often resolved by brute force.[39] A victimized wife more frequently drew public attention to her husband's failure to support—a lapse in his moral obligation—than to his "cruelty," for society attributed economic responsibility but not conjugal violence to men. Though "cruelty"—the phrase at the time—began to replace adultery as the most common ground for divorce in the twentieth century, it frequently was a commiserating relative or a neighbor who first shared a woman's pain and informed an agent, "He treats her cruelly."[40] One-sixth of the three hundred women eventually spoke of threats, blows, and of being afraid. Some were women who on earlier occasions had defended their husbands, and the records showed marriages deteriorating in stages.

Thirty-nine women spoke specifically about husbands "changing"; they had not always lived with nonsupport, drunkenness, cruelty, infidelity, or with a man who was "crazy" and ranted around the house threatening to kill others or himself.[41] A dramatic fusion of these elements appear in excerpts from a lengthy record in which the woman ultimately sought relief in divorce, but the agency initially got involved when the man lost a job owing to drunkenness.

> 1907—[The landlord reported] #1 drinks and gambles and is out late every night, then in the day #1 and #2 stay in bed with shades drawn. #2 recently emerged with a black eye but still clings to #1. . . . When #41 [landlord] asked #2 what they were living on she said "love" and that they were bringing #3 up on it.
>
> 1912—[AC/FWA wrote to another agency about the family and this assessment came back.] It is difficult to accomplish much with such a family as the wife defends the husband's attitude [referring to drinking and gambling].
>
> 1914—[#2 sent a note to AC/FWA asking for help two weeks before Christmas, it read:] Just when he need work worst he was lay off and hasnt found work since has look all over and is willing to work at [any] thing for as little as a dollar and 1/2 day or anything but can't fine none. So if you can possibly help us I would be very happy.
>
> 1915—[Agent reported meeting with the couple.] [husband] had not found work but knew it was no use trying. . . . Man walked up and down floor hurtling accusations at world in gen. [general] and AC . . . Woman has been clerking since man's dismissal . . . explained that man had no training whatever, could not read or write, could not even distinguish street car signs. . . . Man had always refused to go to night school because he feared jeers of younger men. Agent advised man to visit NE Neigh Ho [North East Neighborhood House] for Eng. instruct. He seemed anxious to avail himself of [this] oppty.
>
> 1922—Father [husband] has not lived with her since Sept. In July she had him in court for assault and battery and very soon afterward for non-support. He is on Probation now to Mr. F. at the Court House.

> 1922—Mother had father arrested for non-support, he was given thirty days, became disorderly in court so sentence was increased to ninety days. Before the expiration of the term mother [his wife] secured his release; he was told to keep away from mother but he has not done so, he has gone there and "raved" a great deal, constantly threatens to kill mother, and to kill John [#3].
>
> 1923—Mother had filed papers for divorce—3–23 was divorced. . . . Father was not paying alimony, but Mother was not going to bother him. Everything is going all right, so case may be closed.[42]

The Frequency of Violence and Infidelity

Throughout the thirty years of this study, women's inferences and stories about sexual estrangement, violence, and infidelity greatly outnumbered saucy assertions about "living on love" behind drawn shades. Men's sexual demands carried the threat of pregnancy to women, but in cases where females expressed this fear, records show conception nonetheless, suggesting men's physical dominance at home regardless of their economic status in the community beyond.[43] A few women described their own rebellion against the expectation that they dutifully submit; intimacy with drunkards repulsed them, and one complained: "Mr. P. had had 5 baths in 18 mos. She refused to live with him as his wife."[44] Other female objections to sexual claims or abuse appeared in more vague statements such as, "Her husband's demands for intercourse were entirely impos. [impossible]." Agents wrote such comments into records but without further qualification, because of their own unwillingness to delve into family relationships, or because of unspoken agreement among social workers and wives as to what was meant by "impos. [impossible]."[45]

Some women feared the contagion of venereal disease through sex with spouses, and medical reports in a limited number of cases suggested transfer of infection. A few mothers blamed children's congenital health problems on the husbands' disease and immorality with prostitutes. Social workers were alert to telltale physical symptoms of syphilis in their concern for public hygiene and social purity.[46] Men's sexual power at home also carried the potential of child molestation, but incest was a problem that Minneapolis social workers referred to the Humane Society/Children's Protective Society rather than AC/FWA. Therefore these case records included very few references to this, presenting it occasionally as fear rather than fact, a hint only in second marriages where a stranger moved into a home with youngsters. The mother of adolescent and grown children related the dilemma of her own situation.

> She had been happy with Mr. O. until 8 wks. after their marriage when he had been arrested for indecent exposure. He had insisted to her that he had not been guilty but pled guilty at court. This had almost killed her and she had felt such extreme repugnance for him since that time that she could scarcely live with him. For over a year she had had no relations with him and absolutely never would again. She was approaching her change of life and was nervous and upset fearing that she would go into a decline. . . . Mrs. O. hated him and simply waited for the time when she could get away from him. . . . The children hated Mr. O. . . . Altho he was disagreeable towards the daughter he had never done anything objectionable and Mrs. O. watched him closely.[47]

Mothers could be fearful and watchful, but lacked much power to protect their own children except by leaving with them.[48]

Far more often than making references to sexual fears, women spoke of a general dread of physical abuse. Their vulnerability and the need to escape husbands and fathers appeared in phrases such as being "scared of him" and "we [wife and children] ran from the house." Forty-two women lived with men who were charged with combinations of drunkenness, fighting, cruelty, "immorality," and theft, but these wives confronted the daily dilemmas of domestic violence without overt expression of concern from most social workers or AC/FWA. While agents regularly asked wives: "Is he looking for work," or: "Is #1 still drinking?" the records failed to indicate that agents conscientiously questioned: "Is he still beating—threatening—or scaring you?" The staff at family casework agencies paid minimal attention to this issue as compared to the monitoring they did of men's drinking or men's willingness to bring home wages. In this arena poor women were denied conscientious "professional" assistance and were left largely to solve their own problems or submit to victimization.

Among the personal indignities and violence that some husbands inflicted on poor women, infidelity was the practice most broadly acknowledged in community gossip. Adultery rarely seemed the hidden sin that abuse or incest could be. Observers included neighbors and relatives who talked to social workers who wrote in turn, "He's a rake," or "he spends money on other women." Some wives denied this was true, but more could supply details; they knew the other woman to be a waitress in a local café, a neighbor, or the sister of his friend. And wives resented that "all his wages for the past two years have gone to buy finery for her." Almost 10 percent of the three hundred women made such accusations, and a few described bigamy. On occasion a furious wife confronted the lovers or called the police to do so as men flaunted disregard for their families' economic plight. Some of the unfaithful men escaped challenge by leaving the city with the new companion.

Agents at AC/FWA assumed that casework efforts strengthened decency and morality in Minneapolis, but their own priority and expertise was to promote development of a family's economic self-sufficiency. Nonsupport could cause a woman to come in for material relief, and drunkenness could lead to unemployment, but cruelty—in spite of its frequency—was "private" and without direct economic repercussion. Thus, regardless of the pain to adult females, the social workers in these records appeared quietly oblivious. The deserted wife, unlike the beaten women, however, was a common topic of conversation among social workers. A husband's and father's willful abandonment of his family vexed social reformers far more than women's physical victimization.

What Kind of Man Would Abandon His Home?

The husband who failed to support his wife was guilty of a simple misdemeanor under Minnesota statues, but the deserter was a felon who could be extradited across state lines. In spite of the possibility of punishment, a number of "natural breadwinners" left their Minneapolis homes without word to wives and children. Their male counterparts did likewise throughout the country, which caused reformers and charity workers to define this cavalier disregard of duty as a "growing evil" that warranted professional scrutiny. Not only did desertion create economic problems for individual women who might call on assistance from agency coffers, but when men behaved in that manner they violated the natural order of moral responsibility inherent in gender roles.[49] When those in social welfare focused on the problem, analysis of male behavior elicited professional curiosity to a far greater extent than the survival of those left behind. While charity work was overwhelmingly an enterprise between female social workers and female clients, with desertion the missing husbands were put on center stage.

Mary Richmond first drew attention to desertion at the National Conference of Charities and Correction in 1895. During the next several years social welfare advocates took it up regularly when they met.[50] At AC/FWA the 1913 *Annual Report* claimed, "The men who have failed to support their families [are], the central task of the charity," meaning that men must be made to resume family responsibilities and to lessen women's dependency on others.[51] The first step, however, was to understand those men who walked out of their homes without warning, for a caseworker's only acquaintance with the missing spouse might be limited to an earlier glimpse of him in a back room, or in a wedding picture. To aid in this research, workers organized statistical tables quantifying the characteristics of deserters and their families. Some large COS compiled detailed studies giving little attention to the fact that middle-class men also deserted.[52]

In 1903 a special committee at the Philadelphia COS constructed a classification of deserter types and the appropriate response to them. In "Spurious" desertion a man and woman connived together to create the appearance of separation in order to win unwarranted charity. Such a family deserved little financial support, but the "Reclaimable" deserter loved his family and could be made to see and accept his duty. The "Un-get-at-able" man had gone too far away too long ago to merit attention, and likewise the "Chronic" deserter who came home but left again was to be ignored. In some households fault was seen to lay with the wife—her own offensive behavior, slovenliness, and perhaps intemperance, had driven away the "Half-excusable" deserter.[53] When middle-class ladies in the Minneapolis AC/FWA Friendly Visiting Committee considered "Treatment of Deserted Wives" in 1912, the guest speaker Courtenay Dinwiddie, general secretary of AC in Duluth, Minnesota, employed this set of morality laden concepts to explain the desertion taking place in northern Minnesota.[54]

Sociological explanations over the next several years depicted deserters themselves as victims. A study from the University of Chicago pointed to the "spirit of discontent" in urban anonymity and isolation that encouraged some husbands to depart. Young men in "ill-advised" shotgun marriages were simply running from commitments they never sought. The "Gradual" deserter left his family to search for work and then began thinking less and less about home as weeks away lengthened into months.[55] The relationship between working-class men's employment and their flight perplexed many; some studies showed the chronic or intermittent deserter to be younger and more able-bodied than the general lower-class male population.[56] Dinwiddie had noted these characteristics among deserters from Duluth, and a series of articles in the AC/FWA *Bulletin* lamented the apparent "industrial capacity" of male deserters in Minneapolis. "Contrary to all expectations," a large number of the men were "capable of earning at least $18 a week and some considerably more." Such facts seemingly confused an easy analysis of what went wrong in a home.[57]

Researchers who had extended experience with family casework saw men as immature in avoiding accountability. Lilian Brandt from the New York City COS noted how the "desertion habit" took hold of young men just before or after the birth of another baby, after a serious quarrel with the wife, or after trouble with the law. "If he returns the probability is that he will leave again whenever it suits his convenience. . . ."[58] Before Joanna Colcord came to direct the Minneapolis AC/FWA, she had published *Broken Homes*—a study of desertion based on New York City families—and she dismissed direct correlation between low income and desertion. Instead Colcord had seen a series of interrelated "presignals" that identified families in danger. The woman who worked for wages while her husband spent hours in the neighborhood tavern or found a "woman friend" down the street, could easily find herself deserted. And according to Colcord, marriages became most vulnerable after three to five years when the call of "carefree youth" beckoned. "By this time there are usually one or two babies, the wife's girlish charm had gone, and the romance of the first attraction has vanished, and the steady force of conjugal affection that should smooth their path through the years ahead has not come to take its place . . . [the] last bit of gilt crumbles off the gingerbread."[59] When these men departed, according to Colcord, it was not the equivalent of divorce, but of "vacation" or "self-therapy." Years of casework had taught her, "There are few things less permanent than desertion."[60] Wives knew this best.

Marriage to a Deserter

More than one-third of the 300 women in these cases knew intimately what kind—or kinds—of men deserted. For older women, desertion was frequently an experience remembered from the past; their marriages had since altered for better or worse. For younger women with small children, desertion created a current crisis. Sixty-four of the 300 wives first came to the AC/FWA office needing help to handle the aftermath of problems created by a disappearing husband. A worker would record, "She was very anxious to talk about her husband." With desertion more than any other family occurrence, friends and relatives were likely to accompany the woman in requesting aid, acting in acknowledgement that she had been wronged, and that she both needed and deserved assistance. Reflecting this same sympathy, the corner grocer, a visiting nurse, or the city Poor Department were all more likely to extend support to the young deserted wife and mother than to any other class of potential clients. Such assistance was in demand—for even while casework was underway in 25 conjugally *intact* households, the husband took off. "She says he left last night. "

Among these husbands in the Minneapolis case records only a few abandoned steady skilled jobs. Equal numbers were young and middle-aged, but the "presignals" that Colcord identified had plagued many homes. Desertion exaggerated the unpredictability and insecurity that a man's nonsupport and drinking already had brought home, and wives identified unwanted pregnancy and quarrels as precipitants to flight. An unattributed poem in the 1917 AC/FWA *Bulletin* reflected this painful combination of domestic issues with its opening lines:

The Deserter

Her world had crashed about her, all she knew
Was that her man had left her in a rage,
Growling, "Another Kid!" and then was gone,
Had left his job and them, what could she do?
Her scrubbing might have brought a meager wage,
Or washing at the tubs from early dawn
Till dark would pay the rent and something more,
But another one had come, and she,
She could not understand, all was a blur.[61]

The man who expected sex as part of the marriage contract was not always prepared to be responsible for the baby that followed—even when his wife might be ready to assist economically, to take jobs charring or doing laundry. The poem shows more sensitivity to the interwoven dilemma of sex and the family budget than social workers often indicated in the course of writing records, and it dramatically puts forward the exhaustion and conflict about marital obligations that poor women often expressed in less direct fashion.

Women were rightly *angry* when husbands "punished" them in such a manner, but many wives were simply overwhelmed and surprised when the spouse disappeared—particularly the first time it happened. In the following case a young widow had married her boarder but continued cleaning rooms in a hotel to help with family support. Her supervisor at work called AC/FWA when the husband deserted.

> Mrs. McIntosh of the Leamington Hotel reported the Newton family destitute. Mrs. Newton expects confinement [delivery of a new baby] any time. Mr. Newton deserted. . . . The oldest girl called her mother from the bed room, and after some minutes Mrs. Newton appeared. She was crying so hard that it was almost impossible for her to talk.
>
> [Four days later] Mrs. Newton was very cordial and glad to see visitor, but cried a great deal during the interview. She had recently concluded that her husband had probably gotten in trouble and left town. She knew his hasty temper would get him into trouble in some time and felt something had arisen at the oil station which had disgusted him and he had left in a hurry. She was certain he had never made any mention of leaving before; neither did she feel she was to blame because during his outbursts of temper she had always been very lenient with him and had

> given in to him. . . . She could not understand how he could be so heartless as to go away deliberately know[ing] she had no money and that there were bills to be paid. . . . He provided very well for her before leaving. He worked at the Soldiers' Home as cook and at the Central Lunch in the same capacity.[62]

The first desertion shocked some women into a frantic search for the missing spouse. In spite of presignals, confused wives questioned neighbors seeking information as to where "he" might be and why. Some feared foul play or sudden illness, put notices in the newspaper, and aggressively sought clues asserting to others that the missing husband was no more discontent with home life than were other men.

> No one of whom Mrs. Garfield knew had heard of him. . . . All the neighbors liked and respected him and were very much surprised to hear the news of his disappearance which Mrs. Garfield had had broadcasted over the radio Saturday night. . . . She notified the Police and went to the GH [General Hospital] and to the City Morgue.[63]

Desertion abruptly ended marriage if the man never reappeared. A few wives were at first shocked and then furious to discover the husband had created a nest egg for his new future by borrowing money or remortgaging the home. One man withdrew a small account from the bank and then spent it at a soft drink/bootleg parlor on Hennepin Avenue before disappearing. On learning of this, his wife "had gone over to the Court House and tried to swear out a warrant against him. . . . They told her there this could not be done, because Mr. T. had a right to draw out his own $ from the bank."[64] A few husbands staged departures that led others to temporarily deduce an accidental death by drowning. Most deserters, however, unwittingly left traces behind or rumors circulated as to their whereabouts. Wives contended with the ambiguity of their own status, curious about a man's whereabouts but often with mixed feelings about his return.

Before disappearing a man might have talked with friends of joining a harvest crew in Dakota or even of gold mining in Alaska. Without warning a Russian immigrant left the city but in three weeks sent his wife a note saying he would not return; his friends got cards saying he had gone to Montana. Word filtered back. If infidelity had expanded into desertion with the man and new woman finding lodging on the far side of the city, some neighbor eventually would recognize them on a streetcar and spread the story. Young men went home to their own mothers who had never approved of the wife's religion, housekeeping, or habits, and a cousin would report such gossip to someone who told it to someone else. If home was in rural Minnesota, information of a man's whereabouts took longer to sift back to the city, but if the deserter was in Minneapolis, eventually he would show up at the same job site or saloon as before, and his status become known. At times the missing husband helped out his family by sending a few dollars, not predictably but haphazardly, usually noting it was for the children. And some fathers who remained in Minneapolis consciously tried to meet their youngsters on the sidewalk.

Almost one-fifth of the deserters—those who might be categorized as "gradual" deserters—initially left the city to find work in order to better support the family. For six months one particular wife received letters signed, "Lovingly your husband" before an ominous silence set in; he later appeared in a Minneapolis hotel with a strange woman and child. A can of maple syrup and one dollar came through the mail to another woman from her husband at work in the state's northern lumber camps, but then she, too, heard nothing more. Most commonly when a husband went in search of employment, his wife waited hopefully in spite of having gotten a few discouraged notes saying no job had yet been found or no profit made, and then communication often stopped.[65]

Doing Without a Man

A husband's departure could be cause for celebration—a "divorce" demanding no lawyer's fee—and after her study of desertions in New York City, Lilian Brandt cautioned social workers not to make a "fetich" of keeping families together, as some wives correctly insisted he was "not worth looking for." In *Broken Homes* Joanna Colcord made a similar point that if the deserting husband was irresponsible or cruel, uniting the couple was a foolish goal.[66] Yet a man's earning power complicated the ease of disregarding him in a family unit.

In these case records, wives responded in a variety of following ways. They were surprised, missed, and wanted their husbands home; they sought their husbands' return because the children needed support; they expressed relief and joy at the absence of a man who made life hellish; or they were ambivalent, expressing all these feelings at different times.[67] These four reactions were equally common, but whether a woman cried in a neighbor's kitchen or welcomed relief from marital conflict, she faced the need to develop what agents called "a plan" for the economics of a female-headed household. Almost one-sixth of the women adjusted to a husband's absence not once, but *repeatedly*, as men with the "deserting habit" came and went. For these wives the quandary over what had driven—or lured—a man away lost salience as periodic desertion became a fact of life. While deserted women experienced the same needs and deprivation as widows and wives of men who were ill, unemployed, or nonsupportive, in this sample they appeared the most driven to seek refuge in a sister's home or enter the labor market.

A deserted woman's status could shift—usually at the man's behest. Sometimes children brought word that Father wanted to come home or relatives sent messages through the grapevine. Notes—with little explanation—came from husbands who desired the comforts of home again. Forty-seven women took action leading the court to locate the husband and press charges, but other men simply returned without overture. Neighbors would report to the agent, "#1 [husband] seen going in back door."[68] Many women toyed aloud with whether or not "to let him come home," and it is unclear to what degree this reflected a woman's own mixed feelings or was said for the agent, who had heard the wife condemn the man and now was about to welcome him back. When questioned by an agent about a husband's return, a wife often took an apologetic tone defending her decision to resume married life. One explained, "He made such great promises to be good and care for them." In the following case the wife's views vacillated in the course of a week:

> May 24th 1913—#2 does not think she will let #1 come back. Would rather care for children herself. Says #1 was married before. . . . #2 does not know whether #1 was divorced from her [first wife] or not and evidently did not care. His cousin Elmer T. . . . has helped her a little.
>
> May 28th—HG [agent] meets #2 on street car. . . . #1 wants to come back to her but [she] has not decided whether to have him or not.
>
> May 31st—#2 is not at home. Visits neigh. next door. Said that #2 had gone to spend this afternoon with a friend. #1 has returned and is working.
>
> July 2nd—#1 is still at home. . . . He gives #2 a large portion of his wages and treats her a great deal better than he formerly did. #2 is still doing laundry work to support the family.[69]

Although a man could resume a family role and treat his wife a "great deal better" than usual, she might still have to work at back-straining labor and care for a new baby in addition. And it was tempting fate to assume that a returned deserter would stay around permanently. A missing husband sent a telegram from Duluth, Minnesota, asking his wife if she wanted him to come home, or if he should just send support money from there. In spite of a history of unemployment, desertion, and drinking she wanted him back. The future looked hopeful when he took the "drink cure" at a sanitarium and began working nights. "She believes #1 is going to be all right now." Within a year, however, she described him as a "beast." He deserted again taking all their money and breaking probation. In a few years she had divorced him.[70]

Women "Who Get Themselves Deserted"

When marital troubles drove a woman to seek aid and counsel beyond the walls of her own home, her own behavior was exposed and held up for judgment against accepted notions of what good wives did. Her neighbors, relatives, social workers, and lawyers could speculate on where the "fault" lay in a bad or broken marriage.[71] The social and economic industrial environment contributed as fault in the trials of all laboring-class families, but these case records—relying in the largest part on women's own reporting—point to men whose decisions and actions victimized both wives and children. Sometimes, however, agency investigations swept up information from gossip that suggested that certain women also were guilty of bad tempers, bad housekeeping, or bad morals.[72]

No doubt this sample of three hundred women included some with sharp tongues, but poverty contributed to an inclination to harp upon the flaws of a male partner. Unemployed men who were "useless" at home with nothing to do were eventually open to verbal attacks and resentments that might previously have lain dormant. A limited number of women showed a meanness usually attributed in the records to men.[73] An adolescent daughter summarized the dynamics in her home. "#1 is drunk and disagreeable and #2 keeps on talking and always provokes him."[74] This was the behavior that a "Half-Excusable" deserter used to justify his actions; he could not "stand the quarreling" and had "beat it out for the West." Two husbands retreated for a time to live in the basement to avoid scolding wives, and a spiteful spouse relegated a third husband there forcefully. In a few cases neighbors alerted AC/FWA to the homes of older couples where they judged wives as failing to render the care they felt elderly men deserved.[75] Probation officers often came to know wives, owing to the illegal and nonsupportive behavior of their husbands. One reported, "#2 is the most unreasonable and most ungrateful woman he ever knew, that it is his business to be neutral both to the man and to the woman, but he cannot see any reason why #1 should not take to strong drink [and this husband also deserted] having to live with a woman like that."[76]

Just as women described husbands as "changed" for the worse since the wedding day, men repeated the charge. The house might have been orderly during courtship, but then the young groom discovered that she "knew nothing and cared even less about homemaking." Neighbors and relatives could be found who testified to a woman's domestic incompetence that made life miserable for a family, and the records describe certain household scenes dominated by chaos and filth. According to social workers, these homes invited desertion; they "manufacture[d]" nonsupporting husbands.[77] At the University of Chicago Sophonisba Breckinridge encouraged social work students to determine a woman's "domestic competence including her power to hold him in reasonable fidelity."[78] In Minneapolis the agency had hired visiting housekeepers as part of an early "preventive" strategy. In the 1920s, a series of radio spots about family work at AC/FWA pointed to the nagging wife as one of many causal factors in nonsupport. To recapture a husband's attention, caseworkers encouraged women to develop greater housekeeping skills and to use a toothbrush regularly.[79]

Poor housekeeping or careless motherhood opened a woman to criticism by those about her, but this behavior lacked the seriousness of drunkenness that some social workers took as automatic grounds for a man—but not for a woman—to seek marital dissolution.[80] Some females did drink. Literature posited that these women not only ruined themselves and poisoned children's social environment, but they brought down men whose decency depended on the example of moral superiority in women. An outraged probation officer found that "while #1 was on probation, #2 was drinking rt [right] along and naturally #1 broke it [probation] . . . he [the officer] would not consider taking #1 on probation again, unless #2 would likewise be put on."[81] Only the unfaithful or immoral wife surpassed the impropriety of the drinking wife.[82] In *The Family*, a journal to support the efforts of family case workers, a ten-year study of Boston charity cases published in 1930 identified the "improper" sexuality of wives and mothers rather than any comparable male behavior as the obvious indicator separating "broken families" from "other dependent families."[83]

A tally of neighbors', husbands', and agents' accusations from within the Minneapolis case records indicates that inappropriate sexuality was the most common charge made against women. Social workers in these records labeled twenty-five women as adulteresses or, if they were not married, as immoral. In almost as many cases—though not always the *same* cases—neighbors and husbands charged likewise. Just as rumors and half-truths existed about husbands' infidelity, women were indicted in the same vague manner. A few cases contained specific names and events that highlighted women's willingness to be forward in their sexuality, to invite men home with them, and to "steal" other women's husbands.

The females who engaged in sex outside of marriage and violated social norms threatened family stability and alarmed middle-class social workers with whom they had contact. In spite of charges of adult infidelity that flew between persons in family casework, however, social agencies never identified such acts as a focus for interagency research, which they did with the issue of desertion. In a record from AC/FWA, adultery might be listed with bad housekeeping and dishonesty as a set of judgments about a woman but without any obvious follow-up action. It is not that agents were immune to believing hearsay, but other factors played a part in their seeming lack of response. Female adultery did not occur frequently enough, nor did it have a direct impact on family economics, but most of all, husbands—theoretically the victims—did not go to charity agencies or family casework centers asking for help because of it. Instead, a husband accused his wife of bad housekeeping, poor child rearing, drinking, or infidelity as *justification* for his own cruelty, nonsupport, or desertion. When women pointed an accusing finger at men, husbands in turn did likewise. In certain case records, characterized less by physical than verbal abuse between husband and wife, just who was at "fault" was cloudy. Far clearer was the fact that men and women usually responded differently to marital troubles.

Men ultimately dealt with their wives and own dissatisfactions through desertion, neglect, and violence, which led some into the legal system—though not by choice. Fifty-two men were charged and punished for nonsupport; 47 for desertion; and 42 faced fines, probation, or sentences for other crimes. Women, often laboring under responsibility for dependent children, went outside their homes looking for help or a hearing.[84]

Defending Themselves and Their Children

The kin networks that functioned around some women as emotional safety valves, credit unions, grocery stores, boardinghouses, and day nurseries often sat as juries in the matter of marital relations and exercised the social influence available through "gossip."[85] In almost a sixth of the cases relatives—on both sides—voiced a position on the marriage. Many were "fed up" (a favorite expression in case records) with little hope that problems could be resolved. When husbands' relatives elaborated further, they rarely judged their own sons or brothers responsible for marital dissolution—it was the woman whose housekeeping or cooking fell short.[86] Seen from the viewpoint of a woman's kin, husbands not only broke civil or criminal statutes and made wives miserable, but offended relatives' mores with their behavior. Support, though not always sympathy, was forthcoming from women's kin who opened their households to 30 of the 300 women after a marital crisis.

In some cases a wife had worked for years to keep her relatives from seeing the truth of an unhappy marriage, but when it was known, kin provided an opportunity to discuss and argue about the situation at hand. Sisters figured most prominently, but brothers had views as well: "Her brother is fed up with him [the husband] and tells her to leave him and that he [the brother] will take care of her." This particular sibling, as many relatives, had little appreciation for his sister's ambivalence as she reported "affection" of a sort that still existed toward the wayward husband.[87] In the course of discussion, mothers, daughters, sisters, and aunts built and reinforced one another's expectations about both male and female roles.[88]

Motherhood and womanhood were prominent and interwoven identities. Just as women joined the labor market to provide for youngsters, relationships with men often were couched in terms of what was best economically for children.[89] Women stayed with husbands and opened their doors to deserters again and again because they knew how inadequate were their own wages, how fragile the financial options for a woman alone to maintain a family.

> Talked to Mrs. P. in the shed where she was in a large washing. Mr. P. had come back a week before and had promised to give his entire earnings toward the support of the family. She had talked to Mr. Arland, probation officer, before she had allowed him to come back home. Mr. Arland had advised her to try living together again and to report to him every 2 weeks until the last of May. Mrs. P. thought that this was the only way to get along finan. [financially] because she herself would be entirely unable to supt. [support] herself and the five children.[90]

This same priority caused some women to seek agency intervention. A wife whose husband was "in habit of leaving overnight now and then" grew "very willing to have AC or HS [Humane Society] take any action against #1, says he has no business to have so little concern about his family."[91]

Table 14 shows the range of women's actions and reactions coping with difficult marriages. More than a quarter expressed being upset and disappointed—"fed up" with marriage; lesser numbers accused husbands of specific behavior. All of these wives pondered what could and should be done about the difficulties and indignities they knew. Ultimately some made the trip to the court house to press charges and to bring the power of the state to their own advantage.[92]

Table 14
Wives' Judgments of and Actions toward Husbands in 300 Case Records

Wives who complained to agent as being "fed up" with husband's behavior	81
Wives who spoke specifically of husbands as	
nonsupporters	68
drinking too much	62
cruel and abusive	47
changed from how they were before	39
immoral and unfaithful	28
bad or abusive father	20
good husbands	14
good fathers	13
Wives who acted formally in opposition to husband's behavior	
regarding nonsupport	
talked of pressing charges but did not during case	16
pressed nonsupport with help from AC/FWA	11
pressed nonsupport without agency help	49
regarding divorce	
sued husbands for divorce	37*
did so during the case	25†
divorce grounds included charges of	
drunkenness, nonsupport, cruelty	22
desertion	14
infidelity	11

SOURCE: 300 Case Records, FCS Collection.

*At case closings a total of 41 women were divorced, but in a few instances the man sued.

†Divorce in the course of a case did not guarantee that this was the marital status at case closure.

The informality of common law marriages attracted many couples but denied women formal claims to income support or final separation from a man. Married women, however, who held both social and legal rights often hesitated to take public action.[93] Every wife exhibited an individual and sometimes changing sense of limits regarding her husband's desertion or nonsupport. She could easily disagree with relatives or social workers as to whether a stint in the Workhouse would serve as good medicine or if a marriage should legally end. One of the AC/FWA district supervisors spoke before the Minnesota Conference of Social Work in 1924 giving quantitative data on desertions for the last few months of 1923. Among 140 cases that became known to the agency, only 73 wives took action against their husbands for legal abandonment; 28 of these husbands were located, and 22 finally appeared in court. This low rate was troublesome to the agency, which interpreted women's behavior as follows:

> There were many instances of course, where the deserted wife at first feared court action against her husband, dreading to drive him and his support permanently from her, where she was repelled at the idea of such action against anyone so closely associated with her life. She took the initiative only after her antipathy was gradually overcome by the realization and conviction that such action might be the remedy in the end necessary to re-establish the family, for lower or higher ideals of support or normal family life; that her obligation to the children [providing them economic support] superseded her emotional reaction.[94]

A woman might assure the social worker that she intended to sign the necessary papers against her husband "tomorrow," but the day was slow to come. Other wives changed their minds at the end of the legal process and traveled to the Workhouse to plead that a man's sentence be reduced. On occasion a woman sided with her despicable husband amid the courtroom process, which she herself had initiated. Poetry in *The Bulletin* described a woman with a "wan face," a "thin, frail smile," and "blue-white hands," who welcomed the caseworker at the door. Then, however, the agent caught the scent of cigarette smoke and "knew the rest." The husband had returned, and his wife blurted out: "They did not sentence him. I would not go before the judge that day, For I love Joe."[95] The repetition of such incidents in social work files prompted Joanna Colcord to question: "What is it that makes this plant called marriage so tough of fiber and so difficult to eradicate from even the most unfriendly soil."[96]

The resistance to court action emanated from multiple causes. Some women viewed their own appearance in the courtroom as a greater shame than having a husband who failed to provide. For others negotiating the language and process of the legal system seemed too intimidating, as could be a confrontation with husband or kin. Many women had expressed distrust generally of involvement with public institutions of any sort and thus had little confidence in the potential actions of municipal or district court as neither the Workhouse nor probation guaranteed an end to nonsupport or desertion nor warm relations at home. A man's "reform" could be fleeting, and if he moved beyond the city, he was usually considered beyond the reach of the law. For some women religion denied consideration of divorce, and long-term desertion enabled independence from a painful marriage. The disinclination to ever marry again kept others from bothering with legal dissolution; if the man was gone, that was good enough.[97]

While outsiders could view reluctance to use legal processes as a woman's lack of intelligence or moral standards, her weakness or error, this behavior reflected the internal struggle and material dilemma women faced in assessing the best way to answer family need with slim resources. Just as marriages deteriorated in stages, women reconsidered what they sought as remedy. Turning to the law became the ultimate assertion of those who were "fed up." Eventually over one-sixth of three hundred women pressed nonsupport charges, asserting the right of a family to support. Younger mothers were most willing to move family matters to the courtroom. The wife of one deserter said:

> She could not possibly support herself and the children. Her one desire seemed to be to get hold of her husband and make him support them. . . . She would be willing to live with her husband again if affairs could be arranged that way. If not she was going to see that he supported her children at any rate.[98]

Another wife who suspected that her spouse had left town with his Polish female coworker, walked through the ethnic neighborhood asking questions as to their whereabouts rather than following the agency's suggestion of going to the police. The husband returned but left again; this second time the wife hired a lawyer "to make him come back or help support the family."[99]

Case records reveal that courts enabled "justice" not only as defined under the law, but as a sanctioned weapon enabling wives to "get back at" husbands.[100] For years Mrs. T. covered up for Mr. T. who spent loans from her relatives on "booze." Then, "For the last three years she has maintained quite a different attitude and has seemed to enjoy having father [her husband] arrested at various times."[101] An Irish charwoman stated "that when he got drinking and failed to bring his earnings home, she had him arrested for non-sup. The day of the trial they ["they" is unclear] had tried to persuade her to let him off, but she remained firm, and he was sentenced to the workhouse."[102] In another case the husband "had begged her to withdraw her warrant for non-support and help him out. . . . She had told him that she would do everything she could to see that he was punished."[103]

When a dependent wife sought *punishment* for a man who failed at his obligations, she reaffirmed matrimonial duties, but in applying for divorce and *leaving* that same man, she moved outside the clearly defined and approved roles for adult women. In choosing divorce a woman had to seek out a lawyer and manage funds for his fees, but even then unexpected circumstances could create additional obstacles.[104]

> When she was working at the Bon Ton the other girls asked . . . why she did not get a divorce. She finally decided to do so and had hired Charles Asher as her attorney. Her mother was to be her chief witness. Before the div. [divorce] came into court, however, her mother died and Mrs. H. said that her bros. did not approve of div. [divorce], they would not have been willing to testify for her in court, accordingly the case was dropped.[105]

Regardless of social roadblocks, the percent of marriages ending in divorce climbed steadily from the beginning of the century, whereas the number of women in this sample pressing nonsupport charges continued evenly throughout 1900–1930. Those wives who proceeded through divorce said in various ways that they had "suffered enough" and believed it better to rely on their own abilities than continue to take the man into consideration.[106] Records said little about the terms of individual settlements, alimony, or child support; mothers got custody of children, but this meant expenditures for them with payments from fathers slight and irregular at best.[107] Divorce, however, brought a kind of relief; one case record reported that a newly divorced mother "talked in a very different manner than she had before. . . . She shouted and laughed and altogether seemed happy."[108] Women spoke bluntly and derogatorily of the man they had left or were leaving. "I married him 2 yrs. after my lst husband died; now I am getting a divorce from him, wish I have never seen him."[109] Another said that her husband

> had been a rounder [spendthrift] and although he had made a good living she had never seen any of the money. She had divorced him and she thanked the Lord that she had gotten rid of that bum . . . showed the Visitor an enlarged picture of Mr. Evans, which she said she had had made one time for his birthday . . . she saw no reason to do away with the picture as it had cost her good money.[110]

In a male-dominated society where women had little power and poor women even less, where the helping societies had both limited resources and agendas of concern, and where many husbands earned meager wages even in the best of times, wives who followed their convictions with charges of nonsupport or sought divorce were empowered, if only temporarily. Assertions against erring husbands were an extension of both the strength and desperation motivating many women already acting as *de facto* heads of households, doing double work at home and in the labor market. When testifying in the courtroom they were not only acting within the law, but ironically often were speaking in confirmation of traditional expectations for the responsibility of men and women in marriage.[111] Independence from one man, however, did not mean that an ex-wife wanted always to be apart from men.[112]

Sixty-seven women, young and middle-aged, and almost evenly divided among the earlier and later cases, appeared to have romantic attachments with men—not husbands—while the case record was being written at AC/FWA. Some liaisons qualified as the infamous infidelity pointed to by husbands; other relationships were short-term in the absence of a husband. But in the process of reconstructing their lives within a society dominated by heterosexual relations and the nuclear family, many divorced women sought contact with men. A woman whose husband left her for another woman commented as she got her divorce that she "did not want to live with Mr. C. again under any circumstances. . . . 'This marriage has been a failure [but] I'd hate to think I had to live alone the rest of my life.'"[113] Agents found ex-wives with male friends—occasionally designated as "gentleman" friends—sitting together in the kitchen or on the streetcar. They would find notices of remarriage in the newspaper and change last names on the case record. A twice-married woman explained how her first and second husbands differed, and in speaking inadvertently revealed limited expectations for marital harmony. The second man was an old friend she had met again shortly after her divorce. A courtship of four days led to marriage "and" she added, "I haven't received a black eye yet."[114]

Conclusion

Matrimony was *rarely* accompanied by bliss for the women known to AC/FWA. Their marriages shifted, dissolved, and reformed in a hostile environment where spouses suffered debilitating and fatal health problems and inadequate finances left men and women contending for scarce resources with little time or strength for delight. Too often the strain to survive degenerated into conflict that repeated with striking consistency in the three hundred records generated from 1900 to 1930.

Every couple's relationship existed within a social context where the sexes had unequal power and were held to different standards of accomplishment and behavior. Men were dominant, yet almost every husband knew the uncertainties and loss of status that came with urban unemployment and infringed on his expected role as breadwinner. Some men worsened the economic inadequacies within their own homes by physical abandonment or escape into alcohol and a cruelty that scared women and children. It is unclear what differentiated the men who willfully neglected families from those who accepted social definitions of men as household providers and continued trying as they could.

Even the wives of "good men" knew that marriage brought misery to many—if not to them—for they lived in neighborhoods where drunken husbands staggered home in the early morning and shouts came through open windows and thin walls. But not all wives were equally vulnerable; mothers with dependent young children most often were subject to nonsupport, desertion, and abuse. The records of women who had been deserted, divorced, or separated prior to acquaintance with AC/FWA, were disproportionately likely to continue in relationships with men that included conflict and sometimes violence. Husbands, neighbors, and kin testified to certain women being troublemakers themselves, equal partners in drinking and infidelity, and failures at achieving moral and domestic standards. But many more wives appeared to be victims. Women of all ages and situations talked with sympathetic and critical friends, relatives, and agents using informal conversation as a means to clarify what they had and what they wanted. Women compared the present with the past, trying to discern how or when the man had gone wrong; they acknowledged the discouragement of being abused and without support.

Women were unanimous in expecting a husband to work and contribute to his children's needs; some may have assumed, too, that the marriage contract implicitly included a certain amount of male drinking and brutality. When a husband withdrew from financial responsibilities, however, the contract was violated and called for women to construct their own support and networks to deal with men as they could. No doubt many found ways of influencing, cooperating with, and opposing husbands that never appeared in writing. In dealing with their dilemmas, however, women acted on individual timetables. Tolerance and anger, and assertiveness and despair varied as some hoped to punish men through the courts, and others sought only to escape.

Desertion alarmed social workers, for it illustrated men's willing abandonment of family responsibility. Divorce also was disconcerting as proof that women might decide husbands were inessential for family life. Both could bring a woman relief, but for mothers with dependent children either occurrence meant accepting greater responsibility as the head of household. This was a role many women already played in part, but because of their children, wives and mothers "put up with" husbands, and wanted or accepted them back.

Women also believed in marriage; they called men "bums," beseeched the agent to "scare him into not drinking," used the courts for incarceration, and sought divorce, but male friends and remarriage were common. Experience taught that matrimony was travail, but marriage—whether by license or mutual agreement—was important to these women's identity and often to their survival. As employed workers they took what jobs were available and said little, but as wives they asked for more. With varying strength women spoke with others about what was happening to them, speculated about how men might change or be gone, and created strategies for action using their own resources and those of others. As a minor part of managing these hard times they related to agents at formal charity/social work institutions. This relationship, too, carried obligations, misunderstandings, and judgments, as explored in chapter 5.

5

Women as Charity Recipients: "Why Do You Come to Bother Me Again?"

Shabbily dressed women with children tagging behind were anonymous figures when seen on Minneapolis streets, and the neighborhoods they lived in were avoided by the better sort. Events in their daily lives went without public notice until some pathetic incident appeared in the evening paper. Decked headlines announced one family's plight: "Straw from Tick [Mattress] Their Only Fuel"—"Deserted by 'Daddy' Wife and Five Children Nearly Freeze to Death"—"Help Came Just in Time."[1] Such drama had the power to generate sympathy among the general public, but this was most usually only temporary. Attention, however, to both "need" and "help" was the primary ingredient of the daily activity that occurred between caseworkers at AC/ FWA and impoverished families in Minneapolis. For agency staff, poor women and children were not anonymous, but instead were their "cases."

"Dear Mrs. Bascum," began a written plea directed at the superintendent of agents. The letter continued in one long sentence explaining a desperate mother's situation:

> I am sorry to bother you again but we have sickness in the house again my little girl has Diphtheria there is a sign on the house [quarantine] and we are closed in here for about two weeks she got sick on Christmas eve you are the only one I have to go to when anything happened I hate to bother people but what shall I do when I cant get out of the house and would you try and do what you can for me. Yours sincerely,[2]

If personal resources fell slack, if income from a boarder or doing laundry failed to be enough and relatives lived too far away or neighbors had nothing to share, a woman might consider turning to strangers for help. But when these troubles were brought to the attention of personnel at agencies and institutions, it meant those in need became "cases" available for intervening actions. To be a recipient of charity or of family social work automatically cast one in an inferior position; Mrs. Bascum, the agency supervisor, and the mother with the sick daughter in this letter, were on inherently unequal terms. Ironically, however, the material in the case records emphasizes wives' and mothers' actions not as supplicants (which at times they were)—but as decision makers. Some of the issues women had to handle put them at rancorous odds with social workers who thought middle-class professionals knew best about life. In other instances a woman's activities did not generate conflict or resistance to agents, but simply showed how many avenues she pursued hunting stopgap assistance. Keeping a home demanded that wives and mothers find their way through and to myriad resources within the city, coping with standards set by others.

Making Use of Urban Resources

Page 1 of the AC/FWA case record assumed that poor families might be known to others and space was provided for addresses of an array of professionals and organizations: "physicians, mutual benefit societies, trade unions, ins. companies, pawn brokers, creditors, etc." Visiting nurses, teachers, clergy, lawyers, grocers, probation, or truant officers might typically be added to the list as well. With all of these the agency's intent was twofold: to seek out sources of financial assistance for families (to substitute for and supplement aid from agency funds) and to gather information. The list, however, bore witness to other dimensions in the lives of "case" families; in addition to being "recipients" they could be "customers" or "members." While poverty and limited resources were central issues in many of these contacts, this was not always so. Involvement with a church, for example, put many families in keeping with the religious habits that city fathers advocated for all Minneapolis residents.

Almost half of the 300 women indicated a religious affiliation divided almost equally between Protestant and Catholic faiths. The impact of belief on women's personal behavior was not apparent in the records with the exception of those few who said Catholicism kept them from divorce or that Christian Science told them to reject the medical care encouraged by an agent. However, many mothers incorporated the church into child rearing; in 40 households youngsters were sent to Sunday school and to certain church-related activities.

> She had not been a member of any church since her marriage. She had sent Edmund to the Congregational Sunday school as long as that church had been maintained in the neighborhood. Edmund had not

> been going to Sunday school for about a year or since the time Mr. Duffy [husband] took sick. She thot [thought] it would be wise for him to go back to Sunday school and get in with a class of boys where he could make some good friends.[3]

Attendance at church or Sunday school could give a family the honest name that quickly brought others in the congregation to their aid. Immigrant women, for whom religion and ethnicity often were intertwined, were more likely than those native-born to be helped by churches that considered them part of the congregational "family."

> Rev. Lars Anderson, #2 pastor . . . says he will cooperate with AC [social worker] in every way to help #2. . . . He thinks #2 had better live at #14 [present address] rather than move to town, that he is quite sure she can get plenty of work to do . . . that she is there surrounded by friends and members of his church.[4]

Ninety-nine women received help—often baskets of food or fuel—from the women's auxiliaries and benevolent societies, many of which were attached to various denominations throughout the city. But giving and receiving was not always within the warm context of friendship as just suggested.

By seeking help a woman could easily come up against less sympathetic and more suspicious administrators at the city's institutions. The constant need children had for adequate clothing led mothers to make requests of the Public School Child Welfare program, which distributed used garments, and here a mother's word was not accepted in good faith. For each of the seventy-one families in this study that used the school program, a worker from AC/FWA had to verify children's deprivation.

Almost a third of the women at some point applied for temporary relief at the local Poor Department, later known as the Department of Public Welfare, located in City Hall, and even agents at AC/FWA criticized the slow and niggardly response people usually received there. After Minnesota legislated a "Mothers'" or "Widows'" Pensions to keep certain women out of the work place and at home tending to children's moral development, neighbors passed along word of the program's existence. Women went to apply for the meager funds, but this meant dealing with authorities at the same juvenile court that determined the disposition of delinquent children. A mother's economic means as well as her morals had to match qualifying standards evaluated for the court by the staff from AC/FWA.[5] As the state began expanding program eligibility to include deserted mothers, social workers at AC/FWA encouraged more women to apply, but to do so carried no guarantee of eligibility. Unless a mother had papers to prove the fact of her marriage and the legitimacy of each child's birth, she could leave the office empty-handed; owning property or not yet being a citizen canceled eligibility for others. Talk of the pension—written about in the records as County Aid or "CA"—appeared in thirty-five cases, but only seven women actually appeared to be recipients during the time they were known at AC/FWA. When the calloused treatment, red tape, and meager givings of relief programs were put alongside women's commitment to the work ethic, earning wages appeared the preferable long-term solution to low income. Seventy-nine women registered their names at the employment bureau at AC/FWA or made rounds of private bureaus run by settlement houses and by the public agency in downtown Minneapolis.

While ill health undermined work efforts at home and away, poor women were not unequivocally accepting of available medical services. A nurse walking through the city's shabby housing districts might provide initial access to professional care with varying degrees of sensitivity to the limits of knowledge and resources a woman coped with as care giver or patient. The nurse might also serve as a prod encouraging her to see the doctor some blocks away or to carry an infant to a settlement clinic. Although mothers would seek out this care for children and attempt to follow-up on advice as they could at home, they routinely rejected any recommendation that they themselves receive hospital care.[6]

One or more members from 85 of the 300 families was admitted to City/General Hospital, suggesting the positive correlation between low income and poor health. This institution had out patient and in patient services for those considered charity cases—as did University Hospital, but among that designated clientele, both places were universally *unpopular*. To check into either meant putting oneself in the hands of unknown male doctors and worrying about lost wages and child care. These were powerful anxieties for women, which translated into long-term neglect of their own health and a complication of problems beyond what might have been. Physicians at these places were likely to be a changing group of males whose own roots differed radically from their poor patients; patients in turn felt little confidence:

> She had also been to the City Dispensary [located at GH], the doctor . . . had given her some tablets and told her to come back. She had paid ten cents to see the doctor and 10 cents for her card. Said she does not like the hospital. Has never been to a sanitarium and would not want to go to Hopewell [the city's tuberculosis sanitarium]. When asked

> why, she said "I guess it's the name." She knows many people who went in but no one who ever came out.[7]

> Mrs. C. said that she had been to the dispensary and had been stripped to the waist and examined by five different doctors. Then these doctors wanted her to do some exercises but she was so ashamed to stand naked before them that way and said that they would have to excuse her, perhaps some other time she could it but she did not feel she could then.[8]

> [The] dentist at the infirmary said he had never seen such a bad mouth as Mrs. H. . . . [his plan was to remove her teeth one at a time] but she told him that she was so weak that she could not make so many trips and asked him to take out 8 or 9 at a time. . . . Advised her to go back to the University Health Dispensary and see if they could give her something to strengthen her. She refused to do this saying that she knew they would keep her . . . that she could not go to the hospital on acct. of the children. She would rather die than leave them.[9]

Over time poor women's distrust of hospital services appeared to lessen. Familiar home remedies, the visiting nurse, and private doctors continued to exist but formal medical institutions run by anonymous persons grew to dominate health care. As indication of the change, more and more women from this study gave birth in General Hospital rather than at home, used its dispensary, and had contact with the medical social workers there. In 1927 an agent would record, "The only money Mrs. R. spent was about 4 [streetcar] tokens a month to go to the GH prenatal clinic."[10]

Getting Aid in a Changing Social Work Environment

Women's growing reliance on hospitals rather than on midwives was not simply a shift of habit among the lower class nor a sudden transformation. Throughout the country attitudinal and structural changes were occurring in the social welfare available to those in need. Early century reformers, including some COS personnel, had advocated a greater role for government as a means to overcome the misery caused by industrialization and to pull those living in the lower class up to middle-class standards. Coalitions engaged in strategic lobbying helped bring about a spate of laws affecting such issues as women's work and child labor, mothers' pensions, housing standards, juvenile delinquency, venereal disease, and marriage. These new statutes were understood to be "progressive" reforms that would improve family life, and their implementation often relied on the expertise of professionals with formal training.[11]

As part of these advances the simple good intentions of well-meaning persons diminished as the basis for social welfare in a city. Just as midwives had been losing ground to male physicians, charity was perceived as old-fashioned compared to social casework practiced by a formally trained staff.

For poor people across the country this meant an expansion of formal service agencies and institutions with set regulations and college-educated personnel; conversely, the ad hoc informal resources contracted. The number of ladies' societies and church committees doing charity work shrank, and in records at AC/FWA the so-called "Benevolent Individual" appearing in early cases almost disappeared. When Associated Charities adopted its new name—the "Family Welfare Association"—in 1922, "charity" as a governing concept had met its official demise. Table 15 illustrates quantitatively how Minneapolis families experienced these changes in the social welfare system.

Regardless of its name, AC/FWA experienced a relatively steady flow of needy people through its own doors but changes were taking place in the services people received at this agency. Partially as a result of new thinking in the field of social work, the woman whose case opened in 1920 was treated somewhat differently than her sister had been ten years earlier.[12] Whether this was positive or negative depended on one's perspective.

By the 1920s, publications written by social work leaders and educators were describing a "modern" direction for practice. Rather than investigating the client's empirical experience at home or work, social workers were urged to pose questions focusing on the "meaning" of events using language and techniques adopted from psychiatry and psychology. While this change was obvious in professional literature, the work of young agents in the field at the time showed little more attention to individual psychology than in the previous decade. But for the staff at AC/FWA, concerns about "professionalism" translated into heightened attention to rationality, training, and supervision—a reflection of growing respect for the "expert" that was occurring in other fields as well. Clients, in turn, were to profit as the recipients of more efficient intervention.[13]

Because the agency claimed that family problems needed the skilled approach of trained staff, the role of a visiting housekeeper or volunteer from the Friendly Visiting Committee diminished. Other tasks that agents had assumed—for example, walking the streets to locate a For Rent sign for a homeless family—were seen anew as an unwise use of valuable time. And given the public employment bureau and free ones at the settlements, AC/FWA's own bureau was discontinued as a duplica-

Table 15
Families' Contact with Social Welfare Aid and Institutions by Time of Case Opening in 300 Case Records

	150 Cases Opened 1900–1910	150 Cases Opened 1920–1930
Increasing number of families in contact with		
General Hospital	26	59
Public School Welfare	29	42
Legal Aid Society	8	31
Decreasing number of families in contact with		
Benevolent individuals	23	5
Churches	65	34
Private relief societies	40	18
Ethnic Aid societies	17	1
Stable number of families in contact with		
Poor Department/Dept. of Public Welfare	43	49
Private doctors	29	29
Visiting nurses	61	59

SOURCE: 300 Case Records, FCS Collection.

tion of services. As a result of these measures, poor women began receiving fewer practical services from AC/FWA than they once had as shown in Table 16.

The expanding social work literature implied that a case family experiencing *less* direct help would enter a "partnership" with the agency, taking on *more* responsibility for its own support.[14] Ideally family members would be appraised of, and in agreement, with actions taken on their behalf. In accord with these standards, the first sheet of case records at AC/FWA was modified to include space for individual's "assets" in addition to the traditional category of "problems," and the practice of publicly advertising the plight of worthy cases—particularly at Christmas—was deemed too intrusive.[15] For the agency these changes in casework had an internal consistency; for the client the result was more complex. What seemed to be the loss of practical assistance could

Table 16
Families' Experiences with AC/FWA by Time of Case Opening in 300 Case Records

	Cases Opened 1900–1910	Cases Opened 1920–1930
Families receiving		
undefined relief	105	82
food, grocery orders	81	48
fuel orders	69	31
help finding employment	76	39
help dealing with landlord	32	17
extra agency service—friendly housekeeper or volunteer visitor	34	13

SOURCE: 300 Case Records, FCS Collection.

be interpreted as freedom from outside meddling, but none of the changes removed the inferior status from the client's role.

Articles in new journals affirmed families' right to respect from a casework agency and to privacy from public view, but in contradiction to these principles—caseworkers heightened investigation as further means to exclude sentimentality from their work. The first recognized casework text, *Social Diagnosis* by Mary Richmond in 1917, had emphasized inquiry into a family's social environment. Workers in the field eagerly endorsed the book as a means out of "amateur chaotic method." Supervisors at AC/FWA urged the staff to consult the dog-eared copies in the office for a systematic way to make pertinent inquiries and to study family functioning.[16]

To poor women, Richmond's method meant answering more questions. And a mother's own words about marriage and children, and about mortgage and employment often carried little weight and had to be "verified" by legal records at the courthouse and by calls to other professionals around the city—or country.[17] In 1922 AC/FWA mailed a letter to the Minnesota State Children's Bureau requesting information about a widow with young children who had moved into Minneapolis from a rural town where she had received a widow's pension. The letter included the following list of technical and distrusting questions:

> What were her real reasons for coming to Mpls. [Minneapolis]? For how long was she receiving mother's pension?

Was the county aid [mother's pension] allowance adequate for her needs?

How did she supplement this?

How was she able to get along subsequent to her husband's death?

Can this death be verified for us?

Did Mr. Nielsen [the dead husband] ever take out naturalization papers?

When and where was this accomplished?

Also would it be possible to give us the exact date of birth and birth places of all the children?

She told us Walter is two years old. Was he a posthumous child or an illegitimate one?

The letter closed with the following, "We know that to answer all these questions will be an imposition on some busy man or woman, but we are asking that it be done as we do not feel competent to advise Mrs. Nielsen until we have full information considering her."[18] Social workers at AC/FWA were increasingly concerned with myriad objective data in a case, but the operational goal continued to be self-sufficiency, and the crucial element determining level and form of assistance was the needy woman herself.[19] Regardless of the time period, most families received assistance from AC/FWA because the woman in the household was willing to participate to some extent with a designated agent.

Evaluating the Woman in Need

"Begging" was a job allocated to women in the family. Many men were absent from these households, but even when the husband was home, his wife was twice as likely than he to first appear for assistance in the AC/FWA office. Daughters were sometimes substituted, carrying handwritten pleas and asking for help on behalf of hungry siblings. In sixty-seven cases other females—friends, kin, and neighbors—accompanied the woman and bolstered her while she explained her situation. Some women came as advocates on the behalf of another. Frequently the agency intervened without that invitation.

Personnel from societies and institutions about the city could simply place a call asking for "investigation and aid" and a household would find itself within the purview of AC/FWA. A physician could write "To Whom It May Concern" about an ailing patient and get a similar response; a pastor could request material outreach to sheep who preferred to be lost. In these instances a social worker would follow-up by making her way to the family's front door and expecting to be let in. The landlord, grocer, or woman across the street also could draw agency attention to a family, to "assist"—or "meddle"—in its affairs. The fact that other persons so frequently identified need testifies to the obvious deprivation of some households and denies the notion that families routinely *sought* dependency on others. However, it also makes clear that in these cases a poor woman's life was interwoven with those of many others, and this was not always her choice.

Women with children but who lacked spouses were subject to suspicion throughout a society that touted the superior nature of the nuclear family life. Any woman who came into an agency or opened her door to a social worker, however, was subject to even greater scrutiny. Many case records began with the worker's first and critical impression.[20]

> She was a very stolid unintelligent appearing person, unattractive and dirty.
>
> She was dressed in a simple dark, blue voile dress and was neat and clean. She appeared to be a typical farmer's wife.[21]
>
> Mrs. B. was a rather coarse looking woman with light bobbed hair, blue eyes and fair skin. She gave the appearance of trying to appear much younger than she was.[22]
>
> Well preserved and spry looking old lady, with white hair wearing a garden hat, a small sealskin neck piece and a good looking suit. Mrs. W. gave an odd impression of well breeding coupled with very bad lapses of grammar.[23]

A woman was often hastily and subjectively judged. Social workers freely applied the adjective "nervous" to describe females who had every reason to be uneasy about their future, but agents also defined more than a tenth of the women as "feebleminded" without recording behavioral evidence to substantiate the view. This was a common appellation by middle-class social workers who confused lack of education and cultural differences with intelligence. Women's ethnicity, which might have explained some of the behavior at which agents looked askance, was given little regard.

Early annual reports listed the number of cases by nationality and drew attention to the largest percentage being "American," but this accounting of the caseload ceased. The front page of the case record asked for information about "Nativity" or "Birthplace," but in one-third of the cases studied here agents neglected to record this data. The available information indicates that most women were native-born; another one fourth came from Germany or Scandinavia, with far smaller numbers distinguished by two dozen other nationalities. A scant handful were "Colored." Immigrant status created problems for some families while the bonds in ethnic neighborhoods could function as resources for others, but the content of case records and social work intervention showed a general disregard for the issue of cultural diversity. Agents *did* make infrequent referrals to language and citizenship classes and sometimes commented that a child functioned as translator, that the home smelled of sauerkraut, or that relatives in Norway would send money. However, as reflected in these records, ethnocentric social workers rarely considered that American ways might not be the only ones, or that poverty was aggravated by the task of trying to survive in an alien culture.[24]

Certain poor women were obviously more facile and less vulnerable than others, but all were experiencing difficult circumstances at home, and none embraced the status of being a recipient. To ask for or receive help carried the likelihood of being treated brusquely by "professional" agents.

Relations with the Social Worker

With the first suggestion in the late nineteenth century that charity work was a *job* rather than a volunteer enterprise, Mary Richmond portrayed the ideal candidate for this occupation as a married woman with children (who understood basic female roles). She would be a "good citizen" with a "good general education," be sympathetic, incorruptible, imaginative, and have a sense of humor.[25] This was not the professional who developed, however; the staffs of charity organizations and family casework agencies were dominated by young, single women who over time began their jobs with more and more formal education but rarely with experience grounded in marriage and motherhood. While Joanna Colcord wrote that she trusted such workers could "vicariously" comprehend the difficulties others faced, she cautioned the staff to listen carefully to the language of clients as the "spirit of life" was often expressed in terms different from those learned in school or through reading.[26] Other experts in the field advised young agents to have a "patient hand and discerning eye," and to feel the "unique importance" of each situation, not to rely on relief but on themselves, not to make promises they could not keep, not to show horror or surprise or to allow duty, complacency, or condescension to replace a "scientific mind that asked questions."[27] The important question, however, was whether a worker could make a difference in someone's life. Richmond wrote that charity agents had "no right to meddle with the lives of the poor unless they can better them."[28]

While many poor women became proficient at finding their way to and through certain urban resources, they could not compete with the reputation of AC/FWA and the tools of middle-class background and education that social workers could use in negotiating the social welfare "system" in Minneapolis. Some of the benefits and services available had to be pried loose or the paperwork straightened out before a family could profit. Agents were better positioned to deal with the bureaucracies controlling medical care, workman's compensation, mother's pensions, veteran's pensions, property deeds, and registration for vocational training or citizenship classes. Families received transportation from the railroads and goods from the wealthy because agents put forward their names.

The caseworker known by some women was a helpful female who not only used formal agency connections to make things happen, but who reached into her own purse on occasion. Some of the laundresses trying to profit from washing took on agents as customers who in turn recruited more business for them. The woman sewing, knitting, or weaving at home could sell handwork to the social worker and ask her to pass along word of the crafts' availability. Mothers encouraged agents to stop at the funeral home after the death of a child or to visit City/General Hospital to crow over a newborn infant and were pleased when the worker did so.[29] In appreciation, a woman might press the social worker to accept garden produce or flowers.

When female isolation, anger, and despair made any listener welcome, wives and mothers gladly opened their doors to the agent's knock.[30] This representative from AC/FWA brought the possibility of tangible material relief and sometimes functioned as a listening ear and commiserater.[31] Frequently the agency-outsider wanted to hear past and present grievances about husbands, children, neighbors and relatives, and some women wanted to talk about what they knew and felt. Just as evidence existed of certain workers giving genuinely of themselves, on some occasions 40 of the 300 women—the majority being divorced, deserted, or separated—spoke or wrote to the agent in a genial manner.

> Both [a deserted woman and the brother living with her] were very cordial also on this visit and showed visitor pictures of their family and asked visitor to visit them again later on.[32]
>
> Mrs. S. immediately inquired for SAE [agent] and said that no one understood her condition so well as she had. She was eager to see her again as it was such a relief to have someone with whom she could talk over her troubles and who understood exactly what was the matter with her.[33]

> She was very glad [agent] had stopped in and asked her to come again. Walked out to the gate with [agent] and told her all about her chickens.[34]

In 1906 a woman contacted an agent at AC/FWA after her husband's employment on the Iron Range evolved into desertion; five years later she left Minneapolis to live with relatives but was still sending notes to the social worker in 1913 describing her youngster's experiences in school.[35] At times communication between mothers and agents reflected a shared female sensibility—particularly regarding the needs of children—but other dynamics were more noticeable within the records. Class differences, the lopsided access to resources, and worker turnover limited the possibilities of mutual appreciation.

Agents at AC/FWA worked under supervisors and directors whose names were respected in social welfare circles nationally, but their own daily assignments with large caseloads took long hours at low salaries. With heavy work and little remuneration the majority of social workers acted expediently with the case families they knew, and then left employment at AC/FWA. In a 1905 record, entries in four sets of handwriting appeared in the space of one month; in another case five sets of initials identified the agents and students assigned to investigate a single family during 1923. The director of AC/FWA sent an apologetic letter to this household. "Again let me say how sorry we are that the change in our staff here has made it impossible for one person to have kept in touch with you as we should have wished."[36] This confusion was not uncommon in social service settings, and its negative repercussions were discussed in directors' reports and at board meetings.[37] In 1927 the director Joanna Colcord, bluntly acknowledged: "Staff turnover had been heavy, it has been often a problem to hold workers long enough to complete their two years of training. . . . To charges that our staff is too young, that it changes too rapidly we are obliged to say yes."[38]

While employees at AC/FWA worked within personal and organizational limitations, their jobs *did* give them access to an authoritative stance when dealing with clients. In a crisis, the worker who authorized the delivery of a load of coal or arranged credit for groceries could be hailed with gratitude, and on becoming a "case" a woman and her family often received assistance beyond their initial request. As time progressed, however, many women felt the case worker assumed the right to know too much information and asserted agency direction over family affairs.

In the course of investigating a household, an agent would spread word of the misfortune and solicit contacts to tell what they knew in order to generate "insight" into both the problem and potential for change. Sympathetic neighbors, a grocer, or landlord might already have been aware and extended credit and offered remedy as they could. But an agent might locate some new source of relief in the process of poking around, or she could draw out slander or grievances as well. The grocer might inform her of a family's cigarette purchases in spite of its low budget; a landlord could draw attention to irregular rent payments and liquor bottles in the trash can. When agents came around, the neighbors most likely to be at home were women themselves. If living on the other side of a thin wall, they could air annoyance with someone else's unruly children or with relatives lounging on the back steps. Understanding the strength of gossip and grapevine, many applicants for aid were indignant when they learned that agents had been seeking additional information about them. A few demanded the right to decide just who was to know of their troubles.

Mary Richmond, whose books and articles were guides in the development of casework method, cautioned social workers against taking "an autocratic role in center stage" of a family's life.[39] However, agents' terse descriptions of their own actions throughout case records affirm what Richmond sensed. "Sent 1/2 T. [ton of] coal"; "said Lucy must attend school or [else the] mother would be taken to workhouse"; "made apt GH [appointment at General Hospital]"; "advised she press charges." These phrases show the range of workers' intervention, but also suggest the assumption of a definitive role. Workers were likely to put forward decisions rather than alternatives. When a wife or mother vented her anger with the way life was going or disagreed with agency directives, she was often labeled "too independent," "stubborn," or "insolent."[40]

The Struggle over Family Autonomy

One of every ten records noted that a woman expressed gratitude for agency help but another tenth complained saying they had expected something different. A client once described as "good" might be redefined in the course of her case as "uncooperative." At some point almost a third of the women were accused of withholding information, coloring the truth, or acting irresponsibly. The longer a case was open—and for one hundred eighty families this was more than six months—the greater the possibility that the wife/mother/homemaker/recipient would clash with the social worker as to how she ought to conduct herself in these multiple roles. Beleaguered by many realities in her life—a woman was inclined to hold on to what she could regarding decision-making within the family. While resistance to suggestions from a caseworker did not result in automatic case closure, it did mean that disagreements and stalemates appeared within records mitigated little by the trend over time toward "professionalism." Even when a worker and woman did not directly and sharply disagree, ample evidence pointed to the confidence with which an agent regarded the client as incompetent and involved her own self in the family's matters, sowing seeds that could blossom into antagonism.

The role of kin often emerged as the first point of direct conflict that quickly surfaced during the initial home visit. A majority of families had relatives within the city limits of Minneapolis or St. Paul that created networks essential for survival, but many women were reluctant to draw this part of family into the formal "casework" by identifying them to strangers. Forty-five of the three hundred women were less than forthcoming with names and addresses, explaining that relatives already had given what they could and were not to be bothered by the agency. In fewer of these cases kin were uninvolved because the woman wanted it that way, saying she was ashamed of her situation or felt that relatives with more money would look down on her need.

Social workers disagreed among themselves as to expectations for relatives; the concern was not that women had a right to privacy but a question of how valuable relatives actually were as a resource in casework. Theoretically kin functioned as the "natural" defense in economic emergencies, but very often they themselves were poor and at best were an inconsistent source of aid and information. In *Social Diagnosis* Richmond argued that relatives could be "partisan and prejudiced," could make "mischief," and did not always know what was going on; some relatives, however, knew about family illnesses and had great insight into problems. Thus Richmond concluded that a worker should enlist their aid for, "if they are not with us, they may easily be against us."[41]

A woman could find it hard to sustain her resistance as a worker repeated the request for information in visit after visit. In the cases from 1900 to 1910 an agent might go so far as to seek out relatives' names from clues neighbors might have and then visit or write to them regardless of how that intrusion might upset family equilibrium. As casework developed, workers were more likely to "consult" a woman before proceeding with kin, but agents still wanted their own way in this matter. "Number 2 resists this ["this" being the intent to contact relatives] because they're better and arrogant but after much persuasion she was impressed apparently with the explanation of the confidential nature of FWA's work."[42]

Relatives in the city were solicited not only for financial help but for details about character and background. Those at greater distance were petitioned by mail. Fifty-seven sisters, 49 brothers, and 36 parents all received letters similar to the following, which varied mainly in the degree to which a worker sounded sympathetic and trusting of the client:

> Mr. Arthur Buehle
> Beach, ND
> Dear Sir:
>
> Your sister, Mrs. Lilly Franklin [a divorced mother of young children] living at 2103 4th Ave. So. of this city has been called to our attention. She has been sick for some time, absolutely helpless with no relatives as you know, in this city and with friends who have helped her as much as they have been able but which naturally enough has often been insufficient. She has suffered more than can be expressed in words, but has borne up cheerfully under the most trying circumstances. . . .
>
> From these facts perhaps you may conclude that it will be best for you to return to Minneapolis and help your sister in the future as you have in the past, or at least to send her as much aid as possible. With best wishes for you and your sister's welfare, we are
>
> Very truly yours,
> Associated Charities[43]

> Mrs. A. Hanson
> Underwood, ND
> Dear Madam:
>
> Your sister and little boy have come to us for assistance. She tells us that her husband has deserted. . . . She has lost her place [job] in Mpls. [Minneapolis] and it seems impossible for her to find another. We ourselves are searching for places for a number of women in her position and can find nothing, so it seems that she will have a pretty hard time if she tries to stay in Mpls. [Minneapolis] this winter. Do you think your mother could give her a home for the winter?
>
> Very truly yours,
> Associated Charities[44]

As a case developed it often became clear that on her own with relatives, a woman often was pursuing alternatives for survival. Caseworkers, however, usually failed to get replies to the letters they sent, with the exception of apologetic regrets from kin saying economic hardships prevented compliance with the written request. Other relatives grew annoyed that an unknown outsider was presuming to direct family affairs, and they called or sent word saying *not* to contact them again. This seemed to have little impact on agency procedures. When a woman and her immediate family became a "case," many elements in their lives were exposed for discussion and description; relations with kin were simply one area. A woman also could find herself on the defensive regarding where and how she lived.

AC/FWA never had confidence in the business acumen or thrift of the poor. Some of the skepticism related to problems with mortgages and credit that exploited families brought to the Legal Aid Bureau. Early in the century the agency responded by making arrangements with a local Equitable Loan Association so that "at least one company" in the city would make "loans on household goods at a moderate rate of interest" and treat "the patrons decently in the doing."[45] Among clients, the purchasing habits of a woman without a man to negotiate for her were susceptible to greater scrutiny—even when she was buying the humblest items for daily use.

The principles of homemaking practiced by many poor women included juggling needs, going without, or making do; professionals, however, held homemaking to standards of the developing "domestic" science and to the home economics movement.[46] As family work became more formalized over time and as the agency was anxious to move away from identification with "charity," the monetary relief distributed by the staff came to be described as part of a "treatment plan" that taught the housekeeper how to budget.[47] Thus a homemaker who received a few dollars would be monitored to document her efficiency and rationality in handling not only money from the agency but the entire budget she put together. To the agency this became empirical evidence that she was "trying"; to the woman it was an example of distrust and being held in the role of child.

Regardless of prices in the marketplace and the limited resources with which they worked, women often resisted the imposition of this dollars and cents accountability. They disagreed with social workers as to the cost of necessities and which corners to cut. One who was judged as "too independent" said: "If they did not want to help her without telling her just how the money should be spent [then] FWA could keep away from there [her house]. She was getting tired of having to acct. for every cent."[48]

> [The social worker] inquired about Mrs. Hiazdon's having to borrow $4 from Mrs. Sipac. She said that $5 could not possibly pay their grocery bill for one week. Inquired how much she thot [thought] would be the amount and she said their groceries would come to about $9 a week. Told her that $5 should take care of groceries but she said it would not. She had her accounts carefully kept. They were kept in Polish but she

> went over them with visitor. She buys three quarts of milk a day. . . . She had bought Joseph and Franz each a pair of stockings and had to buy a broom. The rest of the money she could not account for . . . gave her $4 in cash and a $2 milkbook and told her she would order a sack of flour . . . told her to try to get along on $4 cash this week and not borrow any money, and HBA [agent] would be over her accounts with her the following week.[49]

> Went over Mrs. Taylor's budget with her and told her she could live comfortably and well on the budget figures visitor gave, but that such figures did not include $38.00 for suits for the boys or expensive silk hose for herself and Winnie. Mrs. Taylor said the only kind of stockings she could wear was silk stockings or rubber stockings, and that she had not bought them herself anyway.[50]

Mothers were called on to defend choices in buying for themselves as well as for children. Both price and quality were at issue; an agent could criticize a woman's purchase of new overshoes for children rather than finding used ones, of buying bright material for a new garment rather than using a secondhand piece. Housing costs and location were debatable as well. An agent and her "case" would argue as to whether a neighborhood with a "bad" reputation was indeed an unsatisfactory place to live, whether the house was unsafe or unreasonably large and taking too much from a meager paycheck. Fifty-six women were advised to move, often being pushed to look for residences closer to a settlement house that offered a nursery providing "wholesome" child care that could facilitate the mothers' own employment. Women, however, resisted the tidy solutions offered them. They particularly opposed the use of nurseries presided over by strangers and could find themselves bargaining with an agent about how to proceed.

> #2 is told that by Jan. 1st she must move over in that neighborhood and place the children in Wells-Memorial nursery and take up day work. . . . #2 says that she is going to try to get a place at housekeeping for the winter where she can keep the two children and if she cannot do this by Jan. 1st will then consider Wells-Memorial.[51]

The phrase "must move over" is a prime example of what Mary Richmond meant by "autocratic role." While the records never made clear how an agent would or did enforce such a mandate, it *was* clear that many mothers stayed put even after such dictum. Others went along grudgingly with plans they disliked and became angry at the outcome. A deserted mother who "gave in" to the worker's suggestion that she put two preschool children into a settlement nursery had this experience:

> #2 comes to the nursery, finds #3 [the oldest of two children] eating behind a screen as punishment for naughty action. #2 very angry, abuses nursery matron and refuses to take children there any more. . . . Comes to the agency. . . . She is told [she] will have to learn to take advice and allow children to be cared for by someone who knows as much as she about the care of children.
>
> [Two months later at the settlement] #4 was caught in nursery so was punished. #2 became *very angry* think would have struck Miss Smith [resident director] if door had not been closed between [them].[52]

The importance society attributed to women as mothers carried with it serious indictments if women fulfilled the role poorly. As household heads within the purview of a public or private social welfare agency, mothers were particularly vulnerable to judgments of inadequacy—that they were not caring correctly for youngsters, that juvenile willfulness stemmed from their own behavior, and that others knew better than they.[53]

Discord over the Place of Youngster's

When the staff at AC/FWA suspected or defined child neglect, they called on the Humane Society/Children's Protective Society to deal with those parents. However, children's school attendance versus truancy was a common issue they dealt with in many households, and agents gave contradictory messages about what was best.

Arguments took place in kitchens, but the issues were broad and competing—public education, child labor, and a household economy. Youngsters were more likely to be absent from classrooms owing to work obligations at home and elsewhere, than because of hanging around on the street for fun. Parents were indicted as collaborators in their children's behavior, and in this conflict poor women all over the country found themselves opposing not only individual social workers but the national social welfare "establishment" as well.

At the 1903 National Conference of Charities and Correction, Jane Addams delivered a paper entitled, "Child Labor and Pauperism," in which she refuted the claim that families ultimately were helped by children's wages. In the years to follow the status of child labor legislation repeated as an item on the conference agenda. At the 1907 meeting in Minneapolis, Owen Lovejoy—then the acting director of the National Child Labor Committee—outlined the negative effects brought on by youthful wage work and the short-sightedness not only of parents but of social workers who leaped at these wages as the "immediate, easy solution for certain cases of poverty." The result, according to Lovejoy, was a "worse disease" that denied children the right to go to school and develop.[54] Increasing family income in the short term was to take second place to the long-term advantage of educating children who then could become more than common laborers. Needy families and exploitive employers weighed on one side of the debate, and laws about school attendance and their enforcement were on the other.

Most parents knew well that life was unpredictable, which made hollow any promises about education's future payoff. Far more obvious were the needs for the day. Mothers kept children home from school to care for younger ones so they might themselves work; in other families adolescents joined parents—or replaced them—in the work force. Either reason for absenteeism could arouse the social worker who saw the mother defying her domestic obligations—leaving children without proper supervision and robbing them of their youths. With little sensitivity to the shortage of alternatives mothers had, agents threatened that in allowing youngsters to miss school mothers were asking to be sent to the Workhouse. Truancy continued, and agents rarely took the matter further, but such threats were part of the repertoire in family work.[55] In the following case the wife of a frequently unemployed man had a permanent job cleaning the Munsingwear factory at night, but she hoped to give it up and apparently got little sympathy for the proposed alternative:

> Mrs. T. complained it was quite hard on her to have to go to work [she was ill] and she thought her place was at home. She knew if Stella was working she would not have to work herself and thought it was the child's place to work and not the mothers. FE [agent] talked to Mrs. T. quite a while on the advantages of educ. and of the Min. law that gov. the attendance of children until age 16.[56]

While children freely worked after school and on weekends, legislation in 1909 made it illegal for youths under sixteen to be absent from the classroom during the day without a special permit.[57] The school board designated AC/FWA to investigate families and assess if need was severe enough to warrant absence. Records showed both ayes and nays, depending on whether the agent judged there to be other actual or potential wage earners in a household.

> [To] Principal Washington School—
> Welde, James, 508 9th Ave. S. James will be fifteen in August. The

father died in August, 1904. The mother is a janitress in Temple Court [office building] and earns $25.00 a month. Their rent is $17.00 and they sub-let for $18.00. There is a girl nineteen working in the Cream of Wheat [factory] and earning $6.00 a week. There are two children younger than James making five in the family. After talking with the mother, she said that she had a friend in the National Biscuit Co., and she would see him and see if she cannot obtain a position for James when school closes, in order that he may have work during the summer months. In case she does not, she will call upon us. She has promised to keep him in school, if possible, the rest of the year. No certificate [permit] will be necessary.

ASSOCIATED CHARITIES[58]

This family was doing better than many known to the agency, and the daughter's industrial earnings matched her parent's charring wages. The caseworker apparently "convinced" Mrs. Welde that an alternate plan should be designed to keep James out of employment. Usually mothers were very upset with the denial of a permit for they had calculated that family survival depended on one more income.

When children turned sixteen, social workers brushed aside the importance of education to enlist these young people full time in a family's self-sufficiency. The "good," clean, well-mannered child who was no older than his or her classmates might have been encouraged all along to stay in school, but "slow" children who had fallen behind (sometimes owing to ill health) were to become laborers. Not only agents, but volunteers from the Friendly Visiting/Relief and Service Committee, made this clear as they unhesitatingly formulated plans for a family's future. These female volunteers, many of whom had enjoyed education at an eastern college, raised and allocated certain relief funds. Regardless of the meager amount given to a household as pension, the Committee in return claimed rights in family decision-making. And as they designed the relief budget, child labor was usually figured into the equation with little question. Middle- and upper-class women whose own children escaped employment easily accepted it in the lives of other young people.

March 5, 1913—Reported by Mrs. Martin [member of the committee] that Mr. B. was sick and lost a week [of work] therefore Julian [son of Mr. and Mrs. B.] feels he should stop school and go to work. Will be 16 in 2 weeks. There are 2 possibilities open; a milk wagon job at $10 a week; a machine shop job at $9 a week where possibly there is a chance for advancement. . . . Conference advises against milk wagon job, if there is a chance for advancement in machine shops.[59]

In this case the committee's advice about the preferable job likely was sound, but even good counsel could infringe on families' independence.

When mothers sought to keep children away from work, it was rarely because they saw the positive impact of education, but because they feared for the child's health. Even in these situations an agent with an eye on the budget could be insensitive.[60] Children were not to forsake learning for wage earning, yet it did not apply to all children at all times. Social workers' various interventions vacillated between the competing goals of education for youngsters and of self-sufficiency for families. Parents, too, felt conflict—but usually of a different sort—for them it was the constraint others placed around strategies for survival. In some cases a woman's own employment engendered conflict between the agent and herself.

Oversight of Women's Employment

When children left home to work, as when the mother herself did, their actions unwittingly put them amid a national debate about the sanctity of the home and the future of America.[61] At AC/FWA the 1905 *Annual Report* cautioned; "Great care must be taken in giving employment to married women, lest more harm than good be done by depriving young children of their mother's care and relieving the man of his responsibility in supporting the family."[62] An extreme view of this hypothesis cast these husbands as degraded and demoralized, victims of women who upset natural laws of dependence and support.[63]

Sentiment was strong, but policy was unclear at this family casework agency. The staff fluctuated between "keeping"—and thus supporting—a woman in the role of homemaker versus "letting" her seek essential employment. At the New York City COS Edward Devine weighed the effect of accepting widows and deserted mothers as dependents on relief as opposed to encouraging them to take jobs as laundresses, seamstresses, office cleaners, or housekeepers. He hoped those with "energy" and "adaptability" might find employment with both a "demand" and "sufficient reimbursement," but he believed children had first claim on a mother's time.[64] This was hard to honor—and to implement. Agents at AC/FWA simultaneously tried to link women to employment opportunities with the hope of self-sufficiency *and* to circumscribe that experience so as not to weaken socially endorsed maternal obligations.[65]

As practice this meant some women were pushed into a worker status with job searches so as not to develop unrealistic "dependency" on agency relief; others were held back. And the exploitive nature of all the available female employment went unchallenged. In spite of the agency's longtime participation in citywide coalitions discussing unemployment individual social workers spoke to job seekers as if a good hunt guaranteed discovery of employment, which would then eliminate family privation. Any individual woman and her social worker could disagree as to what work was best, when, and where, and whether a working mother was giving her children due consideration.

"Work" for women was easiest for the agency to support when it took place in a private home without the appearance of wage labor. Social workers particularly encouraged seamstresses to continue at their efforts. An agent at AC/FWA wrote to the COS in Grand Rapids, Michigan, inquiring about the wife of an enfeebled Baptist minister whose grown sons had left home.

> Mrs. G.G.W. Baxter has applied to our employment bureau for sewing. She tells us she had a good deal of work through your employment bureau and that you know her very well. She does not state why she is obliged to work, but gives us to understand that she has met with some disappointments since coming to Minneapolis.
>
> Would you kindly give us what information you may have concerning the family? In the meantime, we shall do all we can to furnish her with sewing.

In quick response the female head of the Michigan charity wrote back: "I sent her to the best people in the city, and she was a great favorite. She is the dearest old lady." This older woman acknowledged that the Grand Rapids agency had convinced her to "use my needle" for self-support and she thanked that agency saying, "You got me started." Learning that she was a legitimate recipient of assistance, AC/FWA intended to continue finding customers for her.[66]

Many of the 300 women had "started" work on their own. By the 1920s women who came to the agency were twice as likely as those before them to have had job experience, but earlier in the century, agents arranged many women's first encounter with the labor market without discussion as to conditions, wages to be earned, or the reality of the labor surplus.[67] And when AC/FWA paid the bill for fixing women's teeth in the 1920s, health was only half the concern. A more respectable-looking woman was a more employable woman. Thirty-six of the 300 women got into arguments with social workers who accused them of being slow at locating positions and perhaps being lazy. In the following excerpt the woman was married to a drunkard who beat their children. She admitted her own weakness was "bad" housekeeping but disagreed with the social worker that if she found employment, family life would improve.

> Woman says she realizes she has made a failure of bringing up the family but said if her husband had done the right thing and they had lived in a decent neigh. [neighborhood] she thinks matters would not be as they are now.
>
> [Next month] talked to Mrs. R. about getting work. She said she is afraid to leave the children alone. The older ones all went wrong so young that she [feels she] ought to stay at home with them now.[68]

Female volunteers on agency committees—who themselves were supported by husbands, fathers, and brothers—directed women into and out of jobs as they similarly gave advice for working children. Pensions distributed by the Friendly Visiting/ Relief and Service Committee were "not intended to be full support" as "the mother is permitted to do something toward her support, provided it is no detriment to the home life." Reports such as the following regularly appeared in minutes from their monthly meetings:

> Reported by Miss Wheeler [volunteer] that Mrs. Y. seems to be very much better now; does not get nearly so much washing from the Boarding House as she did. Is working only 2 days a week. . . . Com. [Committee] suggests to Miss Wheeler that it might be well for Mrs. Y. to work three days a week and not to try to take washing home as it will be better for the children not to have the washing hanging about the house.[69]

While mothers alone with little ones were cautioned to be dutiful of child care responsibilities, if these women lacked an adolescent earner they often appeared to be the most desperate for employment. Thus when jobs were in least supply in Minneapolis, social workers at AC/FWA "rationed" the domestic positions they knew of to distribute them among these younger mothers. A deserted wife who had gotten work referrals periodically over twelve years was refused any more when her children reached adolescence. The worker "explained we needed work for mothers of very young children where there were not so many working at home; felt we could not give her any more at present."[70] While progressive social welfare coalitions were using legislation and litigation to constrain working mothers' experiences in certain employment settings, social workers at places such as AC/FWA were encouraging young mothers' entrance into wage earning.[71]

In seeking or opposing employment, a mother could find herself without an understanding ally at the agency. But when the work experiences of all 300 women are considered together over time, figures suggest that AC/FWA preferences were *not* the deciding factor in many households. While social workers had an impact on individual women's work at various points, 129 identified themselves as wage-earners (though perhaps unemployed) *before* they had contact with the agency, and 130 women fit that status at case closings.

Intervention in Relations with Men

Economics—as well as morality—encouraged social workers to be directive in women's relationships with men. A husband could be the best and natural source of support—or a leech allowing his wife to work and the agency to offer assistance. And the woman alone—who in so many ways was assumed to be incapable of making good decisions—might be too susceptible to sexual advance. Casework oversight could begin by soliciting information about an unknown man who might visit a woman. Did neighbors know him? Did it appear that he was welcome? These were not written up as issues in the majority of cases, and such concerns lessened in records from the 1920s; however, earlier in the century a few agents went so far as to enlist neighborhood women as lookouts to check for men's union suits on the clotheslines of unmarried or deserted women.

Accepting boarders carried special dangers as men could take advantage of landladies—and agency largess. To a woman receiving limited assistance whose two male boarders were eating but not paying, the agent warned, "AC cannot feed able-bodied men who do not pay their way and if these men do not pay up she must get rid and take just room by herself. " Yet boarding arrangements *did* carry financial potential. Mary Richmond proposed a compromise position for COS workers. "For moral reasons it has been the general policy of the societies to discourage the keeping of male boarders or lodgers other than relatives." Then she added that social workers could only "influence" behavior, not "control" it. Therefore, the best solution was to encourage only the "moral" women with extra rooms to make appropriate matches with the right sort—ideally a female boarder.[72]

Sexuality—or rumors of female "immorality"—disturbed agents, but at AC/FWA the larger question about relations between men and women was whether a husband would stay around and act as provider. In the nineteenth century, charity workers were stingy with deserted families, being convinced that "too much" aid only perpetuated men's neglect of their duty as providers. So as not to give errant men the wrong message and encourage irresponsibility—the thinking went—wives and children might have to go without relief. If the "innocent" had to "suffer," so be it, for to do otherwise would allow males of weak character to hold "society by the throat."[73] As family work developed in the twentieth century, social workers came to appreciate better the complexity of marriage and the injustice of holding wives completely accountable for husbands' behavior.[74] But social workers *did* want women to be firm with husbands in their duty of providing economic support. One deserted woman reported experiences at another Minneapolis agency. "They refused to help her unless she would allow them to have Mr. N. found and made to support the children and she was so glad to be rid of him that she did not wish to have anything to do with him."[75]

The woman herself had to decide when to continue with a negligent husband, when to seek a lawyer for divorce, when to remarry. And her decisions and their timing could annoy the social worker. As described in chapter 4, agents did little to respond to many of the abuses women suffered at the hands of men. The two principle strategies caseworkers employed for dealing with erring husbands at home were the threat of incarceration—with which wives did not always agree—and a lecture meant to provoke a cooperative spirit between husband and wife.[76] The legislation and social ethos about motherhood that easily blamed women as inadequate parents was accompanied by assumptions that if only women were better homemakers, men's behavior would improve. On rare occasions seen as victories by the agents, caseworkers presided at debates between husbands and wives, which ended with reconciliation—if only short-lived. "After some more argument the scene was closed by #1 and #2 making up. They both promised to be good now and will try to do the best for the children."[77] For the deserter beyond the bounds of the admonition, wives and others—priests (with the advantage of native tongue) and policemen (with the advantage of the uniform)—were instructed to spread the agent's word that the man "must take care of his children . . . or he would go to the workhouse."[78] From the agency's view generally—though not always from the women's—marital obligation and reconciliation were preferable to women being on their own. However, when records opened on the 300 families, men were present as spouses in 120 households; when these cases closed, this figure had fallen to 91. Limits existed to the power of agency preferences.

As a poor woman became known at AC/FWA, an agent often exerted effort to pull this "client" temporarily under her own aegis. Having accepted professional employment, the caseworker took comfort in patterns that maintained her own dominance and a subordinate position for the recipient. In spite of genuine concerns about poverty, many social workers found it impossible to step beyond their own middle-class mores or consider options beyond the existing exploitive economic and gender relations. While agencies eschewed client dependency, they had difficulty conceptualizing how poor women could design *in*dependence from men or from AC/FWA. Once a needy wife or mother accepted assistance, she could find herself alternately treated as a child and blamed for problems rooted in privation. Such treatment poor women often resented and resisted.

Saying "No" to Assistance

Few women ever rejected grocery orders or jobs made available through the AC/FWA employment bureau; many repeatedly asked for more, but only the very aged, too infirm to work and in need of housing, ever willingly left their lives in an agent's hands. Women were very unlikely to tell all, or do all, in response to professional urging. When they knew their lives ran contrary to the principles of behavior voiced by an agent, women shut up. The additional boarder, the deserting husband's return, a male friend, borrowed money, drinking, school truancy, ill health, illegitimacy, the missed doctor's appointment, or the purchase of cake were private matters women gave social workers little help in discovering. Wives and mothers equivocated and refused to follow the advice given them to go to the hospital or send children to the nursery, or to demand more money from a child's wages or to throw out the boarding relative. Each woman's life was broader than her role as "client." To an outsider reading the case records, her resistance and periodic conflict with the social worker is more apparent than any substantive improvement in family life arising from agency intervention.

The case of a woman's struggle with social and economic problems as well as with the agency might continue for months, even years, and then the record ended abruptly. No mutual contract existed between the two parties, either could withdraw at will, and both did. Staff turnover, which worried agency administrators, guaranteed that case continuity was frequently splintered. A woman might explain and then reexplain her circumstance to a series of agents. When the final parting occurred between family and worker, it went without fanfare.

A stamp-lettered "CASE CLOSED" was added to office equipment in the 1920s and used on the last page of records along with a summary paragraph stating the initial reason for contact, a very abridged version of problems, and the final situation. But such formality was employed in only 35 of the 150 records used here from that decade, and available administrative materials suggest little about policy determining case closure. While agency public relations materials affirmed the impact of casework, few records ended with anything identifiable as "success." In some cases where the initial request had been very specific, for example, nursing for an old woman or a work permit for a fifteen-year-old, an agent might write that the goal had been accomplished—and say nothing about intervention in other issues that had consumed time but had not been so neatly resolved.

Some records contain initial interviews and an agent's collection of extensive information from outside sources and then—no further personal contact. At other times a variety of activities underway suddenly ceased. Certain of these records were transferred to another service agency—the Humane Society or Poor Department—but usually AC/FWA integrated other agencies' services into their own work while maintaining the file; thus it is unlikely that referral explains the outcome of most cases. Nor did frustration or distrust of families, which was an element in the midst of many cases, appear in the record as cause for sudden closure. Pearl Salsberry, a supervisor who became agency director in 1929, suspected that many case closings were expedient responses to "the pressure of work," but this explanation was never written into the record.[79]

Clients themselves may have been uncertain or surprised at the final actions of AC/FWA staff workers, but an exasperated woman could hasten along case closure by challenging the worker. By refusing to answer the door, the woman said in effect, "No more."[80] Other families moved away, perhaps to escape further prying by AC/FWA but more likely owing to myriad insecurities and to the ongoing search for more opportunity that characterized their lives. A woman's regard for either her agent or the service was reflected in the mode of departure; sometimes the new destination had been reported and was duly noted in the record. Other times a worker came by one day and found the house empty; neighbors said they knew nothing. Forty-one families achieved a state of economic equilibrium when the number of earners in a household outnumbered dependents. And very occasionally a family seemed to have caught onto adequacy, if not prosperity. An agent went out to visit a couple that had asked for a loan to help them build and she found construction underway on thirty acres at the city's edge. Hay, corn, vegetables, two horses, four calves, and five chickens completed the picture. The social worker suggested to them that they cover the house with tar paper for the winter and went back to write. "This family should be let alone. They are the kind that can get along."[81] This comment was

Table 17
Families' and Agency's Activity and Assumptions at Time of Case Closing in 300 Case Records

Families who:	
move to known destination	24
disappear without informing agency	18
emphasize do not want agency help	24
appear to achieve economic equilibrium	41
Families seemingly judged by AC/FWA as:	
needing no further service	28
deserving no further attention	25
needing referral elsewhere	17
Families whose case ends without deducible explanation	123
Total	300

SOURCE: 300 Case Records, FCS Collection.

unusual in its optimism and certitude. Table 17 shows how *unclear* family disposition was at most case closures as these family records are read by a contemporary researcher. Over time workers at AC/FWA were steadily engaged with a series of new households. Previous case families went their own ways leaving behind the constraints of agency purview and likely continuing with the difficulties inherent in being poor.

Getting Along on One's Own

Theories about family dynamics generated interest within the developing social work profession. Mary Richmond outlined her own understanding in an article illustrated with a series of concentric circles representing resources on which a household could draw. The innermost circle was "Family Forces," with "self-help" the most effective tool for dealing with family problems. "Personal forces" of friends and relatives comprised the next ring; then came the neighborhood where landlords and doctors could provide aid. Beyond this, "civic forces" existed—the truant and probation officers; private charities with benevolent individuals as well as organized services; and lastly, public charity with relief and free institutions such as the county hospital. The latter, she acknowledged, were at the greatest distance from a family's essence.[82] While all available resources were represented in this chart, and charity—or modern family casework—was indeed at a distance from a family's internal operation, the simplicity of the scheme belied how poor women's families worked.[83] The conceptualization discounted how essential wives and mothers were in maximizing resources from all the various levels and how the availability or absence of some options had an impact on others.

The support women had from kin relations, their attachments to ethnic communities with distinct cultural mores, or to rural home places throughout the region was only dimly perceived by agents. For months and sometimes years a family could disappear from view or the worker was too busy to pay them much attention. The woman might have moved in with a sister, or the husband returned home and taken them out West. Sometimes a news clipping or a report from another agency attached to the record would sketch out an accident or streak of good luck that had transpired during this time but was surrounded by unknown history. Poor families never stood still but were coming and going. Women were likely to pull resources from wherever they could be found, picking up what was available and letting it down as need be. Richmond's concentric circles were in fact irregular and overlapping, and daily life was taking place in them concurrently. The orbit of influence that AC/FWA maintained was small though at times intimately intrusive.

In these records family activity was family survival, and survival relied on "women's work." The traditional work ethic was stronger than the willingness to ask—or to keep asking—strangers for charity, and seeking employment was the common and repeating strategy of women and many youths.[84] Aside from accepting or rejecting an agent's direction, mothers on their own sought ways to answer children's needs, oversaw residential moves when finances went up or down, and worked to improve the places they had. Women brought others into their lives; they contacted relatives when they needed help and became acquainted with new men when husbands left. Some eventually packed up youngsters and belongings and left Minneapolis, believing life could be better somewhere else.

Children served as a powerful impetus; their dependency forced many women to overcome hesitation and to take action. When the three hundred cases are considered together, mothers of young children were *most* likely to be engaged with others in the ways just mentioned. When divided by marital status, those found *least* likely to go out on their own during a record's duration were married women whose husbands were present at the case opening. Deserted, divorced, separated, or widowed women had fewer options—and perhaps constraints for their own behavior. The absence of a man may have created the necessity for action initially, and with practice women's ability and inclination grew.

The time period also influenced a woman's options for help and her inclination to use them. Magazines of the 1920s pictured a modern woman as one in shortened skirts with a sassy, self-confident attitude who took and won increased authority to act, even with tasks long assumed to be "men's work." As known by AC/FWA records, the modern but poor woman of the 1920s was more likely to divorce, hire a lawyer, buy and sell property, or dream some entrepreneurial scheme than had been true of her female counterpart earlier in the century.

These efforts as documented in Table 18 appeared to result from a woman's own initiative. No husband was present in the home when they occurred, and the agent who recorded the activity was unaware of related plans until completed. But a larger number of wives had similar dealings as they took over or finished what a spouse began. A man who fell ill or disappeared in the night sometimes left his wife to worry about and deal with an unfair mortgage, overdue bills, and unpaid wages. By choice or necessity she may have asked brothers or a father to be her advocate in these matters, although the agent and case record lacked such details. Women who undertook their own legal dealings made use of the Legal Aid Bureau at AC/FWA, but also consulted lawyers in private practice. Eventually sixty-two women used these professionals to press nonsupport charges, file for divorce, bring lawsuits, and handle property disputes.

To sue another for negligence brought hope not simply for justice and a fair return, but held the possibility of a financial boost. Spurred by cautious optimism one mother brought suit against the driver of the big automobile that injured her son; another took her landlord to court when she broke her shin on a rickety porch. If a settlement or a loan were

Table 18
Women's Independent Behavior by Time of Case Opening in 300 Case Records

	Cases Opened 1900–1910	Cases Opened 1920–1930
Women on their own		
hired a lawyer	21	41
received a divorce	15	26
had a scheme or small enterprise intending to make money	16	32
bought or sold property	17	32

SOURCE: 300 Case Records, FCS Collection.

negotiated, it could yield money for furnishing a boardinghouse, for returning to a farm in the country, or for purchasing yarn to knit and sell. These were very narrow roads to survival. Rarely did women anticipate legal actions as the master stroke guaranteeing comfort. Experiences with charity, poor health, unsteady jobs, growing children, and disappearing men had taught them well about the temporary nature of solutions.

Conclusion

As part of an urban population and as mothers trying to sustain homes, poor women developed relations with a variety of formal and informal city institutions. Between 1900 and 1930 the context for social welfare in the city shifted with the concept of "charity" taking hind place to professional "family work," but in both—to be a recipient carried stigma. Needing help meant that certain aspects of one's life were scrutinized and other important elements ignored. The terms of affiliation with agencies and organizations varied in length, purpose, and mutuality; some contacts were sought—the Sunday School for children and the good-will hopefully to be found there—and others were resisted—the appointment at General Hospital. To become a case at AC/FWA brought welcome but short-term and limited material relief, and it opened the possibility for advice and imperatives regarding family life.

The agency claimed expertise in knowing the poor, reducing poverty, and rehabilitating those families that fell short of the ideals of self-sufficiency and stability. On a day-to-day basis the task of this fell to earnest young agents who carried good intentions and the agency's reputation into poor neighborhoods expecting women to open their doors and listen. Within most of these households, however, wives and mothers were struggling with critical problems: unemployment, illness, drunkenness, and desertion, calamities often beyond an agent's sensitivity and ability to fashion a truly lasting answer. Regardless of intent, many social workers in the field failed even to perceive the basic exploitation of class and sex that female clients routinely experienced. These workers floundered as to practice and policies and in the process many became imperious. Along with well-meaning volunteers, they made unilateral assumptions and decisions as to how daily life should proceed for the lower class and often placed the cause of problems on women's shoulders. Agents were frustrated with uncooperative and willful women and wrote this into the case records; the resistance they recorded is evidence that frustration was felt by both parties.

A social worker was most appreciated if she was willing to follow up decisions the woman had made for herself—to search for a house when a move seemed imperative, to locate used furniture enabling a boarder, or to find a second place for the woman to launder. These were not tasks that required the college training distinguishing family casework from earlier charity, and they did not eliminate poverty, but were simple additional but limited aids to survival.

Women took charity because at the time they needed it. This defined them as "cases" in the record keeping and discussion at social welfare agencies. "Recipiency," however, was not the controlling dynamic in their households, nor did they allow a social worker to set the parameters for all behavior. AC/FWA was only a temporary inset in family life. Women doggedly engaged in activities and initiated relations in self-styled strategies for survival. Pressured by the facts of their existence they frequently could not see far beyond the short-term and as viewed by others, made mistakes. But while the misery they coped with often was great, likewise was their intent to be autonomous.

Conclusion

Bounty from railroads, grain mills, and lumber stands filled pockets and brought civic amenities to Minneapolis, as the nineteenth century rolled into the twentieth. While the city grew rapidly to dominate affairs in the Upper Northwest, not every resident contributed in the same way nor profited equally, and the existence of poverty amid affluence alarmed those with a vision and investment in orderly, progressive urban life. Intent in some measure on alleviating the social ills that plagued impoverished households, city mothers and fathers organized Associated Charities (AC) along lines being pursued by respectable and affluent citizens elsewhere across the country. Many of these organizations would consequently evolve into a Family Welfare Association (FWA) or service agency that intervened in the daily life of the urban lower class. Social workers defined poor women and men as their "clients" whose misfortunes and struggles they translated into entries for case records. The focus in this study, however, is not the city as it was known by the prosperous, nor the agency whose administrators came to enjoy professional reputations, but the dark kitchens, cold houses, and rundown neighborhoods where three hundred women lived at some point. Because they all were known to a degree by caseworkers who kept records, it is possible to interpret the working lives they led.

The Fiction of Traditional Family Wage and Roles

Mrs. Nordheim was described in the Introduction as an exhausted mother with an eviction notice nailed to her door, empty cupboards, and crying children. In the note she wrote to AC/FWA, she asked that someone appreciate what she already had "done and struggled." She knew how hard she pushed herself to hold the family together, and it did not match with the conventional view that the man of the house earned a "family wage" and supported his dependents. Chaos in the Nordheim home reflected contradictions in the larger society that regarded "family" sentimentally but failed to provide opportunities for the lowest class. Industrial capitalism treated laborers with little regard and set many businesses on a roller coaster of boom and bust, which meant that men brought home insufficient pay envelopes—or none—and employed women labored for a pittance. Domestic peace and harmony became fiction in many families; poverty put pressure on both functional and affectional relations.[1] From one poor household to the next, serious difficulties—chronic illness, malnutrition, desertion, violence, and despair—appeared in varying degrees, and the well-being of families and individual family members deteriorated.

Privation pushed women's roles beyond the domestic confines defined in the prevailing family ethic and blurred boundaries of what was appropriate female behavior.[2] To "make" a home challenged poor wives and mothers to be creative with scarce resources and to maintain relations with neighbors and kin in self-styled mutual assistance for times of worst troubles. Many women in this study dealt not simply with a scarcity of household resources, but also coped with neglectful and often drinking and brutal husbands who had the protection of a male-dominated society. For these mothers and their children, home as a refuge might deteriorate over time to become the site of oppression.[3] When women went beyond their own households to work for wages, it was hard to escape a second victimization by the economic system where the lowest-paid jobs of least status were held for them. In the scheme of an urban setting that offered them little respect, poor women could seek material relief by articulating family despair and negotiating needs and wants with landlords, credit agents, and social workers. Dealing with charity institutions—a last resort for many—meant a poor woman had to contend with intrusion in her life as engineered by another female who very likely knew of poverty only through observation.

By design this study included women at different points in the life cycle and with different marital statuses so as to examine how responsibility for children and relations with men impacted on them. While poor women faced many things in common, those who were the youngest and with small children—but who lacked a spouse—were most likely to act in their own behalf and go out to seek help from others. Responsibility for youngsters provided a powerful motivation to act; when even one child reached adolescence a woman was less alone in caring for the others and more able to share the task of wage earning. To characterize these women's lives only by the dependency of offspring, however, neglects the role of men. When a case opened at AC/FWA, the ages of the children suggested something about the demands on the woman, but her marital status as defined initially in a the record promised little about a man's activity.

Men were granted much authority by society, and through violent behavior they could control others at home, but that authority did not translate into responsibility. The term *female-headed household* as used here is more than a legal definition; it applies to times in the life of many families when a woman was left no options but to take over, not simply owing to death and divorce but to absence and illness and to the debilitation of unemployment. Within painful and powerful economic and social constraints women struggled to do what they saw as necessary.

The larger middle-class population in the city only partially understood conditions of lower-class life, and popular discourse usually described the poor in terms of pity or disdain. This study, however, counters the simple view that the lower class was only helpless, only wretched, or only pawns in destructive social systems. Details written into the case records afford more than discussion of class and gender as variables; they reveal despair but also vitality, and show hopeful people pursuing multiple strategies for survival. Such a narrative has to accompany any quantitative summaries of behavior to give due respect to individual variation and to the idiosyncrasy that reveals itself in daily life and changes with time.

Women's Sense and Use of Self

For many women, experiences with impoverishment and pain tested their individual strength and the need to hold one's own. Other women were worn down and waited impatiently for their youngsters to be independent or supportive; a few died young or disappeared into institutions. A grown child with an open door was someone to count on; the charity of an agency was *not*. Women's definition of self had little to do with being a "client" at AC/FWA but much to do with marriage and motherhood. While certain actions differentiated their lives from those of *middle-class* women—doing laundry for money, hawking a fruit drink outside a theater, or pleading for a load of coal—the three hundred in this study had a strong sense of themselves as women. Many forces contributed to the constancy of this female identification in the midst of tribulation.

The staff at AC/FWA urged many women to become wage earners while simultaneously reaffirming them in prescribed domestic roles. A man's status in any one family was likely to change over time, but agency case records distinguished him as "#1" and the woman as "#2." She was always classified according to marital status: divorced, widowed, or the wife of a man—deserted, ill, unemployed, or nonsupporting. Because a mother's care of children tied intrinsically to the future of America, women with youngsters commanded more public awareness and assistance than did a single adult. In contacting kin the agency was more likely to seek shelter and money from a male relative than from a female—though the evidence shows help came more frequently from women. Social workers often encouraged married couples to stay together in spite of economic failure and physical abuse and pushed for legitimization of marriage relations. Thus women getting assistance at AC/FWA received the message that they were principally wives and mothers and subservient—not only to men but to agency direction. And while they often rejected the suggestions and mandates social workers gave for carrying out household responsibilities, they usually agreed with the basic assumption that homemaking obligations were a chief priority.

Identification and reinforcement of female roles also came to women from sources closer to them than the agency. Frequently they operated within a female subculture in which women came to the aid of one another over "female" issues: pregnancy, child care, and marital conflict. Assistance was possible among and between women because to a great degree they shared traditional ideas about women's responsibility to children and home. It is obvious that women discussed their marriage problems with one another. When a wife was criticized by other women she knew, it was owing to her failure to keep a house clean, make hot meals, or be faithful to her husband.

At times when women spoke hopefully about the future, their common wishes were for their children. When they expressed pride, it was most often over handwork, gardens, or the development of well-behaved youngsters. Experience stripped them of assumptions that a family could rely on men's salaries or goodwill and they realized, too, the dangers of of pregnancy and abuse as a result of relations with men. But aware of their own economic vulnerability, many women sought the added support that marriage to a wage-earning husband had the *possibility* of offering. A small number spoke in favorable terms of marriage and *wanted* to live with a man, but most women indicated acceptance of the practical *need* to be married.[4]

As wage earners themselves they often hired out to do cleaning and serving that resembled their work at home, though positions elsewhere put control in the hands of others.[5] In industry they labored in settings that offered little pay and no advancement, where female company might be the only redeeming element. Thus women's identity as "workers" was rarely with these irregular jobs secured at employment bureaus and bringing in a driblet of wages, but with the persisting tasks of making and sustaining home and children. Society offered little opportunity to reject marriage or motherhood, and poverty denied resources for complying with social norms governing these roles, but women in this study labored hard to accomplish what they did. In this, ironically, they conserved traditional gender roles.

Poor women lacked "power" and visibility in the greater society but felt the obligation of struggling for family well-being, which made them an active force. They milked resources and determined the openings and boundaries in dealings with men, children, neighbors, and kin. Case records show most clearly how these women established limits with the social workers who knew them and who sought to link the offering of material relief and opportunities with directives for behavior. Poor women distinguished between the elements of relief and advice; they sought and accepted practical assistance while often rejecting the instructions for family life that accompanied it.

On the national stage, social critics, reformers, settlement residents, and social work educators were documenting and debating various public ills. Extensive private programs were established to intervene in family life. But in the day-to-day work at local agencies, however, young workers failed to advocate remedies for real problems confronting families. Yet these employees were also clear that AC/FWA itself could not and would not provide long-term financial support of any adequacy for a family. Thus social workers conveyed the confusing imperative that the poor were to be "cooperative" with actions at some midpoint between being "too dependent" and "too independent." For many women such counsel led to conflict because the "self-sufficiency" expected from them was not to be achieved simply with the success of one action. Rather, it relied on interlocking strategies, which might be more—or less—acceptable to onlookers. Women had to make a series of demands on those within their families and neighborhoods and on persons beyond. Survival often meant choosing from among various poor alternatives, living for a time with the outcome, and then trying new strategies.

The Presentness of Past Experience

Minneapolis grew and changed between 1900 and 1930, but these case records reflect basic changes in only minor ways over time. Social welfare procedures moved from amateur volunteer services toward professionalism. In keeping with the "modernization" of the 1920s some poor women—as many other females—appeared more assertive in using and creating resources for themselves.[6] But the majority of factors in poor women's lives rendered little evidence of change during the first third of the twentieth century, thus lending support to the conclusion that characteristics of privation alter at a slower tempo than do many other elements in our society. When the Great Depression forced the middle class to learn and adopt new strategies in eking out survival—shared housing among families as an example—they were practicing what the lower class already knew how to do.[7] The *real* strategy change in the

1930s involved the role of federal government in response to widespread economic insecurity.

As hardship worsened in the early depression, the director at AC/FWA documented the growing demand for relief and the agency's inability to respond with either money or staff energy. All over the country social workers experienced the same phenomenon, and in spite of private agencies' basic skepticism about public institutions' ability to do family work, they eventually welcomed federal relief moneys and then passage of the 1935 Social Security Act, which authorized Aid to Dependent Children (ADC) to replace existing state pension programs for mothers.[8] When the economy finally picked up, agencies such as AC/FWA furthered developed their family casework function but *without* the relief element. They understood ADC to be the economic support available to mothers whose incomes qualified under a means test and whose behavior qualified under a rigid but less than precise morals evaluation.[9] In 1962 ADC became Aid to *Families* with Dependent Children (AFDC), known today as the controversial public assistance program dealing directly with poor families although many financially eligible households never apply. The virulent public debate surrounding AFDC is over an old set of questions: Which mothers should be supported? What should be their relationship to men? As mothers, and as poor mothers, what responsibility do they have to earn wages?[10]

Society in the United States today accepts even greater imbalance between upper-and lower-class wealth and income than ninety years ago, and the minimum wage falls far short of being a "family wage." Fathers continue to leave mothers as the parent principally responsible for child-rearing, and if parents are living apart, men's rate and consistency in paying child support is notoriously low especially in the absence of effective government surveillance.[11] Documentation grows of men's at-home physical abuse of wives and mates, which makes women desperate for alternative economic and social supports for themselves and children.

At its best, however, financial assistance through AFDC is accompanied by policies and paperwork embedded with intrusive judgments, and the income granted leaves recipients below the poverty line. If a woman seeks services, help is negotiated by means of a "service contract." The ethics of professional social work dictate that attention be paid to "self-determination" in this process and that providers be sensitive to the multiple disadvantages of women in a sexist world. Yet class and cultural differences still generate misunderstanding between social workers and the poor. Elements in the lives of women prior to the 1930s persist for their counterparts in the late twentieth century.

Whether being a client at AC/FWA in the past or today on AFDC, for most women and their families receipt of organized assistance was and is a temporary experience. A family crisis that lessens resources or increases needs, or uncertain employment and low wages, are likely to have created the demand for assistance. However, approximately half the families on AFDC leave within two years, and dependence on governmental aid is only one of multiple strategies these poor mothers employ.[12] As in the past, women receiving formal assistance survive because they manage to supplement it by loans and exchanges with neighbors and kin. Many recipients do part-time wage work, preferring self-sufficiency to dependency, but the minimum wage available in the secondary labor market is insufficient for families; it scarcely allows payment for child care and lacks benefits such as provision for health care, which does accompany AFDC. Congressional legislation titled the "Family Support Act" in 1988 dealt with the relationship of public-assistance and individual initiative in supporting family well-being; the result for many women, however, is a tightened association between assistance and willingness to work for wages. Contemporary jargon refers to this as "workfare," wherein a recipient maintains program eligibility by participating in job training or low-paid, low-skill employment that may or may not ever lead to permanent and adequate income.

The phrase "feminization of poverty" reflects current statistics showing the disproportionate and *growing* number of females, both AFDC recipients and nonrecipients, whose incomes do not bring them *up* to the federally defined poverty line. While older women who are widowed or never married make up part of this population, the majority are mothers raising children in the absence of a financially supportive male parent and of employment that carries a living wage.[13] What women say today about their lives echoes past voices.

Three hundred seven female heads of household across the country were interviewed in depth in 1985 and 1986 as part of a study commissioned by the National Association of Social Workers. Only a third were poor by the government's poverty line standards, but "economic concerns were uppermost for everyone." Mothers spoke of their inability to purchase food, housing, clothing, and health care and of the time they spent searching for bargains. Finding jobs was difficult and led to the negative self-perception of being "unemployable," while the financial and emotional absence of a second parent added to the unending responsibilities of raising children. A woman interviewed in California wrote, "If my parents and close friends didn't help with food, clothing, paper goods, money on occasion, I think my sons and I would be homeless, regardless of AFDC." However, the title of this NASW study is *Helping the Strong: An Exploration of the Needs of Families Headed by Women.* The author, Dorothy Miller, differentiates between "being in need of money and services and being capable and strong. While the women are quite aware of their problems and needs, they do not see themselves as victims." Sixty percent of the women indicated they believed their families had "more strengths" than other families, and these assets included the support of family, friends, and neighbors, and perseverance and independence as survival skills.[14]

Lacking value in the eyes of society or in the labor market, poor women now and in the past demonstrate and value their own perseverance and ability at making do in raising youngsters against the economic odds. These women and children, however, pay a criminally high physical and emotional cost that challenges our nation's claims to be as just and caring. Ideally parts of the stories presented in this book will eventually be told only as examples of an archaic past.

Notes

Introduction

1. Case 4,285 on Reel 130, FCS, Social Welfare History Archives, University of Minnesota, Minneapolis.

2. This prescription for domestic life and women's dependency in the 1800s was first interpreted by Barbara Welter, "Cult of True Womanhood," *American Quarterly* 18 (Summer 1966), 151–74. See also Nancy F. Cott, *The Bonds of Womanhood, Woman's Sphere in New England, 1780–1835* (New Haven, Conn.: Yale University Press, 1977), which relates changing economics and new gender roles. Carl N. Degler, *At Odds, Women and the Family in American from the Revolution to the Present* (New York: Oxford University Press, 1980), breadwinners and homemakers are roles within the "Modern American family." In Alice Kessler-Harris, *Out to Work: A History of Wage Earning Women in the United States* (Oxford: University Press, 1982), 49, middle-class ideology values women's "moral and spiritual presence in the home" rather than in the labor market. Catherine Hall, "The Early Formation of Victorian Domestic Ideology," in Sandra Burman, ed., *Fit Work for Women* (New York: St. Martin's, 1979), 15–32, discusses the same phenomenon in Great Britain.

3. Robert L. Griswold, *Family and Divorce in California, 1850—1890, Victorian Illusions and Everyday Realities* (Albany: State University of New York, 1982), passim; also Mimi Abramovitz, *Regulating the Lives of Women: Social Welfare Policy from Colonial Times to the Present* (Boston: South End, 1988), 119; Jane Lewis, "The Working Class Wife and Mother and State Intervention, 1870–1918," in Lewis, *Labour and Love: Women's Experience of Home and Family, 1850–1940* (London: Basil Blackwell), 10, 100–103; Ann Vandepol, "Dependent Children: Child Custody and Mothers' Pensions," *Social Problems* 29:3 (February 1982), 227, 228.

4. Robert Bremner, *From the Depths, The Discovery of Poverty in America* (New York: NYU Press, 1956), passim; John Ehrenreich, *The Altruistic Imagination: A History of Social Work and Social Policy in the United States* (Ithaca, N.Y.: Cornell University Press, 1985), 29–32, 43, emphasizes activism among the poor, which drew attention to issues of poverty.

5. See the bibliography of early century wage studies in Dorothy S. Brady, "Family Budgets : A Historical Study, *Monthly Labor Review* 66:1 (January 1948), 171–75; for a contemporary critique of these studies, see Heidi

Hartmann, "Capitalism and Women's Work in the Home 1900–1930" (Ph.D. Thesis, Yale University, 1974), 141–47, 190.

6. A "family wage" begins as a working-class claim in the nineteenth century; social reformers in the twentieth century endorse it for social stability according to Martha May, "Bread Before Roses: American Workingmen, Labor Unions and the Family Wage," in Ruth Milkman, ed., *Women, Work and Protest, A Century of Women's Labor History* (New York: Routledge, 1985), 2–10.

7. Crystal Eastman, *Work Accidents and the Law,* Pittsburgh Survey (New York: Russell Sage Foundation, 1910), found almost no "thorough" investigation of accidents underway in the country. For a contemporary interpretation of the impact of industrial accidents with some mention of Minnesota, see Robert Asher, "Industrial Safety and Labor Relations in the United States, 1865–1917," in Charles Stephenson and Robert Asher, eds., *Life and Labor: Dimensions of American Working-Class History* (Albany: SUNY Press, 1986), 115–30. For an example of businesses' resistance to responsibility for injured workers, see Carl Gersuny, " New England Mill Casualties: 1890–1910," *New England Quarterly* 52:4 (1979), 467–82. For a feminist interpretation of accidents' impact and prevention for female workers, see Vilma Hunt, "A Brief History of Women Workers and Hazards in the Work Place," *Feminist Studies* 5:2 (1979), 274–85.

8. The negative impact of "family wage" for men and women is interpreted by May, "Bread Before Roses," 11–16; and Natalie Sokoloff, *Between Money and Love: The Dialectics of Women's Home and Market Work* (New York: Praeger, 1981), 228–36. Also Karen Bodkin Sacks and Dorothy Remy, eds., *My Troubles Are Going to Have Trouble with Me: Every Day Trials and Triumphs of Women Workers* (New Brunswick, N.J.: Rutgers University Press, 1984), 22; and Lewis, *Women in England 1870–1950: Sexual Divisions and Social Change* (Bloomington: Indiana University Press, 1984), 145. For unions' opposition see Alice Kessler-Harris, *Women Have Always Worked* (Old Westbury, N.Y.: Feminist Press, 1981), 66–68.

9. Linda Gordon, *Heroes of Their Own Lives: The Politics and History of Family Violence, Boston 1880–1960* (New York: Viking, 1988), Gordon interprets case records from Boston agencies involved in child welfare; see 1–12 for an introduction to an analysis of shifting politics of family violence as part of a struggle within and beyond homes. Elizabeth Pleck, *Domestic Tyranny: The Making of American Social Policy Against Family Violence from Colonial Times to the Present* (New York: Oxford University Press, 1987), defines violence, broadly looking at motivation and at the impact of related social policy over time. Lewis, *Women in England,* 45–47, when victimized, working-class women received more public "sympathy" than did men.

10. For a Marxist feminist analysis that women's domestic role results in victimization by capitalism and patriarchy, see Sokoloff, *Between Money and Love,* 180, 222–227. The theoretical relationship of family wage, capitalism,

and patriarchy is discussed in Heidi Hartmann, "The Unhappy Marriage of Marxism and Feminism: Towards a More Progressive Union," in Lydia Sargent, ed., *Women and Revolution: A Discussion of the Unhappy Marriage of Marxism and Feminism* (Boston: South End, 1981), 21–25; Susan Yeandle, *Women's Working Lives: Patterns and Strategies* (New York: Tavistock, 1984), 14, 15; Myra Marx Ferree, "Sacrifice, Satisfaction, and Social Change: Employment and the Family," in Sacks and Remy, *My Troubles Are Going to Have Trouble with Me*, 62, 63; and James Dickinson and Bob Russell, eds., *Family, Economy, and State: The Social Reproduction Process under Capitalism* (New York: St. Martin's, 1986), 8. Mary McIntosh, "The Welfare State and the Needs of the Dependent Family," in Burman, *Fit Work for Women*, 155, 156, women were exploited as a reserve army of cheap labor and as mothers "reproducing" a new generation of laborers.

11. Louise A. Tilly and Joan W. Scott, *Women, Work and Family* (New York: Holt, 1978), passim. See also Winifred Wandersee, *Women's Work and Family Values, 1920–1940* (Cambridge: Harvard University Press, 1981), passim. Elyce J. Rotella, "Women's Labor Force Participation and the Decline of the Family Economy in the U.S.," *Explorations in Economic History* 17:2 (1980), 95–112, contrasts the influence of the "household variable" on single and married women's labor force participation.

12. Stephan Thernstrom, *The Other Bostonians: Poverty and Progress in the American Metropolis, 1880–1970* (Cambridge: Harvard University Press, 1973), first assessed the working-class economic and social mobility using U.S. Census materials and quantitative measures. Women are scarcely visible in his households.

13. For an historical analysis of work within a cultural context that integrates women's home and paid labor, see Louise Woodcock Tentler, *Wage-Earning Women, Industrial Work and Family Life in the United States, 1900–1930* (New York: Oxford University Press, 1979); Lewis, *Women in England;* and Diana Gittins, "Marital Status, Work and Kinship, 1850–1930," in Lewis, ed., *Labour and Love: Women's Experiences of Home and Family, 1850–1940* (Oxford: Basil Blackwell, 1986), 250–67. Gittins writes of paid work, unpaid domestic work, and marriage as three interrelated and overlapping "occupational spheres." For a theory on the interplay between work and home, see in Tamara Hareven, "Cycles, Courses and Cohorts: Reflections on Theoretical and Methodological Approaches to the Study of Family Development," *Journal of Social History* 12 (Fall 1978), 97–109; and Hareven, "Introduction: The Historical Study of the Family in Urban Society," *Journal of Urban History* 1:3 (May 1975), 259–67. See also Sokoloff, *Between Money and Love*, 178.

14. Quantitative analysis of census materials with attention to women as household heads and urban family development are discussed in Theodore Hershberg, ed., *Philadelphia: Work, Space, Family and Group Experience in the Nineteenth Century* (New York: Oxford University Press, 1981); particularly

Claudia Goldin, "Family Strategies and the Family Economy in the Late Nineteenth Century: The Role of Secondary Workers," 277–310. Also Steven Mintz and Susan Kellogg, *Domestic Revolutions, A Social History of American Family Life* (New York: Free, 1988), 91, 92; Jack Wayne, "The Function of Social Welfare in a Capitalist Economy," in Dickinson and Russell, *Family, Economy, and State,* 67, 76.

B. Seebohm Rowntree, *Poverty: A Study of Town Life,* 2nd ed., (New York: Macmillan, 1902), 137, pioneer's work relating family budget and needs to worker's age and children. The same approach is used by Robert Hunter, *Poverty, Social Conscience in the Progressive Era* (New York: Macmillan, 1904), 56–58. Robert Kelso, *Poverty* (New York: Longmans, 1929), 146, "the presence of children in the home is an anchorage to poverty." Hazel Kyrk, *Economic Problems of the Family* (New York: Harper, 1929), 193, 194, there's a need for a "moving average budget" for changing families.

15. Michael B. Katz, *Poverty and Policy in American History* (New York: Academic, 1983), passim, 17. "In neither the past nor the present can family life among the poor be disentangled from the practice of welfare." See Chapter 3, "American Historians and Dependence." Lewis, *Women in England,* 52–62, among English women, Poor Relief was used only "when all else failed."

16. For a comprehensive examination of family ethos in social welfare, see Abramovitz, *Regulating the Lives of Women,* Chapter 4, 111–16. Home was women's "exclusive domain" and motherhood the "central responsibility."

17. Addams, "The Subtle Problem of Charity," in *Jane Addams, A Centennial Reader* (New York: Macmillan, 1960), 82, 83. Reprint from *Atlantic Monthly,* March 1899.

18. Gordon, *Heroes of Their Own Lives,* 12–18, discusses shortcomings of case records as a source, 293–99; there's also a discussion of social control as the theory to explain social welfare history.

19. John R. Borchert, *America's Northern Heartland, An Economic and Historical Geography of the Upper Midwest* (Minneapolis: University of Minnesota Press, 1987), 45, 46, 54–61.

20. Contemporary historians have criticized the philosophy and policies of charity organization boards and staffs, for example, M. E. Gettleman, "Charity and Social Classes in the United States, 1874–1900, I, II *American Journal of Economics and Sociology* 22 (April, July 1963), 325, 327, 417–21; Kenneth L. Kusmer," The Functions of Organized Charity in the Progressive Era: Chicago as a Case Study," *Journal of American History* 60 (December 1973), 672–74; Timothy J. Naylor, "Responding to the Fire: the Work of the Chicago Relief and Aid Society," *Science and Society* 39:4 (Winter 1975–76), 464. Others suggest that the COS concept was not as innovative as claimed at the time. Brian Gratton, "The Invention of Social Work: Welfare Reform in the Antebellum City," *Urban and Social Change Review* 18:1 (Winter 1985), 308; Anne Summers, "A Home

from Home-Women's Philanthropic Work in the Nineteenth Century," in Summers, *Fit Work for Women,* 52–57.

21. National Conference of Charities and Correction, *Proceedings,* 1886, 168.

22. For further information about agency development, see David J. Klaassen, "The 'Deserving Poor': Beginnings of Organized Charity in Minneapolis," *Hennepin County History* (Spring 1988), 15–25; and Beverly A. Stadum, "'Maybe They Will Appreciate What I Done and Struggled': Poor Women and Their Families—Charity Cases in Minneapolis, 1900–1930" (Ph.D. Thesis, University of Minnesota, 1987), passim.

23. AC, *23rd Annual Report,* 1907, 6.

24. For evidence of organizing difficulties in AC, see *29th Annual Report,* 1913, 13; Minutes, General Conference Committee, Exhibit B, February 17, and March 16, 1904, Folder–1, Box L.1, and Twin City Investigating Bureau, "In the Interests of the People of Minneapolis Relative to the Policy and Conduct of the Associated Charities," March 10, 1911, 1, Folder–3, Box 1, FCS Collection. Gary Lloyd, *Charities, Settlements and Social Work, Inquiry into Philosophy and Methods, 1890–1915* (New Orleans: Tulane University School of Social Work, 1971), 25, the public criticized charities' "overly zealous" application of rigid methods.

25. Papers from Folder–3, Box 1, FCS Collection, describe changes in the Minneapolis agency. Amos Warner, et. al., *American Charities and Social Work,* 4th ed. (New York: Thomas Y. Crowell, 1930), 204, 207. Consecutive editions show the changing mission of COS over four decades. Verl Lewis, "Charity Organization Society," in National Association of Social Workers, *Encyclopedia of Social Work,* 1977 ed., Vol. 1 (New York: National Association of Social Workers, 1977), 96–100, details the account of the COS concept moving from Britain to Buffalo in 1877; highlights cities' implementation of COS goals and suggests why many COS evolved into family service agencies. Replacement of volunteers with paid staff is discussed in Stanley Wenocur and Michael Reisch, *From Charity to Enterprise, The Development of American Social Work in a Market Economy* (Chicago: University of Illinois Press, 1989), 35–37.

26. AC, *29th Annual Report,* 1913, 24, 13, 28, 29, 31, 18, 43.

27. Minutes, Special Board Meeting, 30 August 1922, Folder 1–23–18 to 12–16–24, Box 5, FCS Collection.

28. For changes in case recording, see Geraldine Lamb, "The Play," n.p., Folder–3, Box 1, FCS Collection; FWA, *Family Welfare Association in Action,* 8; Ada E. Sheffield, *Social Case History: Its Construction and Content* (New York: Russell Sage Foundation, 1920), 7–15, 75–82, the typewriter had a similar

impact in charity offices across the country; Warner, *American Charities and Social Work*, 278.

29. In the 1940s, after FWA merged with the Children's Protective Society becoming Family and Children's Service, administrators destroyed thousands of records after microfilming what they considered a representative sample of cases opened and closed between 1895 and 1945. The resulting microfilm collection at the University of Minnesota Social Welfare History Archives holds approximately 35,000 cases on 398 reels available for use by qualified scholars within conditions related to confidentiality and the disguise of names. Case numbers are consecutive on each microfilm reel, but the date of case opening is only roughly chronological, and no connection exists between case number and type of case.

Purposeful generation of case records within the social work profession and implications for research is in David Klaassen, "The Provenance of Social Work Case Records: Implications for Archival Appraisal and Access," *Provenance: Journal of the Society of Georgia Archivists* 1:1 (Spring 1983), 5–30. Gordon, *Heroes of Their Own Lives*, 12–20, describes case records as source on families. Frank T. Bruno, *Trends in Social Work, 1874–1956, A History Based on the Proceedings of the National Conference of Social Work* (New York: Columbia University Press, 1957), 184–89, comments that records were used for worker training but were "hardly professional." For weaknesses in records also see Mary Richmond, *What Is Social Case Work? An Introductory Description* (New York: Russell Sage Foundation, 1922, 8; Helen Wallerstein, "Purposeful Investigation," *The Family* 1 (November 1920), 18. Nathan Irvin Huggins, *Protestants Against Poverty, Boston's charities, 1870–1900* (Westport, Conn.: Greenwood, 1971), 78, regarding records at the Boston Associated Charities, "theirs was a science of description, not of analysis."

30. Arrangements between AC/FWA and other local institutions regarding jurisdiction over needy populations is in Report, "The City Poor Department and the Associated Charities-December 1908," Folder 1–15–08 to 12–16–08, Box 4; Letter, Frank J. Bruno to Francis McLean, May 27, 1915; July 3, 1920, Folder-8, Box 3; Minutes, Board Meetings, January 18, June 13, 1922, April 15, 1925, January 20, 1926, in Folder 1–23–18 to 12–16–25, and Minutes, Board Meeting, December 21, 1927, Folder 1–20–26 to 12–16–31, in Box 5, FCS Collection. See a modern interpretation of public/private relations in Wenocur and Reisch, *From Charity to Enterprise*, 155, 156.

The Society for Prevention of Cruelty to Children and Animals began 1874 and was renamed the Humane Society in 1891. The staff there lobbied with AC board members for the establishment of a juvenile court, established in 1905. This led to development of a Juvenile Protective League to provide probation officers and a physician for court-referred children; the league and the Humane Society merged in 1917; the two became Children's Protective Society (CPS), which merged with FWA in 1947. At an uncertain date between 1917 and 1938, CPS and AC/FWA agreed that CPS would handle needy motherless families and AC/FWA those that were fatherless; see Edward F. Ebert, "The Historical Development of the Family and Children's Service of Minneapolis" (M.A. Thesis, University of Minnesota, 1958); Minneapolis Council of Social Agencies, Community Survey of Social and Health Work in Minneapolis, Vol. 14 (Minneapolis: Council of Social Agencies, 1938), 17; "Family Service, The Private Family Agency in Minneapolis in 1936," Social Agencies: FWA, Minneapolis Clippings File, Minneapolis Public Library, Minneapolis.

31. Demographic trends in agency caseloads, 1917–26, FWA, *The Family Welfare Association in Action, 1917–1926* (Minneapolis: FWA), 28–32. Stephan Thernstrom, "Poverty in Historical Perspective," in Daniel Patrick Moynihan, ed., *On Understanding Poverty: Perspectives from the Social Sciences* (New York: Basic, 1968), 171; James T. Patterson, *America's Struggle Against Poverty 1900–1960* (Cambridge: Harvard University Press, 1981), 3–19.

32. This interpretation of the first years in AC, *25th Annual Report,* 1909, 16; also Pearl Salsberry, Minutes from a Staff Meeting, May 2, 1931, Folder–3, Box 1, document titled "The Family Welfare Association" includes ten pages of chronological events, 1884 to 1945. Letter, Geraldine Lamb to Council of Social Agencies, July 18, 1935, Folder–3, Box 1, FCS Collection.

33. More information about the sample is in Stadum, "Maybe They Will Appreciate What I Done and Struggled," Appendix. Scarcity of widows as social work clients is in James R. Reinhardy, "Social Casework with the Elderly Between World War I and II," *Social Service Review* 61:3 (September 1987), 499–501.

34. For the diverse impact of the 1920s on women, see Dorothy M. Brown, *Setting a Course: American Women in the 1920s,* Radcliffe College, American Women in the Twentieth Century Series (Boston: Twayne, 1987).

35. Bruno, *Trends in Social Work,* 193–96, explained that Mary Richmond and the Russell Sage Foundation pushed for separation of COS functions and became forces in development of family casework. When cities adopted federated fund-raising—a move encouraged in Minneapolis by the Chamber of Commerce—the broad public did not see why a COS deserved funds unless it had a designated and needy clientele; without funds no professional staff could be hired. See also Lewis, "Charity Organization Society," 99–100.

36. This is based on the 300 sample cases; see also Bruno, General Secretary Reports, October 22, 1919, Folder–8, Box 3, FCS Collection, he reports the average case length as slightly less than six months.

37. Robert Hunter, an early New York City social worker, was among the first to systematically and quantitatively describe the lower class. In *Poverty,* 3, 4, 20, 25, 26, 94, 95, paupers without pride were distinguished from the working poor. Thernstrom, *Other Bostonians,* 42, asserted a high proportion of the male working-class population as very mobile; other labor historians' work has modified this. See Charles Stephenson, "'There's Plenty Waitin' at the Gates': Mobil-

ity, Opportunity, and the American Worker," in Asher and Stephenson, *Life and Labor*, 73–75.

38. Lewis, *Women in England,* xii, xiii, poverty and lack of education created "unstated boundaries" within which working class women acted "independently." Lewis summarizes, "She cannot be categorized as either victim or free agent." Natalie Zemon Davis, "Women's History as Women's Education," from a Symposium in Honor of Jill and John Conway, Smith College, April 17, 1985 (Northhampton, Mass.: Smith College, 1985), 16, 17. Davis writes:

> The best current practice is not looking for universal pattern, sociobiological, psychoanalytic, or other, in the sexual division of labor. . . . Rather it is looking for *varieties* of arrangements, different ways in which hierarchy and equality, power and reciprocity can be mixed. . . . The best current practice is not listening for a single male or female voice over time, but for multiple voices making different judgments of historical experience.

Chapter 1

1. Agency personnel judged twelve dollars to be less costly than most rental housing for clients at the time; price was reflected in condition. FWA *Family Welfare Association in Action, 1917–1926* (Minneapolis: FWA, 1926), 28, 29, 61.

2. See Minneapolis Council of Social Agencies, *Community Survey of Social and Health Work in Minneapolis*, Vol. 41 (Minneapolis: Council of Social Agencies, 1938), 1–19. See also Minutes, Friendly Visitors' Conference, February 3, 1915, Folder-1, Box L.1, Family and Children's Service Collection Social Welfare History Archives, University of Minnesota, here the superintendent of Minneapolis schools outlined "The School; and Children of Dependent Families." See public schools' role in children's health in Robert H. Bremner, ed., *Children and Youth in America, a Documentary History, 1866–1932*, Vol. II (Cambridge: Harvard University Press, 1971), 813.

3. This study quotes material as it appeared in the case records with original abbreviations, misspellings, and grammatical shortcuts. Proper names are disguised for confidentiality but take the same form as in the record with full names or initials; attention was paid to maintaining ethnicity in substitute names. Quotes are footnoted only if a complete sentence or more in length.

4. U.S. Department of Labor, "Women in Industry," *Monthly Labor Review*, XI: 3 (September 1920), 543–47.

5. Case 1,345 on Reel 115.

6. Florence Welles Carpenter (always appearing in the AC/FWA records as Mrs. E. L. Carpenter) was active at AC/FWA 1901 through 1938, being on the board and chairing the Friendly Visiting/Relief and Service Committee. Her

role on behalf of clients appears in some case records; the many hours she put in at the agency were described by her son Leonard Carpenter, Interview, June 18, 1985, Crystal, Minnesota.

7. Case 22 on Reel 106.

8. Case 845 on Reel 112.

9. Efforts to establish AC in *25th Annual Report,* 1909, 16, 17, Folder-Historical, Box 1, FCS Collection. Early histories of Minneapolis elaborate on George Brackett's role organizing charitable endeavors; see Isaac Atwater, *History of the City of Minneapolis, Minnesota* (New York: Munsell, 1893), 240–44; H. B. Hudson, *A Half Century of Minneapolis* (Minneapolis: Hudson, 1908), passim; Marion Shutter, *History of Minneapolis, Gateway to the Northwest* (Chicago: S. S. Clarke, 1923), 110. Brackett's generous spirit and community concerns were discussed in the Carpenter interview, June 18, 1985. The Carpenters and Bracketts had proximate homes on Lake Minnetonka, an area west of Minneapolis originally developed as a summer retreat for the city's elite.

Organizations voting to adopt the AC constitution included the St. Vincent de Paul Society, the 13th Avenue Methodist Episcopal Church, the Open Door Congregational Church, the First Unitarian Society, the Sisterhood of Bethany, the Plymouth Congregational Church Working Band, the Women's Christian Association, the Plymouth Charity Kindergarten, the Tabitha Society, the Women's Exchange, the Aid Society of the Church of the Redeemer, the Gethsemane Brotherhood, the Franklin Avenue Relief Association, the City Missionary Society, the North Western Hospital, and the Hahnemann Society.

For evidence of difficulties in successful organizing in AC, see *17th Annual Report,* 1901, n.p.; *18th Annual Report,* 1902, 7, 15–17; *20th Annual Report,* 1904, 10; *23rd Annual Report,* 1907, 6; *25th Annual Report*, 1909, 23, 44. Also in Minutes, General Conference Committee, Exhibit B, February 17, and March 16, 1904, Box 5. Twin City Investigating Bureau, *In the Interests of the People of Minneapolis Relative to the Policy and Conduct of the Associated Charities*, March 10, 1911, Folder-3, Box 1, FCS Collection.

10. Information about the Anti-Tuberculosis Committee from AC, *20th Annual Report,* 1904, 4; *23rd Annual Report,* 1907, 27, 28; *29th Annual Report,* 1913, 12, and from a periodic agency publication, *The Bulletin,* July 1, 1918, 3; August 4, 1919, 4; see also FWA, *Family Welfare Association in Action,* 54. Recommendations about the committee becoming independent from the agency are in General Secretary Reports, September 1917, Folder-8, Box 3, FCS Collection. Information about the Visiting Nurse program in AC, is in the *Annual Reports* from 1902 to 1913. See particularly, *18th Annual Report,* 1902, 9, 10; *19th Annual Report,* 1903, 13–16; *21st Annual Report,* 1905, 37, 38; AC, *22nd Annual Report,* 1906, 7, 19, and *26th Annual Report,* 1909, 53.

Formation of the Hennepin County Legal Assistance Program in AC, *23rd Annual Report,* 1907, 30; *26th Annual Report,* 1910, 4, 17, 27, 45–47. Bureau opening in *29th Annual Report,* 1913, 59, 60, FWA, *Family Welfare Association in Action*, 57. Discussion of the employment bureau is in E. A. Fay, "Free Employment Bureau," Minnesota State Conference of Charities and Correction, *3rd Annual Conference*, 1895, 88–91; AC, *18th Annual Report*, 1902, 7, 14; *19th Annual Report*, 1903, 17, 18.

11. General history about the COS movement is in Amos Warner, et. al., *American Charities and Social Work*, 4th ed. (New York: Crowell, 1930), 204, 207. First published in 1894, this early standard history went through many editions—all with Warner as principal author in spite of his demise. Alexander Johnson, with experience at COS in Cincinnati and Chicago, chaired the ongoing committee on Charity Organizing at the National Conference, "Charity Organization Committee Report," NCCC, *Proceedings*, 1886, 168; he reported "sixty-seven organized efforts of charitable relief of various kinds" with twenty-six as "charity societies pure and simple." Edward Devine, *The Principles of Relief* (New York: Macmillan, 1904), 77, 471. See also AC, *17th Annual Report*, 1901, n.p., FWA, *Family Welfare Association in Action*, 51.

Frank J. Bruno, *Trends in Social Work 1874–1956, A History Based on the Proceedings of the National Conference of Social Work* (New York: Columbia University Press, 1957) 11, 96, 193; Verl Lewis, "Charity Organization Society," in *Encyclopedia of Social Work*, 1977 ed., Vol. 1 (New York: National Association of Social Work), 96–100, elaborates how COS diversified and transformed into family service agencies.

Reform inclinations in Frank L. McVey, "The Necessity for Constructive Charity," Minnesota State Conference of Charities and Correction, *14th Annual Conference Proceedings*, 1906, 54–58. General progressive reform in Minneapolis is in Hudson, *Half Century of Minneapolis*, 557, 558; Minneapolis Civic and Commerce Association, *Minneapolis Golden Jubilee, 1867–1917* (Minneapolis: *Minneapolis Tribune*, 1917), 15–17. For New York City COS work with housing and tuberculosis, see Emily Wayland Dinwiddie, "The Redemption of 'Lung Block,'" *Charities and the Common* (August 8, 1908), 579–81.

Later assessment of COS reform is in Bruno, *Trends in Social Work 1874–1956*, 102, 103. Gary Lloyd, *Charities, Settlements and Social Work, Inquiry into Philosophy and Methods, 1890–1915* (New Orleans: Tulane University School of Social Work, 1971), 43, found that both charities and settlements had difficulty balancing between "limited, individual change, and more sweeping social action and change," 152, and "while it is true that many charitable agencies around the country were instrumental in increasing state regulation of housing standards and industry, . . . the proportion of social workers absorbed in, and dedicated to these activities were minimal," 127. Kenneth L. Kusmer, "The Functions of Organized Charity in the Progressive Era," *Journal of American History* 60 (December 1973), 657–78, is more critical.

12. Richmond's role is in Joanna C. Colcord and Ruth Z. S. Mann, eds., *The Long View: Papers and Addresses by Mary E. Richmond* (Russell Sage Foundation, 1930), 627; John H. Glenn, Lilian Brandt, and F. Emerson Andrews, *Russell Sage Foundation, 1907–1946*, Vol. 1 (New York: Russell Sage Foundation,

1947), 58, 125, 126, 131. A brief biography is written by Murial W. Pumphrey, "Mary Ellen Richmond," in Walter I. Trattner, ed., *Biographical Dictionary of Social Welfare in America* (Westport, Conn.: Greenwood, 1985), 622–25. The best contemporay account of how Richmond and the Russell Sage Foundation came to dominate the profession is in Stanley Wenocur and Michael Reisch, *From Charity to Enterprise, The Development of American Social Work in a Market Economy* (Chicago: University of Illinois Press, 1989), 46–77, 89; Bruno, *Trends in Social Work*, 193–96. Francis H. McClean (Richmond's assistant), *The Formation of Charity Organization Societies in Smaller Cities* (New York: Russell Sage Foundation, 1910), illustrates foundation publications dealing with COS.

June Axinn and Herman Levin, *Social Welfare: A History of the American Response to Need*, 2nd ed. (New York: Longman, 1982), 151, 156–58, interpreted COS as slow in "moving toward an explicit family welfare stance."

13. FWA, *Family Welfare Association in Action,* 48–51, outlines careers of 100 professionals employed there 1917–26. Many went to teach or work with the Red Cross and 48 were active agency social workers, many functioning as directors and supervisors. David Klaassen, "History of Associated Charities: Family Welfare Association," unpublished paper, 111–19, FCS Collection, describes the reunion and notes the role of Frank J. Bruno (at AC/FWA 1914–25) and Joanna C. Colcord (1925–29) in training these persons.

Early directors with reputations included Frank McVey, at AC 1900–1902 (he also chaired the Board for some time), later president of the University of North Dakota and of the University of Kentucky, Minneapolis Council of Social Agencies, *Community Survey of Social and Health Work in Minneapolis,* Vol. 3 (Minneapolis: Council of Social Agencies, 1938), 2. Eugene T. Lies, at AC, 1907–13, went on to administration in National Playground and Recreation Association of America, *Community Survey,* Vol 1, 2.

14. AC, *25th Annual Report,* 1909, 36–40, and "Twenty-Five Years in Minneapolis," *Survey* 25 (February 19, 1910), 762–64. Eugene Lies to Prof. Frank L. McVey, February 25, 1907, Letter, Jane Addams to Frank McVey, February 25, 1907, and Letter, Edward J. Devine to Prof. Frank L. McVey, March 4, 1907, Box 5, FCS Collection. "New Charity Head Begins His Work," *Minneapolis Journal,* May 30, 1907, 6:2. Higlights of agency innovation in FWA, are in *Family Welfare Association in Action*, 7–14, 17, 33–35, 45, 46, 51.

Indication of Frank Bruno's broad role in Minneapolis welfare matters is illustrated by his direction of a 1920 citywide study of agencies' casework sponsored by the Council of Social Agencies and helped by the American Association for Organizing Family Social Work. Bruno, Annual Reports, 1920, 8, General Secretary Reports; Letter, Bruno to Francis McLean, December 20, 1920, Folder–12, Box 8, FCS Collection.

15. Examples of articles by AC/FWA staff in *The Family*: Caroline Bedford, "The Daily Log," 4:10 (February 1924), 239–44. Bruno, "Family Social Work,"

6:5 (July 1925), 144, 145. Colcord, "The Fabric of Family Life," 5:2 (April 1924), 172, 173. Pearl Salsberry, "Techniques in Case Work," 8:5 (July 1927), 153–57; and "Supervision," 10:10 (February 1930), 291–97. See also Colcord, *Broken Homes, A Study of Family Desertion and Its Social Treatment* (New York: Russell Sage Foundation, 1919), based on experiences with COS families; further information about Colcord's publications and contributions by Beverly Stadum in "Joanna C. Colcord," in Trattner, ed. *Biographical Dictionary,*188–91.

The Family was renamed *Social Casework,* and in 1990 this became *Families in Society.*

16. Bruno, *Trends in Social Work,* 19, 184–89.

17. AC, *27th Annual Report,*1911, 14, 15; see also Sumner K. McKnight, "What Minneapolis Does for the 'Under Dog,'" Minneapolis Civic and Commerce Association, *Minneapolis Golden Jubilee, 1867–1917* (Minneapolis: Civic and Commerce Association, 1917), 38.

18. References to the agency's role with Widows' or Mothers' Pensions in AC, *29th Annual Report,* 1913, 29; Minutes, Board Meeting, March 19, 1913, Folder 1–22–13 to 12–5–17, Box 5, and General Secretary Reports, January 21, 1920, Folder–8, Box 3. Letters, Bruno to Francis McLean, May 27, 1915; July 3, 1920, Folder-8, Box 3. Arrangement to verify need for child labor permits for 28 city schools, AC, *20th Annual Report,* 1904, 12.

19. FWA, *Family Welfare Association in Action,* 18; United Charities of Saint Paul, Minnesota, *Annual Report,* 1928–29, 5, this advice was quoted from other COS sources. and included in a section titled, "Ideals of a Family Service Society."

20. AC of Boston, *36th Annual Report,* 1915, 32, 35. Reports prior to and after this date indicate the same antirelief policy. Nathan Irvin Huggins, *Protestants Against Poverty, Boston's Charities 1870–1900* (Westport, Conn.: Greenwood Publishing, 1971), 62, 63, 70, 71; Wenocur and Reisch, *From Charity to Enterprise,* 54. Edward T. Devine, "Widows Need," *Survey* 32 (April 4, 1914), 27, summarizes case work with widows in six New York City agencies.

21. AC, *21st Annual Report,* 1905, 17 ; *25th Annual Report,* 1909, 17. Eugene Lies, "The City Poor Department and the Associated Charities," December, 1908, also Letter, Eugene Lies to Father Dolphin, December 7, 1908, Folder-3, Box 8; "Report of the Family Welfare Survey Committee," April 28, 1937, Folder–2, Box 8, FCS Collection. Warner, *American Charities,* 171.

22. Budget figures from AC, *19th Annual Report,* 1902, 10; *26th Annual Report,* 1910, 17; and from FWA, *Family Welfare Association in Action,* 61.

23. Minneapolis Department of Charities and Correction, *Annual Reports 1901–1907* (Minneapolis: Board of Charities and Correction, 1908), 24–27. AC,

23rd Annual Report, 1907, 16, 20, 50, 51. Don Divance Lescohier, "Wages, Prices, Rents and Workingmen's Budgets in Minnesota," in Minnesota Bureau of Labor, Industries and Commerce, *12th Biennial Report,* 1909–1910 (St. Paul: State of Minnesota, 1910), 327, 328.

24. FWA, *Family Welfare in Action,* 28, 29, 61. A graph showing the distribution of total relief bill among different St. Paul agencies in St. Paul Welfare Council, *On Uneasy Street, In the Year 1930* (St. Paul: Welfare Council, 1930), 11–26, private agencies provided a quarter of the total. Analysis of grants from states' Mothers' Pensions in Women's Bureau, *State Laws Affecting Women*" #16 (Washington, D.C.: U.S. Department of Labor), Chart X.

25. Inconsistancy of casework in Bruno, September 30, 1917, General Secretary Reports, Folder-8, Box 3; Minutes, Board Meetings, May 7, 1915; November 21, 1917, Folder 1–22–13 to 12–4–17, Box 5, FCS Collection.

26. "Report of the Friendly Visiting Committee," April 14, 1904, Folder-3, Box 1, FCS Collection.

27. Howard P. Chudacoff, *Mobile Americas: Residential and Social Mobility in Omaha, 1880–1920* (New York: Oxford University Press, 1972), passim, records the high rate of residential mobility in the city as measured by census material and city directories and questions the possibility of "community."

28. U.S. Bureau of the Census, *12th Census of the United States, 1900,* Vol. 4, Vital Statistics, 164.

29. John Modell and Tamara K. Hareven, "Urbanization and the Malleable Household: An Examination of Boarding and Lodging in American Families," *Journal of Marriage and the Family* 35 (August 1973), 473, quantitative measures show boarders sought ethnic "matches" with whom they lived and shared similar economic standing.

30. Mildred Lucile Hartsough, *The Twin Cities as a Metropolitan Market: A Regional Study of the Economic Development of Minneapolis and St. Paul* (Minneapolis: University of Minnesota, 1925), 166, 167, 181.

31. James Leiby, *A History of Social Welfare and Social Work in the United States* (New York: Columbia University Press, 1978), 4, "it is reasonable to suppose that most people who needed help turned to their families or neighbors and that formal institutions served relatively few, but we have no definite generalizations on how families managed for themselves." This study answers some of the unknowns about family life to which Leiby points.

32. Mimi Abramovitz, *Regulating the Lives of Women: Social Welfare Policy from Colonial Times to the Present* (Boston: South End, 1988), 36–40, sexism as factor in public and private society.

Chapter 2

1. Conference On the Care of Dependent Children, Washington, D.C. January 25 and 26, 1909, *Proceedings* (U.S. 60th Congress, 2nd Session, Senate Document #721), 9.

2. Edward L. Devine, "The Economic Function of Women," *American Academy of Political and Social Science, Annals* (November 1894), 374, women added pleasure to material objects used in the home; more importantly they determined production by purchasing choices. Contemporary critics observe homemakers "aiding" consumption.

3. Richmond, "Charity and Homemaking," 1897, in Joanna C. Colcord and Ruth Z. S. Mann, eds., *The Long View, Papers and Addresses by Mary E. Richmond* (New York: Russell Sage Foundation 1930), 178. Richmond wrote often about marriage; *Child Marriages* (New York: Russell Sage Foundation, 1925), and *Marriage and the State* (New York: Russell Sage Foundation, 1929). Eli Zaretsky, "Rethinking the Welfare State: Dependency, Economic Individualism and the Family," in James Dickinson and Bob Russell, eds., *Family, Economy, and State: Social Reproduction Process under Capitalism* (New York: St. Martin's, 1986), 86, 87.

4. Charles Stephenson, "'There's Plenty Waitin' at the Gates': Mobility, Opportunity, and the American Worker," in Robert Asher and Stephenson, eds., *Life and Labor: Dimensions of American Working Class History* (Albany: SUNY Press, 1986), 90, 91. Edgar Sydenstricker and W. Jett Lauck, *Conditions of Labor in American Industries* (New York: Funk and Wagnalls, 1917; reprint ed., New York: Arno and the New York Times, 1969), 291. Stanley Lebergott, *Manpower in Economic Growth, The American Record Since 1800* (New York: McGraw-Hill, 1964), 259, home ownership rose nationally from 37 percent in 1900 to 46 percent in 1930. U.S. Bureau of Census, *13th Census of the United States*, 1910, Vol. 1, 1313, an increase in housing occupancy by Minneapolis owners from 28.7 percent in 1900 to 40.4 percent in 1910.

5. Richmond and Fred S. Hall, discussed homemaking attributes in *A Study of Nine Hundred Widows Known to Certain Charity Organization Societies in 1910* (New York: Russell Sage Foundation, Charity Organization Department, 1913), 12; see also Richmond, *What Is Social Work? An Introductory Description* (New York: Russell Sage Foundation, 1922), 63–65, 79. Example in Case 17,277 on Reel 225.

6. Discussion about visiting housekeepers is in Associated Charities AC *25th Annual Report,* 1909, 7; *26th Annual Report,* 1910, 36; *29th Annual Report,* 1913, 48, 49. Also Minutes, Friendly Visitors' Conference, November 10, 1909; March 1, 1916, Folder-1, Box L.1, Minneapolis Family and Children's Service FCS Collection, Social Welfare History Archives, University of Minnesota.

7. *The Bulletin*, October 22, 1917, 1, 2, Folder-3, Box 3, FCS Collection.

8. Case 427 on Reel 109.

9. Case 514 on Reel 110, contains extensive documentation by homemakers.

10. Ross, "Labour and Love," 85; Susan Yeandle, *Women's Working Lives: Patterns and Strategies* (New York: Tavistock, 1984), a study of contemporary families that includes "Child Helpers at Home"; Rubin, *Worlds of Pain*, 27–29; contemporary working-class adolescents understand pressure on parents.

11. Ellen Ross, "Labour and Love: Rediscovering London's Working Class Mothers, 1870–1918," in Lewis, ed., *Labour and Love: Women's Experiences of Home and Family, 1850–1940* (Oxford: Basil Blackwell, 1986), 74, mothers' "caring services" are essential for children's survival. Lewis, *Labour and Love*, 10, 11, 28, women often sacrificed themselves. Louise A. Tilly and Joan W. Scott, *Women, Work and Family* (New York: Holt, 1978), 213, wrote about the early century. "Although a working class married woman's life at home was difficult and time-consuming, it was also of great economic, social, and emotional importance to her family. It could be as well a source of respect and status in the eyes of the family she served and a source of some pride for herself." Leslie Woodcock Tentler, *Wage Earning Women, Industrial Work and Family Life in the United States, 1900–1930* (New York: Oxford University Press, 1979), 175–79, women's emotional and managerial efforts kept the home together giving women "power," and they were rewarded with affection from family members. Robert L. Griswold, *Family and Divorce in California, 1850–1890, Victorian Illusions and Everyday Realities* (Albany: SUNY Press, 1982), 63–66, reviews literature showing the enhancement of women's self-esteem through domestic responsibility. Mirra Komarovsky, *Blue Collar Marriage* (New York: Random, 1962), 49–55. Research in the 1950s revealed "moral consensus" among working-class women regarding domestic roles, but the inherent frustrations prevented it from offering "contentment."

12. Case 10,046 on Reel 170. Arthur W. Calhoun, *A Social History of the American Family, Vol. III from 1865 to 1919* (Cleveland: Arthur H. Clarke, 1919; reprint ed., New York: Barnes and Noble, 1960), 123. Hazel Kyrk, *Economic Problems of the Family* (New York: Harper, 1929), 43–50, cites "management" and "performance" as part of unpaid household production.

13. Case 5,767 on Reel 140.

14. Case 3,368 on Reel 125.

15. Case 3,293 on Reel 125.

16. Case 7,330 on Reel 150.

17. Case 18,153 on Reel 235.

18. Michael B. Katz, *Poverty and Policy in American History* (New York: Academic, 1983), 53, 54, noted constant clothing needs in case records from Philadelphia COS. Robert S. and Helen M. Lynd, *Middletown, A Study in American Culture* (New York: Harcourt, 1929), 62, clothing held the last priority in family budgets.

19. Katharine Anthony, *Mothers Who Must Earn* (New York: Russell Sage Foundation, Survey Research Associates, 1914), 100, 142, 145, most families in her study had sewing machines, which Anthony attributed to market salesmanship. Heidi Hartmann, "Capitalism and Women's Work in the Home, 1900–1930" (Ph.D. Thesis, Yale University, 1974), 349, 167, in 1925, 90 percent of all sewing machines were sold on time, as little as 10 percent down and an average of 18 months to repay. By 1900 most men's and children's clothing was ready to wear, but working-class women continued to make their own and children's clothing; see also Susan Strasser, *Never Done: A History of American Housework* (New York: Pantheon, 1982), 141–43. For sewing machines that were common in lower-class English homes, see "Elizabeth A. Roberts, "Women's Strategies, 1890–1940," in Lewis, *Labour and Love,* 233, women "altered" or "ran up" garments but few sewed to sell.

20. Case 733 on Reel 150.

21. Case 1,859 on Reel 118.

22. Lewis, *Labour and Love,* 8, British working-class women sought information about female biology and health.

23. Twin City Federation of Settlements, *Self Analysis Survey of Minneapolis Settlement Houses* (Minneapolis: Twin City Federation of Settlements, 1934), passim, many settlements had baby clinics, some with visiting nurses from COS. Between 1924 and 1929 eight prenatal and child health centers were built in Minnesota through the Children's Bureau, United States Children's Bureau, *18th Annual Report, 1930* (Washington, D.C.: 1930), 1–3, in Bremner, *Children and Youth in America, 1008–1010;* midwives were related to infant mortality and blindness, *Ibid.*, 814. For the hardship of pregnancy, see Ross, "Labour and Love," 78, 79.

24. Anthony, *Mothers Who Must Earn*, 154, 155, "abortions are common, and unsuccessful attempts are even commoner"; mothers perceived abortion as economically justified. Jane Lewis, *Women in England, 1870–1950: Sexual Divisions and Social Change* (Bloomington: Indiana University Press, 1984), 15–20, British working-class women aborted for family limitation; little information or privacy limited other forms of birth control. Barbara Brooks, "Women and Reproduction, 1860–1939," in Lewis, *Labour and Love,* 157–63, emphasizes women's control in spite of church and legal prohibitions. Calvin Schmid, *Social Saga of Two Cities* (Minneapolis: Bureau of Social Research, Minneapolis Council of Social Agencies, 1937), 410, between 1927 and 1936, 109 women in

Minneapolis died from abortion, half were married, facts frequently were "suppressed or falsified."

25. Women's Cooperative Alliance, Joint Commission on Social Hygiene, *Attitudes of Mothers Toward Sex Education* (Minneapolis: Women's Cooperative Alliance, 1926), 4, 20, 81, 89, Minneapolis Clippings File, Minneapolis Public Library.

26. Case 5,040 on Reel 135.

27. Absence of contraceptive information among the working class is noted in Robert and Helen Lynd, *Middletown*, 123; Wally Seccombe, "Marxism and Demography: Household Forms and Fertility Regimes in the West European Transition," in Dickinson, *Family, Economy, and State*, 44, 45; legal prohibitions and working-class ignorance and lack of access to contraception is noted in John D'Emilio and Estelle B. Freedman, *Intimate Matters, A History of Sexuality in America* (New York: Harper, 1988), 174–76, 243–46. Linda Gordon, *Heroes of Their Own Lives: The Politics and History of Family Violence* (New York: Viking, 1988), 199, withdrawal was a common attempt at contraception. Norman Hines, *Medical History of Contraception* (Baltimore: Williams and Wilkins, 1936), 385, 386, by the 1930s a "democratization of contraceptive knowledge " had occurred throughout the country, but advice varied from medical knowledge to "back fence" information. In 1935 the archbishop of St. Paul declared any Diocese Catholic affiliated with an association that "endorsed, advocated, or facilitated contraception" would be denied Church sacraments, from David M. Kennedy, *Birth Control in America; The Career of Margaret Sanger* (New Haven, Conn.: Yale University Press, 1970), 149, 150. Gordon, *Woman's Body, Woman's Health; A Social History of Birth Control in America* (New York: Grossman, 1976), 256, "social workers were converted to birth control [as a social good] only slowly in the 1920s." Individual national social welfare figures were supportive earlier, but it took the depression "to win over the profession as a whole."

28. Case 17,290 on Reel 225.

29. Mark Schneyer, "Mothers and Children, Poverty and Morality: A Social Workers' Priorities, 1915," *Pennsylvania Magazine of History and Biography* 112:2 (April 1988), 213, similar experiences occurred in the Yiddish-speaking community of Russian Jews.

30. Ann Vandepol, "Dependent Children: Child Custody and Mothers' Pensions," *Social Problems* 29:3 (February 1982), 231–35.

31. Case 4,285 on Reel 130.

32. Colcord, "Strengths of Family Life," *The Family* 11:7 (November 1930), 214.

33. Case 6,477 on Reel 145. Dangerous additives in children's candy are noted in Louise Eberle, "Penny Poisons," *Colliers* (July 8, 1911), 18–19; reprinted in Bremner, *Children and Youth in America,* 883–84.

34. Case 4,946 on Reel 135.

35. Case 15,890 on Reel 215.

36. Attitudes toward children with TB is in, John Lovett Morse, "The Protection of Infants and Young Children from Tuberculosis Infection," in National Association for the Study and Prevention of Tuberculosis, *Transactions* (1906), 624–26; public schools' activity in children's health Research Division, American Child Health Association, *A Health Survey of 86 Cities* (New York: 1925), xiv–xv, 175–78, 184–87; both reprinted in Bremner, *Children and Youth in America*, 890–92, 924–29.

37. Case 6,477 on Reel 145. In four years two children died from whooping cough, a daughter developed heart trouble, a son had bowed legs and needed glasses, another developed pneumonia and blood poisoning, the home was quarantined for chicken pox, and the father tested positive for venereal disease. Further information on children's health and responding institutions in Bremner, *Children and Youth in America,* 811–1092. Also Ross, "Labour and Love," 79, 83, 84.

38. Case 4,285 on Reel 130.

39. Anthony, *Mothers Who Must Earn*, 155; a different view is in Margaret Jarmon Hagood, *Mothers of the South, Portraiture of the White Tenant Farm Woman* (Chapel Hill: University of North Carolina Press, 1939; reprint ed., New York: Norton, 1977), 155, "it seems that more value attaches to children when they represent about all a man and his wife can call their very own."

40. Vandepol, "Dependent Children: Child Custody and Mother's Pensions," 221–35, social welfare advocates argued over home versus institution for needy children. Mimi Abramovitz, *Regulating the Lives of Women: Social Welfare Policy from Colonial Times to the Present* (Boston: South End, 1988), 166–68, theoretically child caring institutions provided the discipline of an ideal home.

41. Case 10,023 on Reel 170.

42. Case 4,256 on Reel 130.

43. Case 2,398 on Reel 120.

44. Case 1,355 on Reel 115.

45. Case 2,398 on Reel 120.

46. D'Emilio and Freedman, *Intimate Matters*, 181–83, 194–201.

47. Class and commercial amusements is in Kathy Peiss, " Dance Madness: New York City Dance Halls and Working-Class Sexuality, 1900–1920," in Asher and Stephenson, *Life and Labor*, 184–89. See also Dorothy M. Brown, *Setting a Course: American Women in the 1920s* (Boston: G..K. Hall Twayne, 1987), 29–32, 105. Rubin, *Worlds of Pain,* 41, 43, 57, marriage was an "escape" for working-class girls. See Mintz and Kellogg, *Domestic Revolutions,* 118, for an analysis of youth culture in the 1920s.

Joanne J. Meyerowitz, "Holding Their Own: Working Women Apart from Family in Chicago 1880–1930" (Ph.D Thesis, Stanford University, 1983), 2–7, 64, independence of young working-class women was supported by gifts and support from men; Meyerowitz writes that these women were neither "victimized" nor "liberated."

48. Case 17,339 on Reel 225.

49. Case 16,418 on Reel 220. Working-class emphasis on split of "good girl" and "bad girl," is in Rubin, *Worlds of Pain,* 57. "Sexual delinquency" as an encompassing indictment included women's victimization, Gordon, *Heroes of Their Own Lives,* 21, 22, 49–52, 241–47; Pleck, *Domestic Tyranny,* 130.

50. Juvenile court's perception of social problems is in Ellen Reyerson, *The Best-Laid Plans, America's Juvenile Court Experiment* (New York: Hill and Wang, 1978), passim. Women's sexual behavior—even when men are involved—has greater potential to "offend" public morality. Records from Hennepin County Juvenile Court, *Report 1926–1928,* 14, 15, 20, 21; crime and gender is in Schmid, *Social Saga*, 353.

51. Case 14,332 on Reel 200. See R. E. Denfield, "The Delinquent Parent," Minnesota State Conference of Charities and Correction, *20th Annual Conference*, 1911, 67–69. Also Mark H. Leff, "Consensus for Reform: The Mothers' Pension Movement in The Progressive Era," *Social Service Review* 47:3 (September 1973), 400, discusses juvenile delinquency as it was blamed on working mothers; Abramovitz, *Regulating the Lives of Women*, 192; Pleck, *Domestic Tyranny*, 126–35; Vandepol, "Dependent Children: Child Custody and Mothers' Pensions," 227.

52. Case 440 on Reel 109.

53. Case 10,140 on Reel 150. Diana Gittins, "Marital Status, Work and Kinship, 1850–1930," in Lewis, *Labour and Love*, 262–64, discusses sexist family expectations about who provides caring services.

54. Case 2,810 on Reel 105. James R. Reinardy, "Social Casework With the Elderly Between World Wars I and II," *Social Service Review* 61:3 (September 1987), 509, the elderly were defined socially as obsolete.

55. Case 1,332 on Reel 115; Case 2,360 on Reel 120.

56. Case 15,521 on Reel 210. Abramovitz, *Regulating the Lives of Women,* 51, few elderly had pensions, savings, or insurance policies during this period. Rubin, *Worlds of Pain*, 27–29.

57. Case 353 on Reel 108.

58. Case 2,385 on Reel 120.

59. Case 637 on Reel 111.

60. Robert and Helen Lynd, *Middletown,* 459, 460; Lois Rita Helmbold, "Making Choices, Making Do: Black and White Working Class Women's Lives and Work During the Great Depression" (Ph.D. Thesis, Stanford University 1983), 182, landladies fed poor tenants and gave free rent. James Leiby, *A History of Social Welfare and Social Work in the United States* (New York: Columbia University Press, 1978), 4.

61. Yeandle, *Women's Working Lives*, 154, 155, women relied on friends and neighbors for day care. Helmbold, "Making Choices, Making Do," 177–84, in the Great Depression middle-aged and older women relied on friends in various exchange agreements. For other relations between women, see Lewis, *Labour and Love,* 10.

62. Richmond, *Social Diagnosis* (New York: Russell Sage Foundation, 1917), 187–89, 196, 197, 467–69, COS agencies in three cities show relatives as the most frequent resource for families, but social workers debated whether agencies should press kin for support. Also Winifred Wandersee Bolin, "Past Ideals and Present Pleasures, Women, Work and Family, 1920–1940" (Ph.D. Thesis, University of Minnesota, 1976), 275, kin were the "first barrier" against hard times. Relatives in the economy of the poor is in Gittins, "Marital Strategies, Work and Kinship," 251; Lewis, *Women in England,* 9.

Mintz and Kellogg, *Domestic Revolutions*, 104, marginality of working-class economic security should prevent romanticizing about assistance available among kin; Rubin, *Worlds of Pain,* 166, 197. Also Elizabeth Bott, *Family and Social Network: Roles, Norms and External Relationships in Ordinary Urban Families* (London: Tavistock, 1957), 118–26, within industrial society elementary families could not stand alone, but kinship systems varied. Working-class families had more kin contact than other classes, but it depended on physical accessibility, genealogical relationship, and perceived similarities and differences in social status and economic ties.

63. Case 1,205 on Reel 115.

64. Case 3,394 on Reel 107.

65. Case 15,464 on Reel 210. Lewis, *Labour and Love*, 19, 20, female kin could give mutual support *or,* at worst, be rivals.

66. Karen Brodkin Sacks and Dorothy Remy, *My Troubles Are Going to Have Trouble with Me*, 30,: *Everyday Trials and Triumphs of Women Workers*

(New Brunswick, N. J.: Rugers University Press, 1984) 30, 31, working conditions force women to rely on such networks: Robert Smuts, *Women and Work in America* (New York: Columbia University Press, 1959), 57. Carol B. Stack, *All Our Kin: Strategies for Survival in a Black Community* (New York: Harper, 1973), passim, discusses complex patterns in the reciprocity of goods and services among contemporary black urban female-headed households, kin and fictive kin. Yeandle, *Women's Working Lives*, 151–54. Helmbold, "Making Choices, Making Do," 138, 142, relief records from the Great Depression showed daughters, not sons, helping mothers. Jerome Skye Stromberg, "The Family and Its Kinship, Quasi-Kinship and Friendship Network: An Exploratory Study of Middle and Working Class Families" (Ph.D. Thesis, University of Minnesota, 1967), 106,167–69, working-class kin networks are more localized than are the middle class, and women's relatives are in closer contact than men's for both classes.

67. Case 360 on Reel 205.

68. Case 7,254 on Reel 150.

69. Case 17,784 on Reel 230.

70. U.S. Bureau of the Census, *15th Census of the United States, 1930*, Vol. 4, 856; Vol. 5, 389.

71. Josephine Schain, comp., *Laws of Minnesota Relating to Women and Children* (Minneapolis: Minneapolis Civic Improvement League, 1908), 62–66. (Schain was the first lawyer employed at the AC/FWA Legal Aid Bureau.) Minnesota Bureau of Labor, Industries and Commerce, *12th Biennial Report, 1909, 1910* (St. Paul: State of Minnesota, 1910), 73; State of Minnesota, *Session Laws of Minnesota for 1917, Passed During the Extra Session of 1916 and the Fortieth Session of the State Legislature 1917* (St. Paul: State of Minnesota), 352.

72. U.S. Bureau of the Census, *15th Census of the United States, 1930*, Vol. 4, 856; Vol. 5, 389.

73. Anthony, *Mothers Who Must Earn*, 46, adolescents were working in 46 percent of the families studied, and at "the first job available." Robert A. Woods and Albert J. Kennedy, eds., *Young Working Girls: A Summary of Evidence from Two Thousand Social Workers* (Boston: Houghton Mifflin, 1913), 11, most girls worked but with little preparation. Robert and Helen Lynd, *Middletown*, 48–52, initial jobs rarely responded to individual ability. Tentler, *Wage-Earning Women*, 107, youth drifted between jobs with "lack of calculation."

74. Case 15,508 on Reel 210, the grandmother's suggestion of fumigation was her acknowledgement of differences in class standards. Anthony, *Mothers Who Must Earn*, 60, only 5 percent of the girls in her study initially went into domestic work, but after marriage they drifted into it.

75. "Child Labor," *Monthly Labor Review* XI:6 (December 1920), 129–31. See Manuel C. Elmer, *A Study of Women in Clerical and Secretarial Work*

(Minneapolis: Women's Occupational Bureau, 1925), Introduction, 5, 6, 12, 18, 33. With advice from women's groups and the Board of Education in 1925, the University of Minnesota Sociology Department studied secretarial work, females' number one choice at the city's Occupational Bureau. One hundred ninety-one businesses employed 8,200 clerical workers with fluctuating demand and high unemployment; 25 percent of the women left annually owing to seasonal layoffs or failing business; 20 percent married. Four-fifths earned less than $25 weekly. Tentler, *Wage-Earning Women*, 96, by the 1920s working-class girls competed with middle-class girls for jobs.

76. Calhoun, *Social History of the American Family,* 136. Sacks and Remy, *My Troubles Are Going to Have Trouble with Me*, 20–29.

77. Case 17,806 on Reel 230; Case 7,338 on Reel 150.

78. Case 277 on Reel 108.

79. Literature disagrees as to the disposition of children's wages. Anthony, *Mothers Who Must Earn*, 44–46, daughters were more compliant than sons in sharing wages; Woods and Kennedy, *Young Working Girls,* 34, 35, 56–58, parents allowed girls to keep some wages to prevent them from leaving home; Paul H. Douglas, "The Changing Basis of Family Support and Expenditure," in Margaret E. Rich, *Family Life To-Day,* Papers Presented at a Conference in Celebration of the Fiftieth Anniversary of Family Social Work in America, 1927 (Boston: Houghton Mifflin, 1928), 109, sons left when mothers demanded too much; Kyrk, *Economic Problems of the Family*, 137–40, and Women's Bureau Studies agree that various arrangements existed.

In contemporary monographs, Tentler, *Wage-Earning Women,* 108, found parents less likely to interfere with sons' wages than daughters'. Work turned a son into a "man," but a working daughter remained a "daughter." Tilly and Scott, *Women, Work and Family*, 186, 187, twentieth-century European working-class adolescents were "assumed" title to some of their earnings. Lynn Jamieson, "Limited Resources and Limiting Conventions: Working Class Mothers and Daughters in Urban Scotland, c 1890–1925," in Lewis, *Labour and Love*, 49–65, emphasizes sexism in treatment of children: daughters did more work in the home and had less control over their own wages. Mintz and Kellogg, *Domestic Revolutions*, 88, 118, after the 1920s parents expected less of children's wages.

80. Case 17,302 on Reel 225.

81. Case 4,946 on Reel 135.

82. Case 2,398 on Reel 120.

83. Woods and Kennedy, *Young Working Girls*, 54, 55, boarding meant the noxious involvement of outsiders in family affairs and could potentially break down morality; certain settlement workers sought regulation of boarding by law. Organization for such reform in Roy Lubove, *The Progressives and the Slums: Tenement House Reform in New York City, 1890–1917* (Pittsburgh: University

of Pittsburgh Press, 1962). Jacques Donzelot, *The Policing of Family* (New York: Pantheon, 1979), 44, in theory, correct housing helped to supervise children.

John Modell and Tamara K. Hareven, "Urbanization and the Malleable Household: An Examination of Boarding and Lodging in American Families," *Journal of Marriage and the Family* 35 (August 1973), 467–79, "fear of family breakdown" motivated late century reforms; the increase in immigration and developing concepts of family privacy lessened the respectability of boarding.

84. The U.S. Census Bureau separated "boarders" who received food and room, from "lodgers" who received room but took meals apart from the family. Much literature describing boarding as an earning strategy misses the emotional content and variation in arrangements.

Kyrk, *Economic Problems of the Family,* 14, 15, 17, studies by Home Economics and Economics program at University of Chicago showed one-fifth to one-fourth of families with boarders. Stanley Lebergott, *Manpower in Economic Growth, The American Record Since 1800* (New York: McGraw-Hill, 1964), 252, 253, census materials and federal labor reports suggest 23 percent of all urban households had boarders or lodgers in 1900, 17 percent in 1910, 11 percent in 1930, (lower figures than Kyrk's for the same period). Incremental costs of feeding another mouth could be minimal, but women bore the psychological hardship of another in the house. Alice Kessler-Harris, *Out to Work, A History of Wage Earning Women in the United States* (New York: Oxford University Press, 1982), 124, 125, boarders were a favorite means of income among immigrant blue-collar families as it allowed women to stay home, but census materials still described these women as "Keeping House," thus disregarding their labor. Frequency of practice varied with regional employment opportunities for single men. Roberts, "Women's Strategies," 233, more family than nonfamily boarders were in British households. Leonore Davidoff, "The Separation of Home and Work, Landladies and Lodgers in the Nineteenth and Twentieth Centuries," in Sandra Burman, ed., *Fit Work for Women* (London: Croom Helm, 1979), 69, 70, lodgers were a "social indicator" reflecting a family's loss of privacy, part of the domestic ideal.

Strasser, *Never Done,* 145–61, boarding arrangements flourished within an American capitalism that valued private homes and worker mobility, particularly between the Civil War and World War I. "Nearly all working class people lived with nonrelatives at some stage of their lives." The practice varied—even within the same household—but work fell to women as "surrogate mothers, wives, and sisters."

Modell and Hareven, "Urbanization and the Malleable Household," 467–69, aging of the household head, departure of adult children, and changes in household income were associated with the decision to take in boarders; it particularly enabled "widows and single women in their forties, fifties and sixties an opportunity to maintain their own households rather than to live with kin." In Modell's study occupational similarities between head of household and boarder suggested design; when match did not occur, boarders usually lived with families "less well placed" than themselves." In female-headed households with male boarders, as in this study, such a match was less clear given transiency and insecurity of employment of both boarders and families. See also Claudia Goldin, "Family Strategies and the Family Economy in the Late Nineteenth Century: The Role of Secondary Workers," and Michael R. Haines, "Poverty Economic Stress, and the Family in a Late-Nineteenth Century American City: Whites in Philadelphia, 1880," in Theodore Hershberg, ed., *Philadelphia: Work, Space, Family, and Group Experience in the Nineteenth Century* (New York: Oxford University Press, 1981), 264, 265, 292. Steven Mintz and Susan Kellogg, *Domestic Revolutions: A Social History of American Family Life* (New York: Free, 1988), 89.

85. Case 585 on Reel 110.

86. Case 14,906 on Reel 205.

87. Linda Gordon, "Single Mothers and Child Neglect, 1880–1920," *American Quarterly* 37:2 (Summer 1985), 183, records from the Massachusetts Society for the Prevention of Cruelty to Children suggested "common-law" spouses may have been boarders "disguised" by women who wanted to avoid conflict with moralistic social workers.

88. Case 659 on Reel 111.

89. Elizabeth A. M. Roberts, "Women's Strategies, 1890–1940," in Jane Lewis, *Labour and Love: Women's Experiences of Home and Family, 1850–1940* (Oxford: Basil Blackwell, 1986), 231–35, deals broadly with family income strategies describing women as "penny capitalists" with schemes for earning. See similar material in Lewis, *Women in England,* 53, 54; also Helmbold, "Making Choices, Making Do," 348–58, discusses independent efforts to earn money during the depression.

90. Case 685 on Reel 111.

91. Case 7,930 on Reel 105.

92. Don Divance Lescohier, "Wages, Prices, Rents and Workingmen's Budgets in Minnesota," in Minnesota Bureau of Labor, Industries and Commerce, *12th Biennial Report, 1909–1910* (St. Paul: State of Minnesota, 1910), 327, 328; "Minimum Wage," *Monthly Labor Review,* 7:4 (October 1918), 184, 185. Commercial laundries were an alternative to laundresses, Strasser, *Never Done*, 104–24; Heidi Hartmann, "Capitalism and Women's Work in the Home 1900–1930" 280–99.

93. Case 277 on Reel 108.

94. Robert and Helen Lynd, *Middletown,* 170–74, compared class differences in time spent washing clothes, 1890 to 1924; half of the business class families hired someone to do the wash in both time periods. Half the working-class families spent over nine hours weekly with wash in 1890; by 1924 technolo-

gy lessened the task by a few hours but it still consumed most of a day for 75 percent of the wives.

95. Strasser, *Never Done*, 104–24, nineteenth-century women complained about washing more than other household chores. Laundresses were usually the "poorest of the women" who "sacrificed the independence of working in their own homes, usually because they lacked the equipment to do so." Strasser noted a Russell Sage Foundation study early in the century that found 60 percent of 391 working men's families in New York City hired others to do laundry as the task was so onerous.

Chapter 3

1. Edward T. Devine, *The Principles of Relief* (New York: Macmillan, 1904), 29–33; Edward T. Devine, *Social Work* (New York: Macmillan, 1922), 46–51. A Marxist approach to theories of need is in Mary McIntosh, "The Welfare State and the Needs of the Dependent Family," Sandra Burman, ed., *Fit Work for Women* (London: Croom Helm, 1979), 163.

2. Social welfare literature, 1900–1930, contains many studies, for example: Robert Hunter, a New York City social worker who was among the first to systematically and quantitatively describe the lower class, *Poverty, Social Conscience in the Progressive Era* (New York: Macmillan, 1904), 3, 4, 25, 94, 95, he distinguished paupers without pride from the working poor reluctant to apply for charity but who were "a few weeks from distress when the machines are stopped." He calculated that this was 14 percent of the population in "good" times, in "bad times" 20 percent.

The Charity Organization Department of Russell Sage sent Margaret Byington to study households in Homestead, Pennsylvania, as part of the Pittsburgh survey. *Homestead: The Household of a Mill Town* (New York: Charities Publication Committee of Russell Sage Foundation, 1910; reprint ed., New York: Arno Press and the New York Times, 1969), 98, she concluded that a man could not marry and have children without dropping into poverty. "No individual family income keeps always at its maximum; sick benefits do not equal wages; cuts in rates are declared without warning."

U.S. Bureau of Labor frequently compiled wage and price materials, see, for example, "Minimum Quantity Budget Necessary to Maintain a Worker's Family of Five in Health and Decency," *Monthly Labor Review* 10:6 (June 1920), 1–18. Robert Kelso, head of the St. Louis Council of Social Agencies, reviewed results from federal Bureau of Labor studies and others in *Poverty* (New York: Longmans, Green, 1929), 51–54. The bureau studied thousands of families nationwide in 1901–2 and again in 1918–19, comparing annual incomes and expenditures. "The self-supporting population who represent the solid warp and woof of the American society," approximately a sixth of families in both surveys, ended the year with deficits. From the University of Chicago, the economist Hazel Kyrk wrote *Economic Problems of the Family* (New York: Harper, 1929), 333, cites a bibliography with 180 wage/budget studies since 1869. Chapter II, "The Adequacy of Money Incomes for Family Support—Its Determination," 213, four-fifths of married urban men had adequate incomes. The economist Paul Douglas criticized work based on a family of five as standard; he proposed a wage that varied with family size and need in *Wages and the Family* (Chicago: University of Chicago Press, 1925), 40, 41. A starting place to study this material is Dorothy S. Brady's "Family Budgets: A Historical Study," *Monthly Labor Review*, 66:1 (January 1948), 171–75.

Contemporary discussion of these studies is in Heidi Hartmann, "Capitalism and Women's Work in the Home 1900–1930" (Ph.D. Thesis, Yale University, 1974), 141–47, 190; and Winifred Wandersee, *Women's Work and Family Values* (Cambridge: Harvard University Press, 1981), 9–14. Mimi Abramovitz, *Regulating the Lives of Women: Social Welfare Policy from Colonial Times to the Present* (Boston: South End, 1988), 190, attention to working women in the laboring class was skewed toward single women, widows (perceived as lacking choices), and middleclass married women seeking careers; working married women were ignored.

3. Fluctuations in American business cycle, 1870 to 1930, are shown graphically in Campbell R. McConnell, *Economics, Principles, Problems, and Policies*, 9th ed. (New York: McGraw-Hill, 1984), 150. Statistics of per capita income by decades are in Simon Kuznets, *National Income, A Summary of Findings* (New York: National Bureau of Economic Research, Inc., 1946), 32–35, emphasizes errors in looking at per capita income increase and assuming equivalent improvement in quality of daily life. See also Paul Brissenden, *Earnings of Factory Workers 1899 to 1927: An Analysis of Pay Roll Statistics,* Census Mongraph 10 (Washington, D.C.: Government Printing Office, 1929), 282, 392, explains the formula for determining the average number of wage earners and wages from census findings considering unemployment in industrial operations. Calculated wages for selected cities show that wages in Minneapolis are slightly higher than for the national average although this does not translate into adequacy.

4. Information on the early city in Minneapolis Writers Project Program, *Federal Writers Project, Minneapolis, The Story of a City* (St. Paul: State Department of Education, 1940), 64. Calvin Schmid, *Social Saga of Two Cities* (Minneapolis: Bureau of Social Research, Minneapolis Council of Social Agencies, 1937), 15, 22, 25, an invaluable source of quantitative sociological and economic information for fifty years.

U.S. Bureau of the Census, *12th Census of the United States*, 1900, Vol. 4, Manufactures, 591–94. See also E. Dudley Parsons, *The Story of Minneapolis* (Minneapolis: Colwell Press, 1913), 132–42. John R. Borchert, *Northern Heartland, An Economic and Historical Geography of the Upper Midwest* (Minneapolis: University of Minnnesota Press, 1987), 45–61, details of Twin Cities as regional center, the "Northwest anchor" of primary rail corridor between the Middle Atlantic seaboard and Midwest with a "national image" as the flour center. Minneapolis Civic and Commerce Association, *The Market of the Northwest*, 2nd ed. (Minneapolis: Civic and Commerce Association, 1917), 156.

5. E. Dudley Parsons, *The Story of Minneapolis* (Minneapolis: Colwell, 1913), 155; William H. Bingham and R. I. Holcombe, eds., *Compendium of History and Biography of Minneapolis* (Chicago: H. Taylor, 1914), 267.

6. William D. Washburn, Jr., "Preventive Measures in the Mississippi Valley," National Conference of Charities and Correction (NCCC), *Proceedings*, 1907, 341.

7. Minneapolis Civic and Commerce Association, *Market of the Northwest*, 91.

8. Minneapolis as an employment center is in Mildred Lucile Hartsough, *The Twin Cities as a Metropolitan Market: A Regional Study of the Economic Development of Minneapolis and St. Paul* (Minneapolis: University of Minnesota, 1925), 166, 167, 181; David L. Rosheim, *The Other Minneapolis, of the Rise and Fall of the Gateway, the Old Minneapolis Skid Row* (Maquoketa, Iowa: Andromeda, 1978), 58, 59; and Charles Rumford Walker, *American City, A Rank and File History* (New York: Holt, 1937, reprint ed., New York: Arno Press and the New York Times, 1971), 30. See also Industrial Commission of Minnesota, *1st Biennial Report*, 1921–22 (St. Paul: State of Minnesota 1922), 56, 57, reported problems of placing farm labor to advantage farmer and worker. See also Fred A. Shannon, "A Post Mortem on the Labor-Safety-Valve Theory, *Agricultural History* 19 (1945), 31–37, rural population moved to urban areas, specific mention of Minnesota. The Minneapolis Council of Social Agencies, *Community Survey*, Vol. 3, 3.

9. Parsons, *Story of Minneapolis*, 134; Minneapolis Council of Social Agencies, *Community Survey of Social and Health Work in Minneapolis*, Vol. 3 (Minneapolis: Council of Social Agencies, 1938), 1–3. See also U.S. Bureau of the Census, *12th Census of the United States 1910*, Vol. 4, 443; Schmid, *Social Saga of Two Cities*, 6.

10. Case 4,285 on Reel 130.

11. Stephan Thernstrom, *The Other Bostonians: Poverty and Progress in the American Metropolis, 1880–1970* (Cambridge: Harvard University Press, 1973), 42, asserts the existence of a "floating proletariat," men whose names appeared and disappeared from city directories as they, and sometimes their families, drifted seeking employment in the nineteenth and early twentieth centuries. Labor historians since have modified understanding of insecurity in employment; jobs were irregular, turnover high, and unemployment "endemic" but "floaters" were a shifting group. See a review of this literature in Charles Stephenson, "'There's Plenty Waitin' at the Gates': Mobility, Opportunity, and the American Worker," in Stephenson and Robert Asher, eds., *Life and Labor:*

Dimensions of American Working-Class History, (Albany: SUNY Press, 1986), 82–90. Alice Solenberger, wife of an early director at Minneapolis COS authored *One Thousand Homeless Men, A Study of Original Records* (New York: Charities Publication Committee, 1911), includes research of boardinghouse occupants in Minneapolis and Chicago. Lillian Rubin, *Worlds of Pain: Life in Working Class Families* (New York: Basic, 1976), 155–160, discusses the movement of working-class men in the contemporary labor market seeking better wages and conditions.

12. Case 5,767 on Reel 140.

13. E. A. Fay, "Free Employment Bureau," Minnesota State Conference of Charities and Correction, *3rd Annual Conference Proceedings*, 1895, 88–91.

14. AC, *18th Annual Report,* 1902, 7, 14; see also AC, *19th Annual Report,* 1903, 17, 18.

15. AC, *26th Annual Report,* 1910, 33, 43, 44. Industrial Commission of Minnesota, *1st Biennial Report, 1921–22,* 56, there was a lack of adequate funding for the state's first public employment bureau. See also Minnesota Bureau of Labor, Industry and Commerce, *12th Biennial Report,* 1909–1910 (St. Paul: State of Minnesota, 1910), 570. "Twenty Five Years of the Minneapolis Associated Charities, 1909," Folder-3, Box 1, Family and Children's Service Collection, Social Welfare History Archives, University of Minnesota.

16. Eugene Lies, General Secretary Reports, February 7, 1912, Folder-8, Box 3. "Report of the General Secretary, 1913," Folder-8, Box 3, FCS Collection.

17. AC, *28th Annual Report,* 1913, 38, 39; AC, *21st Annual Report,* 1905, 15; AC, *25th Annual Report,* 1909, 32.

18. AC, *32nd Annual Report,* 1916, 8.

19. Hartsough, *The Twin Cities as A Metropolitan Market,* 167; Industrial Commission of Minnesota, *1st Biennial Report,* 65. Udo Sautter, "Government and Unemployment: The Use of Public Works Before the New Deal," *Journal of American History* 73:1 (June 1986), 59–86.

20. Richmond, "Emergency Relief in Times of Unemployment," 1921, in Joanna C. Colcord and Ruth Z. S. Mann, eds. *The Long View: Papers and Addresses by Mary Richmond* (New York: Russell Sage Foundation, 1930), 510–25; Richmond, *What Is Social Case Work? An Introductory Description* (New York: Russell Sage Foundation, 1922), 51.

21. General Secretary Reports, May 1921, Folder-8, Box 3; Minutes, Board Meeting, January 18, 1922, Folder 1–23–18 to 12–16–25, Box 5; Marion V. DeVoy, "A Study of Jobs Secured by the FWA of Minneapolis During 1932," Folder-3, Box 1, FCS Collection.

22. "Report of Employment Agent," March 1927, Folder-3, Box 1, FCS Collection.

23. Letter, Joanna C. Colcord to Otto F. Bradley, March 20, 1929, Folder 8, Box 3, FCS Collection.

24. Rosheim, *The Other Minneapolis*, 114, graphs show increasing relief demands, 1930–32 in St. Paul Community Chest, *That Lengthening Line* (St. Paul: Community Chest, 1932), 5–21. Futility of private efforts to handle depression poverty is in Stanley Wenocur and Michael Reisch, *From Charity to Enterprise, The Development of American Social Work in a Market Economy* (Chicago: University of Illinois Press, 1989), 157–64.

25. Don Divance Lescohier, "Wages, Prices, Rents and Workingmen's Budgets in Minnesota," in Minnesota Bureau of Labor, *12th Biennial Report*, 1909–10, 327, 328.

26. Walker, *American City*, 32–40, 59, 60.

27. Robert Asher, "Industrial Safety and Labor Relations in the United States, 1865–1917," in Stephenson and Asher, *Life and Labor*, 116–20, includes examples from Minnesota north woods.

28. Minnesota Bureau of Labor, *12th Biennial Report*, 1909–10, 154, 155, details accidents' impact on family life.

29. "Report of Federal and State Workmen's Compensation Experiences, *Monthly Labor Review* 8:3 (March 1919), 257, 258; James Leiby, *A History of Social Welfare and Social Work in the United States* (New York: Columbia University Press, 1978), 202–5, a national movement for workmen's compensation legislation began when New Jersey passed a bill in 1911; see also Kelso, *Poverty*, 307.

30. Minutes, Board Meeting, April 18, 1923, Folder 1–23–18 to 12–16–25, Box 5, FCS Collection.

31. Richard L. Kozelka, *Business Fluctuations in the Northwest, Bulletin of the Employment Stabilization Research Institute*, 1:4 (Minneapolis: University of Minnesota Press, 1932), 223–27, shows cause and effect in the Northwest agricultural economy and business cycle dominated by Minnesota.

32. U.S. Bureau of Census, *14th Census of the United States, 1920*, Vol. 4, Occupation, 691, 692, inconsistencies in the past census make it difficult to compare categories across time; figures for working women assumed to be too high in 1910 and too low in 1920. Claudia Goldin, "Historians Consensus on the Economic Role of Women in American History: A Review Essay," *Historical Methods* 16 (Spring 1983), 77, 78, noted that the census of 1890 and 1900 carried more details estimating the female labor force than three following censuses. For a discussion of census attention to occupation in Women's Bureau, see

Janet Hooks, *Women's Occupations Through Seven Decades*, #218 (Washington, D.C.: U.S. Department of Labor, 1947), 53–63.

Historians agree that married women have been systematically undercounted; work at home with boarders, laundry, and sewing was most often ignored. U. G. Weatherly, "How Does Access of Women to Industrial Occupations React Upon the Family?" *American Journal of Sociology* 14 (May 1901), 740–52, many married women saw their work as "incidental." This same point is made by contemporary historians. Alice Kessler-Harris, *Out to Work, A History of Wage Earning Women in the United States* (New York: Oxford University Press, 1982), 125; Lynn Y. Weiner, *From Working Girl to Working Mother, The Female Labor Force in the United States, 1820–1980* (Chapel Hill: University of North Carolina Press, 1985), 87. Virginia Yans-McLaughlin, "Italian Women and Work: Experience and Perception," in Cantor and Laurie, eds., *Class, Sex, and the Woman Worker*, 102–4, women and men may define their work differently than do census takers and historians.

33. Goldin, "Historians Consensus on the Economic Role of Women," 78, there was an absence of census information linking women's labor force participation and life cycle until the 1940 census. Primary and secondary literature agrees that most married women worked for wages because of families' material needs; lure of independence or money for extras—the motivation attributed to young single women—was unrelated to their situations. See federal Women's Bureau studies, some of which include marital status, family size, and wages: *The Family Status of Breadwinning Women*, #23, 1922; *The Share of Wage Earning Women in Family Support*, #30, 1923; Agnes L. Peterson, *What the Wage Earning Woman Contributes to Family Support*, #75, 1929; Emily C. Brown, *A Study of Two Groups of Denver Married Women Applying for Jobs*, #77, 1929 (Washington, D.C.: U.S. Department of Labor). See also Katharine Anthony, *Mothers Who Must Earn* (New York: Russell Sage Foundation, Survey Research Associates, 1914),19, 20, the "condition of the principal breadwinner determines the family's economic circumstances." More than a third of working mothers in her study were widows but the largest group were wives of men unemployed or in ill health—primarily with tuberculosis. Edward T. Devine, " Widows Needs," *Survey* 32 (April 4, 1914), 23. Robert Smuts, *Women and Work in America* (New York: Columbia University Press, 1959), 51, 52, "most of the married women who worked outside the home had little choice." Winifred Wandersee, *Women's Work and Family Values, 1920–1940* (Cambridge: Harvard University Press, 1981), Introduction, 70, includes information on early century debate and research of women's paid labor. Married women "needed to" work, but "economic need is a concept not easily measured." Heidi Hartmann, "Capitalism and Women's Work in the Home, 1900–1930" (Ph.D. Thesis, Yale University, 1974), 206, found working class married women commonly contributed to family income even when a husband was home. Tentler, *Wage-Earning Women*, 165–69, widowed and divorced women at times preferred work to relief to avoid the intervention of charity workers in child rearing.

34. Claudia Goldin, "Family Strategies and the Family Economy," in Theodore Hershberg, ed., *Philadelphia: Work, Space, Family and Group Experience in the Nineteenth Century* (New York: Oxford University Press, 1981), 277–310, quantitative modeling relates family factors leading to the selection of secondary earners; it suggests more consistency than this study of case records suggests. Tilly and Scott, *Women, Work, and Family*, 126, are more consistent than many historians of women's labor in pointing to "episodic" quality of married women's work related to irregularity of family need, health, unemployment, family life cycle—age and number of dependents. Jane Lewis, *Women in England, 1870–1950, Sexual Divisions and Social Changes* (Bloomington: Indiana University Press, 1984), 149, 150, 166, 168, finds a much higher wage work rate among widowed and divorced women in Britain.

35. Anthony, *Mothers Who Must Earn* 56.

36. Tilly and Scott, *Women, Work and Family* (New York: Holt, 1978), 128–36, lower-class married women in Europe have seen themselves as economic producers creating family livelihood by work within or beyond the home. Middle-class women were bound by cultural mores discouraging wage work except as last resort. Anthony, *Mothers Who Must Earn*, 20, 24, experience taught women that marriage was not an escape from wage work. Lois Rita Helmbold, "Making Choices, Making Do: Black and White Working Class Women's Lives and Work During the Great Depression," (Ph.D. Thesis, Stanford University, 1983), 186, in the depression, "few working class women questioned the propriety of their own employment."

For a working wife as a symbol of disgrace, see in Louise Woodcock Tentler, *Wage Earning Women, Industrial Work and Family in the United States, 1900–1930* (New York: Oxford University Press, 1979), 139; Susan Kleinberg, "The Systematic Study of Urban Women," in Milton Cantor and Bruce Laurie, eds., *Class, Sex, and the Woman Worker* (Westport, Conn.: Greenwood, 1977), 22, "in all settings it became the mark of pride for a man to have a wife who did not work." Because men were so frequently absent or silent in this study of case records, "disgrace" was not evident; obvious was women's assumption that they *would* work.

37. Case 14,332 on Reel 200.

38. Natalie Sokoloff, *Between Money and Love: The Dialectics of Women's Home and Market Work* (New York: Praeger, 1981), 35–44, 55.

39. The secondary literature disagrees as to the relative importance of regional economic opportunities for women versus cultural mores as a principal determinant of work habits. Tilly and Scott, *Women, Work and the Family*, 230, working-class women responded to changing family needs with wage work, but "characteristics of the economy" influenced demand for that work. McLaughlin, "Italian Women and Work," 105, describes Tilly's position elsewhere as one in

which cultural traditions only "mediate or modify" economic roles; her research on Italian women suggests that culture influenced work choices and shaped women's perceptions of work and its importance. This study of case records shows most women taking what the market offered.

Other historians have merged the roles of economics and culture. Barbara Klaczynska, "Why Women Work: A Comparison of Various Groups—Philadelphia, 1910–1930," *Labor History* 17:3 (Summer 1974), 73, women worked because they needed income, but like Wandersee, in *Women, Work and Family Values*, Introduction, Klaczynska found that the perception of the family need complex. It included life-style, material possession, and ambitions for children shaped by ethnic values and available opportunities. Kleinberg, "The Systematic Study of Urban Women," 24, 25, 36, employment opportunities are important, but family economic and demographic factors determined which women would work and under what circumstances. This is helpful in shifting the argument from dealing with women in a cultural aggregate to dealing with individual women. Kessler-Harris, *Out to Work*, 128, 322, "class, ethnic, and racial constraints that influenced a women's work choices were all bounded by sex, making gender rather than ethnicity the independent variable"; technology, general labor force, occupational structure, and family functions needing women were interrelated "like strands in a braid." Lewis, *Women in England*, 170–73, definitions of "appropriate" female work varied from area to area but were shared by employers and women. See also Sokoloff, *Between Money and Love,* 55, poses a theory about dual labor market versus women's socialization as determinants of labor choices.

40. FWA, *The Family Welfare Association in Action, 1917–1926* (Minneapolis: FWA, 1926), 32.

41. Hooks, *Women's Occupations through Seven Decades*, 6. Susan Yeandle, *Women's Working Lives: Patterns and Strategies* (New York: Tavistock, 1984), 5, 6, domestic service was primary employment for British women also.

Kessler-Harris, *Out to Work,* 218, regardless of changes in employment opportunities after the First World War, "production workers, domestic servants, and the poor, whose survival depended on their wages, still faced the old problems of arduous labor." Tentler, *Wage—Earning Women*, 172, women were no more capable of supporting themselves adequately with wages in 1920 than had been true earlier. Klaczynska, in "Why Women Work," 75, many native-born working-class men succeeded in achieving middle-class status in the 1920s, and their wifes left the work force; conversely Robert S. and Helen M. Lynd, *Middletown, A Study in American Culture* (New York: Harcourt, 1929), 27, saw an increase in working wives in the 1920s. Working women are believed undercounted in the 1920 census.

42. U.S. Bureau of the Census, *14th Census of the United States 1920*, Special Report, Occupation, 693. Valeria Kincaid Oppenheimer, *The Female Labor Force in the United States, Demographic and Economics Factors Govern-*

ing Its Growth and Changing Composition, Population Monograph Studies, 5 (Berkeley: University of California Press, 1970), 36, showed that household workers per 1,000 households fell from 98.9 in 1900 to 58.0 in 1920 and then rose to 66.8 in 1930, reflecting women's desperate willingness to work for little during the depression. For domestic work in depression see also Helmbold, "Making Choices, Making Do," 162–64.

43. The number of females in domestic and personal service in U. S. Bureau of Census, *13th Census of the United States, 1910,* Vol. 4, Occupational Statistics, 179. Helmbold, "Making Choices, Making Do," 162, 232, distinguished between "personal service," work as waitress, laundress, chambermaid, institutional housekeeper, etcetera, and "domestic service," work in private homes. Not all sources touching on domestic work are careful about the breadth of this category in the census.

44. Edward Cadberry, M. Cecile Matheson, and George Shann, *Women's Work and Wages: A Phase of Life in an Industrial City* (Chicago: University of Chicago Press, 1907), 110.

45. Bureau of Labor, *12th Biennial Report*, 586, 579, 334, 335, 604, 605.

46. Lescohier, "Wages, Prices, Rents and Workingmen's Budgets in Minnesota," 327, 328.

47. "Minimum Wage," *Monthly Labor Review*, 7:4 (October 1918), 184, 185. Edgar Sydenstricker and W. Jett Lauck, *Conditions of Labor in American Industries* (New York: Funk and Wagnall, 1917; reprint ed., New York: Arno and the New York Times, 1969), 46, 47, women's wages varied more around country than men's, attributed to the lessened mobility of female labor supply nationally. A study of over thirteen thousand women in factories, shops, and laundries in St. Paul and Minneapolis in 1915 showed that 67 percent earned less than ten dollars weekly. Tentler, *Wage-Earning Women*, 17, frequently women worked for wages yielding an income far below subsistence.

48. See the discussion of the Minneapolis study from the U.S. Department of Labor, "Women in Industry," *Monthly Labor Review* XI:3 (September 1920), 543–47.

49. David M. Katzman, *Seven Days a Week, Women and Domestic Service in Industrializing America* (New York: Oxford University Press, 1978), passim, explores the physical and emotional content of job and shift from live-in servants to domestic day workers. See also Donna L. Van Raaphorst, *Union Maids Not Wanted, Organizing Domestic Workers 1870–1940* (New York: Praeger, 1988), 124–54, analyzes employers' personal and organized efforts to maintain control. Susan Strasser, *Never Done, A History of Housework in America* (New York: Pantheon, 1982), 162–79, discusses reformers' attempts to "rationalize" domestic service and housekeeping; Hartmann, "Capitalism and Women's Work," 169–

180, associated a decrease in live-in servants to broader changes in family consumption.

For "advantages" of this work see Frances A. Kellor, a reformer concerned about "Americanization," writing "Immigrant Women," in Edna Bullock, ed., *Selected Articles on the Employment of Women* (Minneapolis: N. W. Wilson, 1911), 54, 55. The concept of domestic work as women's "most praised" use of self in Steven Mintz and Susan Kellogg, *Domestic Revolutions, A Social History of American Family Life* (New York: Free, 1988), 123, 124; Phyllis Palmer, "Housework and Domestic Labor: Racial and Technological Change, in Karen Brodkin Sacks and Dorothy Remy, *My Troubles Are Going to Have Trouble with Me: Everyday Trials and Triumphs of Women Workers* (New Brunswick, N.J.: Rutgers University Press, 1984), 81.

50. Case 5,701 on Reel 140.

51. Anne Summers, "A Home from Home—Women's Philanthropic Work in the Nineteenth Century," in Burman, *Fit Work for Women*, 39, the distance increased between male employers and employees, but female employers continued to have relations with the working class through their servants. Palmer, "Housework and Domestic Labor," 83, women would do light cleaning themselves and leave the heavy work for servants.

52. Case 17,357 on Reel 225.

53. Van Raaphorst, *Union Maids Not Wanted,* 210, 211.

54. Information about the legal aid in many annual reports, see particularly AC, *29th Annual Report,*1913, 59, 60; FWA, *Family Welfare Association in Action*, 57. See similar information about wage claims at the St. Paul COS in Mark E. Haidet, *A Legacy of Leadership and Service* (St. Paul, Family Service of Greater St. Paul, 1984), 21.

55. AC, *26th Annual Report,* 1910, 60, 61, this advertisement is shown as it is within the report.

56. Case 1,355 on Reel 115; Case 427 on Reel 109. Weiner, *From Working Girl to Working Mother,* 102, working women faced physical "debilitation," not "role ambiguity"; Tentler, *Wage Earning Women*, 200, women spent their own health for wages received. Robert L. Griswold, *Family and Divorce in California, 1850–1890, Victorian Illusions and Everyday Realities* (Albany: SUNY Press, 1982), 60, women referred to their own health, not the economic situation, as explanation for work opportunities.

Anthony, *Mothers Who Must Earn*, 69–80, reviewed long hours in jobs classified as domestic work and personal service. Susan E. Kennedy, *If All We Did Was to Weep at Home, A History of White Working Class Women in America* (Bloomington: Indiana University Press, 1979), 104, described the advantages of restaurant work with free meals and physical dangers of commercial laundries with steam and high temperatures. Dangers are also discussed in Women's Bureau, Ethel L. Best and Ethel Erickson, *A Survey of Laundries and Their Women Workers in 23 Cities*, #78 (Washington, D.C.: U.S. Department of Labor, 1920), passim.

57. Case 4,946 on Reel 135.

58. Case 2,432 on Reel 120.

59. Anthony, *Mothers Who Must Earn*, 129, when ill, women would reduce but not eliminate work. Lewis, *Women in England,* 24, responsibility for household budgeting made women "notoriously" reluctant to add their own health need costs.

60. Case 8,518 on Reel 160.

61. Case 553 on Reel 110.

62. Case 707 on Reel 111.

63. Manuel C. Elmer, *A Cooperative Study of Women in Industry in St. Paul* (St. Paul, Minn.: St. Paul Association of Public and Business Affairs, 1925), 5, 6, studied the employment of 14,648 women at 359 establishments; 24 percent were married—the majority at work in restaurants and hotels; the oldest women were in laundries; labor turnover was high; much work was temporary. Anthony, *Mothers Who Must Earn*, 40–44, few married women had regular employment, a New York State Commission on Employers Liability found 40 percent of 1,933 married women had been unemployed for at least ten weeks of last year. Women's Bureau, Caroline Manning, *The Immigrant Woman and Her Job,* #74 (Washington, D.C.: U.S. Department of Labor, 1930), 100–111, measured irregularity of employment.

64. Case 16,386 on Reel 220.

65. Case 17,816 on Reel 230.

66. Case 15,541 on Reel 210.

67. Case 18,153 on Reel 235.

68. Case 17,784 on Reel 230. Kleinberg, "The Systematic Study of Urban Women," 24, while single women competed for jobs, "married women did not compete in the labor force." It is not clear how broadly she asserts this; most married women did not work, but the lowest class who did work often competed with one another for limited positions. Anthony, *Mothers Who Must Earn*, 85, describes "pathetic" middle aged women wearing out shoes by looking for work; aggressive ones were most successful. Tentler, *Wage Earning Women,* 142, women seeking jobs were "supplicants." Lois Rita Helmbold, "Downward Occupational Mobility During the Great Depression: Urban Black and White Working Class Women," *Labor History* 29:2 (Spring 1988), 137,148,151–53, women were kept employed by the willingness to accept downward mobility; discusses "sex-

ual component" of certain jobs—the need to look attractive to compete in tight labor market.

69. Case 18,153 on Reel 235.

70. Case 16,386 on Reel 220.

71. Concern over women's "other job" at home in Women's Bureau publications, see, for example, Manning, *The Immigrant Woman and Her Job,* 60–63. The detrimental impact of mothers' work on children is in Annie Marion Maclean, *Women Workers and Society* (Chicago: A.C. McClurg, 1916), 36. Cadberry, *Women's Work and Wages,* 219–21. Alva Myrdal and Viola Klein, *Women's Two Roles: Home and Work* (London: Routledge and Kegan Paul, 1956), passim, were early and outspoken in concern for the double responsibility of mothers in the work force. They include Children's Bureau investigations, 1920–25, which revealed a higher infant mortality rate for mothers employed during pregnancy. Impure commercial milk in some cities led to the creation of local milk committees concerned with milk production and child-rearing practices.

Kessler-Harris, *Out to Work,* 164, twentieth-century reformers understood and accepted that married women needed work for economic reasons. Mimi Abramovitz, "The Family Ethic: The Female Pauper and Public Aid, Pre-1900," *Social Service Review* 59:1 (March 1985), 129–31, "enforcing the family ethic for women, like enforcing the work ethic for men, also serves wider economic and political goals."

Patricia Branca, "A New Perspective on Women's Work: A Comparative Typology," *Journal of Social History* 2:2 (Winter 1975), 144–47, married women wanted work "in or near a family context," but "when this was not possible they would drop out of work in favor of the home." These case records show that decisions *not* to work were difficult for lower-class women to make; they agree more with Kyrk, *Economic Problems of the Family,*151, saying children had impact on *kind* of job a woman sought, but not whether she sought it; Lewis, *Labour and Love,* 14, "love" in working-class homes meant wage work.

72. Case 4,285 on Reel 130. Weiner, *From Working Girl to Working Mother,* 120, 121, 127, referred to studies at the time that reported that mothers paid neighbors for child care; she also commented that not all mothers felt constant supervision was necessary, and a neighbor who looked in periodically could be sufficient; most children looked after themselves. Carol B. Stack, *All Our Kin, Strategies for Survival in a Black Community* (New York: Harper, 1974), 67–73, studied poor urban black families who survived through patterned exchanges with kin, "the dispersing of children in households of kin [is] not haphazard." Mothers relied most on adult female kin.

73. Anthony, *Mothers Who Must Earn,* 152–54, mothers "dreaded the influence of the streets," but fewer than 10 percent of children in her study were in agencies, institutions, or with relatives; the majority were on their own. Tentler, *Wage-Earning Women,* 154–56, 159, found "casual arrangements" dominated

child care, but noted standards for child care—with or without the mother present—are unknown. It may be an error to assume these changed greatly with the mother at work. Tentler assumed two constants, that working-class children's lives generally were "harsh" but that most mothers "cared." The records here support that but are not complete enough for comparison of children's activities with and without a working mother. Linda Gordon, "Single Mothers and Child Neglect, 1880–1920," *American Quarterly* 37:2 (Summer 1985), 184, many children were left unattended, but night work could be disguised so no explanations need be made to social workers about child care. Mary P. Ryan, *Womanhood in America: From Colonial Time to the Present*, 3rd ed. (New York: Franklin Watts, 1983), 178, factory jobs led to "casual supervision" of children.

74. Case 1,152 on Reel 114.

75. Anthony, *Mothers Who Must Earn*, 148, 149.

76. Samuel Hopkins Adams, *The Great American Fraud* (New York: 1900), 3, 4, 40, excerpted in Robert Bremner, ed., *Children and Youth in America, A Documentary History 1866–1932,* Vol. 3 (New York: Oxford University Press, 1971), 882–83.

77. Case 15,890 on Reel 215.

78. Case 15,541 on Reel 210.

79. Kessler-Harris, *Out to Work*, 180–218, examines polarization of female reformers and feminists in campaigns for protective legislation, and long-term negative impact on women's status as workers. See also Judith A. Baer, *Chains of Protection The Judicial Response to Women's Labor Legislation,* Contributions to Women's Studies, #1 (Westport, Conn.: Greenwood, 1978), details successes and failures of protective legislation into the New Deal.

80. Concern for impact of women's wage earning on housework led to research. Cadberry, *Women's Work and Wages*, 15, 216–17, 222, 223, cross-tabulated mothers' employment, fathers' incomes, and household conditions; homes of men with the largest incomes were cleanest, but Cadberry found less difference between housekeeping of employed and unemployed women than he expected and said this reflected working women's "strength of character." "Whether the state of the home affected the habits of the husbands, or whether those habits caused apathy and indifference on the part of the women must remain an open question, though extenuating circumstances might be pleaded for the occupied women, who, in addition to their factory labours and their home duties, have the drunken husbands in three-fourths of the cases of these untidy homes." As to cause and effect:

> Throughout the tables it is shown that where the women work the habits of the husbands are worse than where the wife stays home. . . . These figures lead to two possible conclusions; either the women are compelled to work because the

husbands are unsteady, drunken or idle, or the husbands develop bad habits because their wives remove the burden or responsibility from them. The former seems the more probable theory, but the influences are apparently interacting and cummulative, the two evils perpetuating each other in a vicious circle.

81. AC, *25th Annual Report,* 1909, 41.

82. Case 7,305 on Reel 150. Frank J. Bruno, *The Theory of Social Work* (Boston: Heath, 1936), 301–6, includes a good bibliography of early classics in many fields. In a section titled "Husband and Wife Relationship," a man might feel proud of a working wife's self-sufficiency and understanding of industrial world, which makes her a better wife and mother. This argument was made one hundred years earlier to justify education for women.

83. Linda Gordon, *Heroes of Their Own Lives, The Politics and History of Family Violence, Boston 1880–1960* (New York: Viking, 1988), 264–71, examines conflicts over alcohol, family finances, work, and sex as factors influencing men to beat women. Lillian Rubin, *Worlds of Pain: Life in Working Class Families* (New York: Basic, 1976), 34, 37, 38, 77, 98, discusses the difficulties of the unemployment for working-class men that is expressed as violence.

84. Heidi Hartman, "The Unhappy Marriage of Marxism and Feminism: Towards a More Progressive Union," in Lydia Sargent, ed., *Women and Revolution: A Discussion of the Unhappy Marriage of Marxism and Feminism* (Boston: South End, 1981), 20; Evelyn Nakano Glenn, "Racial Ethnic Women's Labor: The Intersection of Race, Gender and Class Oppression," *Review of Radical Political Economy* 17:3 (Fall 1985), 105.

85. Case 5,701 on Reel 140. While the sex discrimination in wages is no doubt true, it is unlikely the male cleaners earned this much daily.

86. Case 2,229 on Reel 120. Mirra Komarovsky, *Blue-Collar Marriage* (New York: Random, 1962; reprint ed., New York: Vintage, 1967), 62–73, economics was accepted as a reason for employment of working-class women in late 1950s, but its impact on women's family relations varied. Rubin, *Worlds of Pain,* 176, in contemporary working-class homes half of the men surveyed complained of working wives as "too independent."

87. Wandersee, *Women's Work and Family Values,* 112, 113, 121, 122, did not interpret women's economic responsibility for families as "personal victory" but a commitment to family. Employment had low status and low wages, and while women had the psychological burden of responsibility, "custom" meant that men continued to be perceived as the head of the household. If a husband or older son were at home, it could be difficult for them to acknowledge a wife's authority when they could make higher wages themselves if employed.

Caroline F. Ware, Introduction, in Cantor and Laurie, *Class, Sex, and The Women Worker,* 16–19, contains a helpful discussion of "class" and "sex" regarding women's work experience; class is both *situation* "applied to occupational categories and power relations" and *perception*—"a value system in which horizontal loyalty takes precedence over individual ambition, which seeks upward mobility." Ware posed provocative questions, for example: "What is the meaning of class for women who are in and out of the labor market at different periods in their lives?"

88. Manning, *Immigrant Woman and Her Job*, 62, "the women were disinclined to regard these irregular or part-time jobs as anything that had counted much." Sheila Ryan Johansson, "Herstory as History: A New Field or Another Fad?" in Berenice A. Carroll, ed., *Liberating Women's History, Theoretical and Critical Essays* (Urbana: University of Illinois Press, 1976), 406, the narrow range of occupational choices, sex-differentiated wages, and faint possibility of work leading to economic independence from family or security in old age translates as little "status" for working women. Tentler, *Wage Earning Women*, 24, 81, 157, 147, compared women's autonomy at home and work; the latter reinforced "marginality" through wages, work conditions, and the need to neglect children. Men could reject jobs due to low pay or type; women were expected to take whatever. In contrast, homemaking allowed women authority, independence, and creativity in working. Hartmann, "Capitalism and Women's Work," 2, is more critical about women's status at home, and interpreted patriarchy influencing capitalism to keep women in a dependent status with low wages and child care responsibilties as part of this control. Lewis, *Women In England*, 162, 218–21, working-class British women shared employers' notions of women's work; Lewis, *Labour and Love*, 105, women preferred work identified for women rather than taking jobs that brought higher wages but were commonly held by men.

89. These comments are not to deny the courage and clarity with which some women in industry fought to create labor unions during this period.

Chapter 4

1. AC, *26th Annual Report*, 1910, 32. Linda Gordon, *Heroes of Their Own Lives, The Politics and History of Family Violence, Boston 1880–1960* (New York: Viking, 1988), 86, similar concern about female-headed families was expressed by Boston social workers. Edward T. Devine," Widows' Needs," *Survey* 32 (April 4, 1914), 23, describes the same in New York City.

2. Agreement for British working-class women in Jane Lewis, *Women in England 1870–1950: Sexual Divisions and Social Change* (Bloomington: Indiana University Press, 1984), 8, 11.

3. Case 14,931 on Reel 205.

4. Case 7,330 on Reel 150.

5. Case 621 on Reel 110.

6. "Studies of Breakdowns in Family Incomes: Broken Families," *The Family* 11:1 (March 1930), 3–13, 1 of 6 families known at a Boston relief agency, 1918 and 1928, was broken by desertion or divorce.

7. Peter Uhlenberg, "Cohort Variations in Family Life Cycle Experiences of U.S. Females," *Journal of Marriage and the Family* 36 (1974), 284–92, graphed 150 years of family life cycles. See also John Modell, "Changing Risks, Changing Adaptations: American Families in the Nineteenth and Twentieth Centuries," in A. J. Lichtman and J. R. Challinor, eds., *Kin and Communities* (Washington, D.C.: Smithsonian Institution Press, 1978), 119–44; Paul H. Jacobson, *American Marriage and Divorce* (New York: Rinehart, 1959), 140–44. Steven Mintz and Susan Kellogg, *Domestic Revolutions, A Social History of American Family Life* (New York: Free, 1988), 109, the divorce rate increased fifteenfold 1870 to 1920.

8. Calvin Schmid, *Social Sage of Two Cities* (Minneapolis: Bureau of Social Research, Minneapolis Council of Social Agencies, 1937), 310, 311, 314, in 1936 the "divorce curve for the United States closely parallels that of Minnesota," but the urban Hennepin County rate exceeded the state's. Jacobson, *American Marriage and Divorce* (New York: Rinehart, 1959), 69, the high divorce rate between 1915 and 1925 was credited to the First World War and to postwar depression.

9. William O'Neill, *Divorce in the Progressive Era* (New Haven, Conn.: Yale University Press, 1967), 267, early century debate over divorce appeared "peripheral" to reform concerns of most progressives. See also Minutes, Friendly Visitors' Conference Committee, November 9, 1911, Box 7, FCS Social Welfare History Archives, University of Minnesota; a professor from the university's Sociology Department discussed the "Modern Family and the Danger of Divorce to the Home."

10. Jacobson, *American Marriage and Divorce*, 69–82. Louise A. Tilly and Joan W. Scott, *Women, Work and Family* (New York: Holt, 1978), 52, in preindustrial Europe "remarriage was clearly the happiest solution for a widow since an economic partnership was the best means of survival"; similar analysis is not provided for the industrial period. Katharine Anthony, *Mothers Who Must Earn* (New York: Russell Sage Foundation, Survey Research Associates, 1914), 20, 24, found frequent remarriage.

11. Case 1,109 on Reel 114.

12. Case 14,958 on Reel 205.

13. Case 4,256 on Reel 130.

14. This view of marriage is in Richmond, "Charity and Homemaking," 1897, in Colcord and Ruth Z. S. Mann, eds., *The Long View: Papers of Mary E. Richmond* (New York: Russell Sage Foundation, 1929), 78, 79. Robert S. and Helen M. Lynd, *Middletown, A Study in American Culture* (New York: Har-

court, 1929), 114–18. Robert L. Griswold, *Family and Divorce in California, 1850–1890, Victorian Illusions and Everyday Realities* (Albany: SUNY Press, 1982), 93–106, nineteenth-century divorce records showed "frequent references to work habits"; charges of nonsupport and temperance were more often made by women in the lower class who felt that "work by the husband was a responsibility owed to the wife, and nothing more detrimental could be said about a man than that he did not support his wife and family." Lewis, *Women in England*, xiii; and Lewis, ed., *Labour and Love: Women's Experiences of Home and Family, 1850–1940* (Oxford: Basil Blackwell, 1986), 107.

15. Arthur W. Calhoun, *A Social History of the American Family, Vol. III From 1865 to 1919* (Cleveland: Arthur H. Clarke; reprint. ed., New York: Barnes and Noble, 1960), 326.

16. Pat Ayers and Jan Lambertz, "Marriage Relations, Money, and Domestic Violence in Working Class Liverpool, 1919–1939," in Lewis, *Labour and Love*, 196–219, there was the potential of money problems for creating family tension. Lillian Rubin, *Worlds of Pain: Life in Working Class Families* (New York: Basic, 1976), 34–38, 77, 91, contemporary working-class families were debilitated by unemployment as manifested in violence.

17. Case 621 on Reel 110.

18. Ernest W. Burgess and Harvey J. Locke, *The Family from Institution to Companionship*, 2nd ed. (New York: American Book, 1953), 311, a companionate marriage included "mutual affection," "emotional interdependence," "sympathetic understanding," and "consensus on family objectives." Lynds, *Middletown*, 118, the working class did not regard "companionship" essential to marriage. Agreement exists in studies by Mirra Komarovsky, *Blue-Collar Marriage* (New York: Random, 1962), 334; and Lee Rainwater, *And the Poor Get Children; Sex, Contraception and Family Planning in the Working Class* (Chicago: Quadrangle, 1960), 72, 73, lower class wives saw husbands as dominant, powerful, and unaffectionate. Women would "acquiesce" to "isolation"; to believe in "mutual understanding," required women to have too much faith in men's basic goodness. Mintz and Kellogg, *Domestic Revolutions*, 113.

19. Case 1,122 on Reel 114.

20. E. Wight Bakke, *The Unemployed Worker: A Study of the Task of Making a Living Without a Job* (New Haven, Conn.: Yale University Press, 1940), 196–98, "unemployed workers and the public share an illusion that constant application for any and all jobs is the way to land a job and an evidence of diligent effort—when it is volume of demand and not the character of supply which is requisite for job getting."

21. Bakke, *Unemployed Worker*, 7–11, 155–72, 232, 314, the impact of unemployment varied with a family's size, health, initial resources, and previous employment experiences. In this Great Depression study families progressed

from initially being able to maintain a previous life-style to social withdrawal and acceptance of outside assistance, but unemployment did not change workers' basic behavior—the hard worker continued to be the hard worker, although perhaps directing energy in alternate ways for self-reliance. Bakke assumes a prior state of stability that makes his sample different from many of the families coming to AC/FWA. Komarovsky, *Blue-Collar Marriage*, 282, 292, men became dissatisfied with low-status, low-pay work, but blamed themselves for low achievement and suffered a loss of self-esteem; deprivations that women themselves suffered led them to "a more critical scrutiny of their husbands' personalities." See also Mirra Komarovsky, *The Unemployed Man and His Family, The Effect of Unemployment upon the Status of the Man in Fifty-Nine Families* (New York: Dryden, 1940), 74, without work men not only lost prestige but daily routine. Roy Rosenzweig, *Eight Hours for What We Will, Workers and Leisure In an Industrial City, 1870–1920* (New York: Cambridge University Press, 1983), 46, 51–53, discusses the value of the saloon to working men. John D'Emilio and Estelle B. Freedman, *Intimate Matters, A History of Sexuality in America* (New York: Harper, 1988), 185, 186.

22. Mary E. Richmond, "Charity and Homemaking," 1897, in Colcord, *Long View*, 77. Gordon, *Heroes of Their Own Lives,* 90, 101, social workers found it difficult to distinguish between separation and desertion, and nonsupport and unemployment.

23. Such behavior is described as common in Colcord, *Broken Homes, A Study of Family Desertion and Its Social Treatment* (New York: Russell Sage Foundation, 1919), 149–51.

24. Desertion laws are cited in Lilian Brandt, *Five Hundred and Seventy-Four Deserters and Their Families: A Descriptive Study of Their Characteristics and Circumstances* (New York: Charity Organization Society, 1905), 18–21, 89–91. Also E. G. Steger, "Report of the Committee on the Family on the Need for the Organization of a Family Court in the State of Minnesota," Minnesota State Conference of Social Work, 29th Annual Conference, 1921, *Proceedings,* 112–17; Minutes, Friendly Visitors' Conference, April 9, 1913, Folder-1, Box L.1, FCS Collection, an official from the district court explained the relationship between nonsupport and divorce.

25. Minutes, Friendly Visitors Conference, January 15, 1913, Folder 1, Box L.1, FCS Collection. Elizabeth Pleck, *Domestic Tyranny: The Making of American Social Policy Against Family Violence from Colonial Times to the Present* (New York: Oxford University Press, 1987), 126, family courts like juvenile courts in the progressive era were more likely to assume family members as ignorant and shiftless than "criminal" in behavior toward one another; courts commonly sought conciliation between husbands and wives.

26. AC, *32nd Annual Report,* 1916, 12; Rosenzweig, *Eight Hours For What We Will,* 53, 103.

27. "Studies of Breakdowns in Family Incomes," 10, among one thousand families known to three Chicago relief agencies over a ten-year period, husbands' drinking helped differentiate broken from unbroken homes. Griswold, *Family and Divorce in California*, 6, 8, 16, 100, "drink was the great incapacitator" that destroyed families on all class levels but particularly for the lower class; 48 percent of male defendants in these divorce cases were sued for nonsupport; 21 percent for intemperance and 14 percent for both.

28. Case 3,269 on Reel 120.

29. Case 2,317 on Reel 120.

30. AC, *32nd Annual Report,* 1916, 12. Pleck, *Domestic Tyranny,* 49–66, nineteenth-century temperance organizers assumed alcohol played a causal role in violence against women. Rosenzweig, *Eight Hours for What We Will,* 103, another perspective on role and intent of social reformers against the saloon. See also Judith Lacerte and Donna L. Harris, "Alcoholism: A Catalyst for Women to Organize, 1850–1980," *Affilia* (Summer 1986), 41–52.

31. Robert Kelso, *Poverty* (New York: Longmans, Green, 1929), 209–17, contains statistics from late century studies correlating poverty, alcoholism, and family troubles. See also Edward T. Devine, *Misery and Its Causes* (New York: Macmillan, 1904, 211, 212; and Edward T. Devine, *The Principles of Relief* (New York: Macmillan, 1909), 144, 145, 149. A contemporary empirical study is in Gloria Kaufman Kantor and Murray A. Straus, "The 'Drunken Bum,' Theory of Wife Beating," *Social Problems* 34:3 (June 1987), 213–30, relates violence in the working-class culture to drink and family violence with a good bibliography of contemporary literature. Frank J. Bruno, *Trends in Social Work, 1874–1956, A History Based on the Proceedings of the National Conference of Social Work* (New York: Columbia University Press, 1957), 361, judged in retrospect that social workers had too long neglected the problem of drinking.

32. Speeches in Minutes, Friendly Visitors' Conference, May 1910; April 10, 1912; June 15, 1913, Folder-1, Box L.1, FCS Collection.

33. Dr. Haldor Sneve, "Hospital Treatment of Inebriates," Minnesota State Conference of Charities and Correction, 16th Annual Conference, 1907, *Proceedings*, 92–101. W. J. Rorabaugh, *The Alcoholic Republic: An American Tradition* (New York: Oxford University Press, 1979), passim, related nineteenth-century social destabilization and worker mobility to the great consumption of alcohol; there's also helpful bibliographic sources.

34. David L. Rosheim, *The Other Minneapolis, or the Rise and Fall of the Gateway, the Old Minneapolis Skid Row* (Maquoketa, Iowa: Andromeda, 1978), 123.

35. *The Bulletin*, June 21, 1920, Box 5, FCS Collection.

36. Minneapolis Civic and Commerce Association, *Minneapolis Golden Jubilee, 1867–1917* (Minneapolis: Civic and Commerce Association), 7, high license fees and limited areas for locating bars controlled saloon traffic in MIn-neapolis before Prohibition. A history of local saloon business is in Rosheim, *The Other Minneapolis,* 73, 94–104, 118, 123. The Women's Cooperative Alliance studied Minneapolis neighborhoods in the 1920s finding soft drink parlors selling moonshine; police agreed. See *A Study of Community Conditions, East District, 1923*, 29–31, Minneapolis Clippings File, Minneapolis Public Library.

37. Women's Cooperative Alliance, *Study of Community Condition*, 31.

38. Case 15,890 on Reel 215; Kantor, " The 'Drunken Bum,' Theory," 24, concludes that the "approval of violence" in blue-collar culture is an important factor in the alcohol/family violence equation.

39. Culture, material scarcity, employment, and alcohol appear in various combinations as causal factors in husbands' behavior in primary literature from the period as well as in contemporary literature with historical and current concerns. Many authors hypothesize why men behave badly, but they rarely suggest why only *some* men do. Contemporary analysis includes work by Gordon, *Heroes of Their Own Lives,* 3, 257–71, 286, examines competition over resources that occurred between husbands and wives, often alcohol use escalated conflict; Ayers and Lambertz, "Marriage Relations, Money and Domestic Violence," 195, 200; Nancy Tomes, "A Torrent of Abuse: Crimes of Violence between Working Class Men and Women in London," *Journal of Social History*, 11:3 (Spring 1978), 334, nineteenth-century British records show men as physically abusive when minor issues of privilege and resource allocation were threatened. The incidence of domestic violence decreased toward the end of the century, and Tomes offered various social and domestic explanations, among these improvement in the economic situation of the working class. Elizabeth Pleck, "Challenges to Traditional Authority in Immigrant Families," in Michael Gordon, ed. *The American Family in Socio-Historical Perspective*, 3rd ed. (New York: St. Martins, 1983), 504–17, women's rights threatened role assumptions of many immigrant men in the early century, and the state with police and courts became a third party in marital relations. Pleck, *Domestic Tyranny*, 55–63, reformers' concerns about violence against women peaked in the late nineteenth-century and then disappeared until the women's movement of 1960s and 1970s.

Analysis from the early century is in Mary E. Richmond, *What Is Social Case Work? An Introductory Description* (New York: Russell Sage Foundation, 1922), 185, referred to immigrants' "autocratic traditions" and the "shock" of the new American environment. Helen Bosanquet, *The Family* (London: Macmillan, 1915), 260, 261, observed men achieving and maintaining superiority through physical strength that achieved less in modern society, but still could be effective against wives. An early dissertation from the Sociology Department at the University of Minnesota reflects an ecological approach popular at the time matching desertion, divorce, and family geographic mobility, see Agnes C. Harrigan, "A Study of the Mobility of Members of Disorganized Families in Minneapolis in 1926," (M.A. Thesis, University of Minnesota, 1929), 53. Calhoun, *Social History of the American Family*, 266, cities provided ways for men to escape from community controls and economic pressures. Devine, *Principles of Relief*, 144, 145, 149, "demoral associations" and "debasing appetite" of urban drinking men led not only to cruelty but to crime and suicide.

Research with sample populations includes Rainwater, *And the Poor Get Children*, 77–90, "ineffective" in many aspects of their own lives, working-class men "escaped" by drinking. Komarovsky, *Blue-Collar Marriage*, 220–35, provides diverse interpretations of power in working-class families, as more patriarchal and more matriarchal, than middle-class families. The theory of patriarchy describes home as the last arena for men to act out dominance. In *Unemployed Man*, 66, male unemployment appears as pattern deteriorating into irritability, drinking, infidelity, and emotional instability.

40. Changing grounds for divorce in Jacobson, *American Marriage and Divorce*, 122–27; O'Neil, *Divorce in the Progressive Era*, 28, listed the frequency of charges for 1867—adultery, desertion, and cruelty; the order reverses by 1928. Neither author extensively discussed reasons for change. Local exceptions to this national trend appear in Elaine T. May, *Great Expectations, Marriage and Divorce in Post-Victorian America* (Chicago: University of Chicago Press, 1980), 175, a sample of petitions filed for divorce and annulment in Los Angeles courts; showed increase in desertion and decrease in cruelty charges from the 1880s to 1920. Friends aiding women in making legal complaints, in Gordon, *Heroes of Their Own Lives*, 276–80.

41. *Factors in the Sex Life of Twenty-Two Hundred Women* (New York: Harper, 1929), 39, among women with above average educational backgrounds, 116 were partially or totally unhappy with their marriages owing most frequently to "incompatibility of temperament or interest," with 40 responses, "difficulties of adjustment of sexual life—(on the part of the husband—18, on the part of the wife—5)," "economic reasons—14," "husband unfaithful—12," "husband alcoholic—10." "Cruelty" was a factor less often. Ernest R. Mowrer, *Domestic Discord: Its Analysis and Treatment* (Chicago: University of Chicago Press, 1928), 257–61, "Diagnostic Factors in Domestic Discord," in over one thousand cases from the Jewish Social Service Bureau and the United Charities of Chicago, 1924–25, abuse and drunkenness were the most frequent disruptive factors in family life; immorality, venereal disease, sexual refusal, excessive sexual demands, and sexual perversions were less common. Leslie Woodcock Tentler, *Wage-Earning Women, Industrial and Family Life in the United States, 1900–1930* (New York: Oxford University Press, 1979), 175. Tomes, "Torrent of Abuse," 329, 335, 336, neighbors knew of men beating their wives, but intervention was minimal unless abuse appeared to be leading to homicide. As homes become sounder structurally and more private in location, neighbors became less likely to know of abuse.

Much research exists on contemporary women's reluctance to speak out against abuse, see, for example, Roger Petersen, "Social Class, Social Learning, and Wife Abuse, *Social Service Review* 54:3 (September 1980), 390–406, a study of six hundred women suggested abuse was related to group norms *and* poverty's structural stress. He refers to Richard Gelles's work; for example, "Abused Wives: Why Do They Stay?" *Journal of Marriage and the Family* 38 (November 1976), 659–68, multiple factors affect women's response to abuse but *women with the fewest resources were most likely to continue accepting it. Women often found social services ineffective helpers* (emphasis added).

42. Case 1,252 on Reel 115.

43. Barbara Brookes, "Women and Reproduction, 1860–1939," in Lewis, *Labour and Love,* 158, 159, describes sexual relations in her study as "demand and supply," an area of dominance for males with little power beyond their own homes. Gordon, *Heroes of Their Own Lives,* 199, fear of pregnancy led wives to attempt withdrawal from sexual relations; Pleck, *Domestic Tyranny*, 88–98, late nineteenth-century female reformers attacked the reality of female sexual subservience, and some groups organized service and advocacy programs to provide assistance to victims; Barbara Brooks, "Women and Reproduction, 1860–1939," in Lewis, *Labour and Love*, 158, women often judged the quality of working-class husband as inversely correlated with the degree to which he "bothered" the wife with sexual demands. D'Emilio and Freedman, *Intimate Matters,* 185. Komarovsky, *Unemployed Man*, 122, 131, wives of unemployed men feared pregnancy and the economic demands of another child and therefore shunned sex; for women who never felt sexually eager, unemployment created an excuse for reluctance. *Blue-Collar Marriage*, 227, some women used sex to influence their marriage but many believed in dutiful submission. In these case records there was little evidence of wives "using" sex in marriage. See also Rubin, *Worlds of Pain,* 134–54, which includes description of marital sex among working class in the 1970s.

44. Rainwater, *And the Poor Get Children,* 113, found lower-class women rejected husbands sexually, owing to men's drinking.

45. May, *Great Expectations*, 174, in Los Angeles courts divorce litigation in the 1880s and 1920, men complained of women's refusal of sex, and women complained of sexual abuse from men; such complaints increased over time.

46. Schmid, *Social Sage,* 367, documented veneral disease rates among men and women in Minneapolis in 1936, the "greatest incidence of venereal disease occurs before marriage for both males and females; a relatively greater proportion of females than of males are infected after marriage." Documentation was difficult as most women were treated in clinics, but men went to private physicians and to the medical staff at the city Workhouse.

47. Case 15,531 on Reel 210. Gordon, *Heroes of Their Own Lives,* 204–232, in this study Gordon discusses roles of fathers/stepfathers and the social

politics of incest, which involved 10 percent of the families in the caseload at the Boston Society for the Prevention of Cruelty to Children. It should be noted that that agency was established to deal with such abuse and consequently had case material on it as the Minneapolis AC/FWA did not. See also Linda Gordon, "Incest and Resistance: Patterns of Father-Daughter Incest, 1880–1930," *Social Problems* 33:4 (April 1986); and Pleck, *Domestic Tyranny,* 82.

48. Pleck, "Feminist Responses to 'Crimes Against Women,' 1868–1896," *Signs* 8:3 (Spring 1983), 451–70, traced women's abuse as an issue of nineteenth-century women's movement and their reluctance to suggest divorce for the home was considered private. To infringe on this and on the sanctity of marriage was controversial and could threaten central efforts of the suffrage campaign engaging many activist women. Pleck contrasted public attention to abuse of children with scant attention to women at the same time. Gordon and Wini Breines, "New Scholarship on Family Violence," *Signs* 8:3 (Spring 1983), 507, repeat this observation. Pleck, *Domestic Tyranny,* 126, 145, 146, in the progressive era legal protections to women as industrial workers were unmatched by concern for their domestic safety; neither the new juvenile nor domestic courts created took family violence as a "crime"; such concern was seen as a figment of earlier times when moralism dominated social intervention. Psychiatric intervention followed the progressive approach; it perceived both victim and perpetrator in abuse as likely to be genetically inferior.

49. AC, *21st Annual Report, 1905,* 13, "There is reason to fear that the evil of wife-desertion is a growing evil." National statistics on desertion are incomplete and scattered, relying on the man being charged in court or his family being seen by a charity. Discussion of these statistics in Earle E. Eubank, *A Study of Family Desertion* (Chicago: Department of Public Welfare, 1916), 22–26.

50. National Conference of Charities and Correction, *Guide to Study of Charities and Correction* (Indianapolis: National Conference of Charities and Correction, 1908). Eubank, *Study of Family Desertion,* 6, 7, "the most practical consideration that the matter has received has been at the hands of the National Conference of Jewish Charities. Desertion has been under consideration nineteen times by various state conferences of charities and correction."

51. Agency interest in desertion and related laws in Minutes, Board Meeting, March 19, April 16, 1903, Box 5, FCS Collection; AC, *21st Annual Report, 1905*, 14; AC, *29th Annual Report, 1913*, 33; AC, *32nd Annual Report, 1916*, 11. The St. Paul municipal court judge critiques Minnesota desertion laws, John W. Finehout, "Desertion," Minnesota State Conference of Charities and Correction, 12th Annual Conference, 1903, *Proceedings,* 35–42; Mildred D. Mudgett, "Where the Courts Interlock," *The Family* 4:3 (May 1923), 54, Mudgett was fieldwork supervisor of the University of Minnesota Training Course for Social and Civic Work; her students had internships at AC/FWA.

52. Lilian Brandt, *Five Hundred Seventy-Four Deserters and Their Families: A Descriptive Study of Their Characteristics and Circumstances (New York: Charity Organization Society, 1905),* 23, 14, 43, while the husband was the "most important feature in the situation" (because of his earning power), he was often "an unknown quantity." Devine, *Principles of Relief,* 37, 140; Martha May, "The 'Problem of Duty': Family Desertion in the Progressive Era," *Social Service Review* 62:1 (March 1988), 40–60, traces revision of desertion as a moral issue to one requiring legal treatment with assumptions of maladjustment.

53. Zilpha Smith, *Deserted Wives and Deserting Husbands: A Study of Two Hundred Thirty-Four Families Based on the Experience of the District Committees and Agents of the Associated Charities of Boston* (Boston: AC, 1901), passim.

54. Minutes, Friendly Visitors' Conference, March 6, 1912, Folder-1, Box L.1, FCS Collection.

55. Eubank, *Study of Family Desertion*, 20, 21, 37–45, 64, 9–14, 17; Rubin, *Worlds of Pain*, 60–68; working-class girls who "get caught" with pregnancy are held responsible for the prior sex.

56. Brandt, *Five Hundred Seventy-Four Deserters*, 23–29, 63; Devine, *Principles of Relief*, 137, 138, among 500 deserters, 48 percent were under 35 years; they were skilled, and a large proportion were employed.

57. Minutes, Friendly Visitors' Conference, March 6, 1912, Folder–1, Box L.1. See also desertion as discussed in *The Bulletin*, February 19, December 24, 1917; November 10, 1919; September 23, 1918, 7, Box 3, FCS Collection.

58. Brandt, *Five Hundred Seventy-Four Deserters,* 14, 15.

59. Colcord, *Broken Homes,* 191, 192.

60. *Ibid.*, 8, 9, refuted the popular phrase, "poor man's divorce" to describe desertion.

61. *The Bulletin*, July 23, 1917, Folder-3, Box 3, FCS Collection.

62. Case 14,906 on Reel 205.

63. Case 6,477 on Reel 147.

64. Case 14,332 on Reel 200.

65. Eubank, *Study of Family Desertion,* 27–35, deserting "unanchored husbands" swelled "ranks of anti-social men."

66. Brandt, *Five Hundred Seventy-Four Deserters*, 48, 49; Colcord, *Broken Homes,* 128–30; Richmond, "War and Family Solidarity," 1918 in Colcord, *Long View,* 451, advised that when both spouses were "weak," it was better for the wife to be apart from than with her husband.

67. Eubank, *Study of Family Desertion,* 31, observed that deserted wives were reticent to criticize husbands though glad they were gone; others continued to be loyal, were ashamed, or feared male "reprisal"; however, the absence of some men had the positive effect of "one less mouth to feed," an end to drunken brawls and bad examples before children.

68. Colcord, *Broken Homes,* 73, men returned—without intention to stay—to see children, in jealousy of wives, or came as acts of bravado.

69. Case 732 on Reel 111.

70. Case 1,160 on Reel 114.

71. AC, *23rd Annual Report,* 1907, 16, 17, contains a discussion of "fault."

72. Pleck, *Domestic Tyranny*, 11, makes an important point that individuals' participation in family conflict often precludes an easy assessment of one party being guilty and the other entirely innocent.

73. Komarovsky, *Unemployed Man,* 54, "unemployment made existing dissatisfactions explicit." Tomes, "Torrent of Abuse," 332; in British court cases from the mid and latter nineteenth-century. The "aggravating" of wives—their swearing and insolence—were husbands' justification for beating them.

74. Case 1,317 on Reel 115.

75. Pleck, "Challenges to Traditional Authority," 506, this study included limited instances of women abusing husbands. Gordon, "New Scholarship," 512, 513, the great "asymmetry" of "power" between men and women in public and private relations gives women far less support than men for such behavior.

76. Case 1,600 on Reel 117.

77. Colcord, *Broken Homes*, 31, 153. See also "Housekeeping and Family Adjustment," July 1926, Folder-Radio, Box 2, FCS Collection, the woman had to maintain "her part" for husband's respect.

78. Breckinridge, *Family Welfare Work in a Metropolitan Community* (Chicago: University of Chicago Press, 1924), 560.

79. "When the Head of Household Fails to Provide," August 1926, Folder–13, Box 10, FCS Collection. Gordon, *Heroes of Their Own Lives*, 260, 268.

80. Colcord, *Broken Homes,* 42, the "justifiable deserter" was the man married to an alcoholic. Gordon, *Heroes of Their Own Lives,* 144–46, 265–67, Gordon associates some part of child neglect and domestic violence with women's drinking problems, but these were not publicized as part of the justification for reformers' Prohibition efforts.

81. Case 4,188 on Reel 130.

82. Griswold, *Family and Divorce in California*, 72, 74, 77, 117, the charge of infidelity against a woman had "social and legal significance." A husband could bring "shame" to a wife and obtain favorable court response by charging immorality. Gordon, *Heroes of Their Own Lives,* 269, 270.

83. "Studies of Breakdowns in Family Income," 7, 9, 10.

84. Gordon, *Heroes of Their Own Lives,* 6, 295–98, men's and women's varying access to resources is defined as "political"; the fact that women sought help from agencies challenges certain historians' interpretation that welfare programs have primarily exercized "social control" entirely against the wishes or rights of those experiencing the intervention. She notes that people requesting service often got less than what they wanted or needed. Pleck, *Domestic Tyranny,* 139, when confronted, men accused women of wrong behavior.

85. Elizabeth Bott, *Family and Social Network: Roles, Norms, and External Relationships in Ordinary Urban Families* (London: Tavistock, 1957), 60, among the British working class in the 1950s segregation of conjugal roles was a function not of class but reinforced by social network shared with kin.

86. "Studies of Breakdowns in Family Income," 8, offers statistics of relatives' opposition to marriages resulting in "broken homes"; unfortunately "opposition" was not defined. Mark Schneyer, "Mothers and Children, Poverty and Morality: Social Workers' Priorities, 1915," *Pennsylvania Magazine of History and Biography* 112:2 (April 1988), 211, mothers protected adult divorced sons from having to pay child support.

87. Case 15,944 on Reel 215.

88. Komarovsky, *Blue-Collar Marriage,* 35, 210–18, working-class women's world of intimate communication was with other women, particularly female relatives. Unhappily married women used more confidants than those content in marriage. Bott, *Family and Social Network,* 137, distinct conjugal roles encouraged close ties among female relatives; Rainwater, *And the Poor Get Children,* 64, women learned about sex from female relatives. Gordon, "New Scholarship," 515, 518, women can "learn" to accept abuse if it is within community standards. Nothing in these case records suggested that female friends or relatives approved of abuse, but many acknowledged that a woman in question had faults that made her difficult to live with. Gordon, *Heroes of Their Own Lives,* 276–80.

89. Gordon, *Heroes of Their Own Lives,* 106.

90. Case 38 on Reel 106.

91. Case 1,039 on Reel 113.

92. Tomes, "Torrent of Abuse," 333, wives in her study reacted to abuse in different ways; some accepted it; others fought back.

93. Colcord, "The Relation of Marriage Laws to Family Welfare," Minnesota State Conference of Social Work, 31st Annual Conference, 1923, *Proceedings*, 52.

94. Alice Newbold, "Problems of Desertion and Abandonment," Minnesota State Conference of Social Work, 32nd Annual Conference, 1924, *Proceedings* 53. Devine, *Principles of Relief*, 231, assumed women who placed charges against husbands usually did so for economic reasons rather than in belief that the marriage would improve.

95. *The Bulletin,* July 30, 1917, Folder-3, Box 3, FCS Collection.

96. Colcord, *Broken Homes*, 10; Pleck, "Challenge to Traditional Authority," 508, found few women wanted divorce and many were willing to settle for better behavior from husband.

97. Gordon, *Heroes of Their Own Lives*, 105, found exhausted victims of marital violence were not interested in remarriage. This differs from the longitudinal experience suggested by case records in this study.

98. Case 15,206 on Reel 205.

99. Case 1,480 on Reel 105.

100. Colcord, *Broken Homes*, 156, most nonsupporters had "moral faults" in addition to nonsupport; wives took men to court for revenge. Pleck, "Challenge to Traditional Authority," 510, "state intervention" carried out by municipal courts in cases of wife abuse was used by immigrant women to get "power."

101. Case 14,332 on Reel 200.

102. Case 7,884 on Reel 155.

103. Case 15,464 on Reel 210.

104. Griswold, *Family and Divorce in California,* 191, found nineteenth-century illiterate women taking initiative to press for divorce with its attendant legal forms and processes.

105. Case 10,048 on Reel 170.

106. Calhoun, *Social History of The American Family,* 271, wrote in 1918 that divorce was part of emerging feminism; "new ideals of woman are in conflict with the old despotism of the husband." Women in these cases reflected not ideals of feminism as much as family survival skills. Lynds, *Middletown,* 126, found wives seeking divorce, preferring to earn their own living than adjust to a situation with a husband. Griswold, *Family and Divorce in California,* 29, women sued first in two-thirds of the cases in his study; "plaintiffs had a high rate of success." Elaine T. May, "The Pressure to Provide: Class, Consumerism, and Divorce in Urban America, 1880–1920," in Gordon, *American Family*, 165,

differentiated divorce issues brought to court by the class of the litigant; working-class couples were more concerned with "bread and butter" issues.

107. Jacobson, *American Marriage and Divorce,* 127, women were more likely to get alimony if they brought charges. The increasing "privilege" of mothers to be awarded child custody (vs. earlier custom of assuming children belonged to father) carried heavy obligations for their support, see Carol Brown, "Mothers, Fathers, and Children: From Private to Public Patriarchy," in Lydia Sargent, ed. *Women and Revolution : A Discussion of the Unhappy Marriage of Marxism and Feminism* (Boston: South End, 1981), 239–67; Ellen Ross, "Labour and Love: Rediscovering London's Working Class Mothers, 1870–1918," in Lewis, *Labour and Love;* Pleck, *Domestic Tyranny*, 141–43, judges considered a woman's "morality" in determining support after divorce.

108. Case 7,338 on Reel 150.

109. Case 7,630 on Reel 105.

110. Case 17,294 on Reel 225.

111. Pleck, "Challenge to Traditional Authority," 508, found few women wanted divorce and were willing to settle instead for better behavior from a husband. Also Pleck, *Domestic Tyranny,* 106, 107, 141, divorce was a safer alternative than a violent marriage, but social reformers were reluctant to support this as an option. Those pursuing divorce found access to Legal Aid limited.

112. Brown, "Mothers, Fathers and Children," 248, 249.

113. Case 11,415 on Reel 180. See also O'Neill, *Divorce in the Progressive Era*, 6, 85, who interpreted divorce as means for a "second chance" at an important institution. May, *Great Expectations*, 161, "because most women viewed matrimony as the only place they could truly express themselves, it is misleading to equate desire for marital dissolution with any widespread urge for freedom from marriage itself."

114. Case 3,394 on Reel 125.

Chapter 5

1. News story dated January 22, 1906, *Minneapolis Journal.*

2. Case 277 on Reel 108. Jane Lewis, *Women In England, 1870–1950: Sexual Divisions and Social Change* (Bloomington: Indiana University Press, 1984), 52–62, British working-class women viewed charity as the last resort.

3. Case 15,986 on Reel 215.

4. Case 547 on Reel 110.

5. Mark H. Leff, "Consensus for Reform: The Mothers'-Pension Movement

in the Progressive Era," *Social Service Review* 47:3 (September 1973), 397–417. Scholars agree on how scant were pension benefits but disagree as to the program's relationship to the mother's status; for a feminist critique, Mimi Abramovitz, *Regulating the Lives of Women: Social Welfare Policy from Colonial Times to the Present* (Boston: South End, 1988), 190–206, the program kept recipient mothers from the labor market, oversaw their child rearing, and made them dependent on the state versus a male provider; Ann Vandepol, "Dependent Children: Child Custody and Mothers' Pensions, *Social Problems* 29:3 (February 1982), 221–35, pensions recognized mothers as the primary parent apart from male authority, but left her with obligations as well; Anne Summers, "A Home from Home-Women's Philanthropic Work in the Nineteenth Century," in Sandra Burman, ed., *Fit Work for Women* (London: Croom Helm, 1979), 60.

6. Marion Daniel Shutter, ed., *History of Minneapolis, Gateway to the Northwest* (Chicago: S. S. Clarke, 1923), 206, 207; *Self Analysis Survey of the Minneapolis Settlement Houses* (Minneapolis: Twin City Federation of Settlements, 1934); Council of Social Agencies, *Community Survey,* Vol. 38. Interpretation of North East Neighborhood House (in AC/FWA records as NENH), by Winifred Wandersee Bolin, "Heating Up the Melting Pot," *Minneapolis History* 45:2 (Summer 1976), 58–69. Many settlements had child care facilities, kindergartens, employment bureaus, and dispensary clinics, some staffed with visiting nurses. Margery Spring Rice, *Working-Class Wives, Their Health and Conditions* (London: Penguin, 1939; reprint ed., London: Virago, 1981), 69–76, 97, 1930s study of 1,200 wives by the Women's Health Inquiry Committee of the British National Health Service showed women's tacit acceptance and expectation of tiredness, strain, and ill health. "There is absolutely no evidence of hypochondria." Lewis, "The Working-Class Wife and Mothers and State Intervention, 1870–1918," in Lewis, ed., *Labour and Love: Women's Experiences of Home and Family, 1850–1940* (Oxford: Basil Blackwell, 1986),111, at times nurses' arrogance made them unwelcome in poor homes.

7. Case 8,581 on Reel 160.

8. Case 4,946 on Reel 135.

9. Case 2,432 on Reel 120.

10. Case 4,285 on Reel 130. Steven Mintz and Susan Kellogg, *Domestic Revolutions, A Social History of American Family Life* (New York: Free, 1988), 120, in the nineteenth-century only poor women—often unwed—gave birth in hospitals still reputed as less healthy places than private homes.

11. The assumption that legal remedies existed for social problems is in Mary E. Richmond and Fred S. Hall, *Marriage and the State* (New York: Russell Sage Foundation, 1929). Christopher Lasch, *Haven in a Heartless World, The Family Besieged* (New York: Basic, 1977), 14–18, criticizes expanded intervention by school and social welfare professionals in family life. Jacques Donzelot,

The Policing of Families (New York: Pantheon, 1979), 96, social workers took on the task of "civilizing the social body"; Eli Zaretsky, "Rethinking the Welfare State: Dependence, Economic Individualism and the Family," in James Dickinson and Bob Russell, eds., *Family, Economy, and State: The Social Reproduction Process Under Capitalism* (New York: St. Martin's, 1986), 89, 97–105, disagree that the state invaded or replaced family authority; the harsh urban industrialization made many social reforms supportive to working-class family well-being. Zaretsky also questions the impact of female social welfare workers as effective agents of "social control," given their place in a sexist society.

12. Frank J. Bruno, "The Dynamic Aspects of Liberty and Control," in Margaret Rich, *Family Life To-Day*, Papers Presented at a Conference in Celebration of the 50th Anniversary of Family Social Work in America (Boston: Houghton Mifflin, 1928), 203; also Frank J. Bruno, *Trends in Social Work, 1874–1956, A History Based on the Proceedings of the National Conference of Social Work* (New York: Columbia University Press, 1957), 186–88. Stanley Wenocur and Michael Reisch, *From Charity to Enterprise, The Development of American Social Work in a Market Economy* (Chicago: Univeristy of Illinois Press, 1989), 59, 60, 94–99, record the shift from "personal service" to "professional service."

13. Description of agents' early century training at AC of Boston is in *26th Annual Report,* 1905, 7–10; development of "professional" social work is in Nathan Irvin Huggins, *Protestants Against Poverty, Boston's Charities, 1870–1900* (Westport, Conn.: Greenwood, 1971), 131–35. Frank D. Watson, *The Charity Organization Movement in the United States: A Study on American Philanthropy* (New York: Macmillan, 1922), devotes a chapter to "Tests of Efficiency," 444–91.

Bruno, *Trends in Social Work,* 186, 188, 281, 284, law, medicine, and religion lent ideas to social work; after World War I none gave more than psychology. Bertha C. Reynolds' autobiography, *An Uncharted Journey: Fifty Years of Growth in Social Work* (New York: Citadel, 1963), 13–15, passim, describes experiences at Smith College, the first social work program in the nation to build psychology into the curriculum. Social workers were vaguely aware of psychiatry as early as 1914 but initially discounted its possibilities. Margaret Millar, "Modern Use of Older Treatment Methods," in Fern Lowry, ed., *Readings in Social Case Work 1920–1938* (New York: Columbia University Press, 1939), 345–47, suggests why social workers welcomed psychological explanations of behavior.

Contemporary observations about social work's withdrawal from reform in John Ehrenreich, *The Altruistic Imagination: A History of Social Work and Social Policy in the United States* (Ithaca, N.Y.: Cornell University Press, 1985), 43–83; impact of changes on female workers and clients is in Elizabeth Pleck, *Domestic Tyranny, The Making of American Social Policy Against Family Violence from Colonial Times to the Present* (New York: Oxford University Press, 1987), 147; Summers, "A Home from Home-Women's Philanthropic Work," 56; Dorothy M. Brown, *Setting a Course: American Women in the 1920s* (Boston:

G.K. Hall/Twayne, 1987), 152, social work as career for women changed more than any other during the 1920s.

Variation in casework method and professional expertise is in Clarke A. Chambers, *Seedtime of Reform, American Social Service and Social Action, 1918–1933* (Minneapolis: University of Minnesota, 1963), 87–106, 105, research into actions of both administration and staff at Minneapolis AC/FWA supports Chambers's assessment. See also Gary A. Lloyd, *Charities, Settlements, and Social Work: An Inquiry Into Philosophy and Method, 1890–1915* (New Orleans: Tulane University School of Social Work, 1971), passim; Roy Lubove, *The Professional Altruist, The Emergence of Social Work as a Career, 1880–1930* (Cambridge: Harvard University Press, 1965; reprint ed., New York: Atheneum, 1969), 86–89, 114. Martha Heineman Field, "Social Casework Practice During the 'Psychiatric Deluge'," *Social Service Review* 54:4 (1980), 482–507; case records from Illinois Children's Home and Aid Society show no psychodynamic concepts employed until after 1939.

14. FWA, *The Family Welfare Association in Action, 1917–1926* (Minneapolis: FWA, 1926), 20–21, though changes in casework took place, relief increased owing to larger caseloads. Amos Warner, et. al. *American Charities and Social Work*, 4th ed. (New York: Thomas Y. Crowell,1930), 290–92, between the 1890s and 1920s fewer cases received relief but in larger amounts. Warner quotes Colcord that giving small amounts "on demand" was less effective than creating adequate budgets for families. When Community Chests began advertising agencies' services, asking for relief lost some of its stigma. Frank J. Bruno, "Family Social Work," *The Family* 6:5 (July 1925), 144, 145, an increase in the cost of living justified increases in relief, but workers continued "indiscriminate" giving. Francis H. McLean, *Organizing Family Social Work in Smaller Cities* (New York: FWA of America ,1932), 4, "relief as largess is so hopelessly undemocratic that its disgrace attaches to giver and to the receiver . . . it curses both." Richmond, *What Is Social Case Work? An Introductory Description* (New York: Russell Sage Foundation,1922),172, 173, "patronage has no place in modern social work," nor was it appropriate to do the 'same thing for everybody'."

15. Pearl Salsberry, "Christmas 1924," *The Family* 6:2 (April 1925), 37–40.

16. Salsberry, "Techniques in Case Work," *The Family*, 8:5 (July 1927), 153–57; Salsberry, "Supervision," *The Family*, 10:10 (February 1930), 291–97, supervision was a learning opportunity for workers and supervisors at AC/FWA in Minneapolis. Josephine Strode and Pauline R. Strode, *Introduction to Social Casework* (New York: Harper, 1940), 25–28, 30–39, it is ironic that Richmond would codify social work technique in *Social Diagnosis* as attention was turning to a psychological approach. Two contemporary welfare historians differ on Richmond's *Social Diagnosis*. Chambers, *Seedtime of Reform*, 97, 98, respects Richmond's ability to appreciate multiple factors in human behavior; Lubove, *Professional Altruist*, 20, 47, 121, is critical. See also Ehrenreich, *Altruistic Imagination*, 64, 65, 73.

17. See extended verification in Case 2,241 on Reel 120.

18. Case 14,906 on Reel 205.

19. Economic self-support always appeared the goal at AC/FWA. This was voiced by C. C. Carstens, longtime director of the Massachusetts Society for the Prevention of Cruelty to Children and then director of the Child Welfare League of America, speaking to the AC/FWA Friendly Visitors on "Dependent Families" in 1915; the first goal in working with cases was to create "a spirit of independence and self-support"; morality and decency followed. Minutes, Friendly Visitors' Conference, September 25, 1915, Folder-1, Box L.1, FCS Collection, Social Welfare History Archives, University of Minnesota. Frances McLean, *Organizing Family Social Work in Smaller* Cities (New York: FWA of America, 1932), 3, 4, points to the misplaced centrality of economic self-support, "the work of relief societies in the past—and even sometimes today—was planned largely on the theory that economic dependence in a family was the one and only difficulty to be corrected. . . . but this had little to do with fundamental difficulties and prevention."

20. James Leiby, *A History of Social Welfare and Social Work in the United States* (New York: Columbia University Press, 1978), 185, describes changes in workers' judgments of clients; a person deemed "pathetic" early in the century was later categorized according to mental hygiene, personal autonomy, and growth.

21. Case 14,994 on Reel 205.

22. Case 17,822 on Reel 230.

23. Case 14,932 on Reel 205.

24. Mark Schneyer, " Mothers and Children, Poverty and Morality: A Social Workers' Priorities, 1915," *Pennsylvania Magazine of History and Biography* 112:2 (April 1988), 220, 221, deals with social workers' attention to poor women's "nervousness." A Slavic worker was temporarily hired at AC/FWA in 1913 owing to concern that these immigrants did not know American ways or vice versa, AC, *26th Annual Report*, 1910, 32; AC, *29th Annual Report, 1913*, 11. Linda Gordon, *Heroes of Their Own Lives, The Politics and History of Family Violence, Boston 1880–1960* (New York: Viking, 1988), 11, 15, poverty counted for more than ethnicity as a factor in family violence, as observed in cases from the Massachusetts Society for the Prevention of Cruelty to Children.

25. Richmond, "The Training of Charity Workers," 1897, in Colcord and Ruth Z. S. Mann, eds., *The Long View, Collected Papers of Mary E. Richmond* (New York: Russell Sage Foundation, 1929), 87, 88.

26. Staff lists appeared in AC *Annual Reports*, 1901–13. Agency general secretaries/directors were male until Colcord came in 1925; casework supervisors were always female. The few male agents listed in the very early century

left as the agency grew. FWA, *Family Welfare Association in Action,* 48–50; 88 of 100 people employed at AC/FWA 1917–26 were female. Colcord, "The Fabric of Family Life," *The Family* 5:2 (April 1924), 172, 173.

27. Richmond, *What Is Social Case Work?* 38, 118; Karl de Schweinitz, *The Art of Helping People Out of Trouble* (Boston: Houghton Mifflin, 1924), 61, 62; Warner, *American Charities and Social Work,* 212; Richmond, "Case Worker and the Client," 1916, in Colcord, *Long View,* 385, Frank Bruno, Minutes, Friendly Visitors' Conference, February 2, 1916, Folder-1, Box L.1, FCS Collection. See also Bruno, *Trends in Social Work,*185.

28. Richmond, "Friendly Visiting," 1907, in Colcord, *Long View,* 260.

29. Eudice Glassberg, "Philadelphians in Need: Client Experiences with Two Philadelphia Benevolent Societies, 1830–1880" (Ph.D. Thesis, DSW, University of Pennsylvania, 1979), upper-class volunteers in two nineteenth-century Philadelphia charities "advocated for clients," particularly for lone women. Caseworkers at AC/FWA made little money and may have acted in self-interest in using services provided by clients, but these records suggest it was intended to be mutually helpful.

30. Mirra Komarovsky, *Blue-Collar Marriage* (New York: Random, 1962), 17–20, speculates on the "therapeutic value" of talk in 1950s research; her questions seemed to "stimulate self-analysis" by women about their own marriages.

31. Ehrenreich, *Altruistic Imagination,* 55, when social work shifted emphasis and workers brought less relief, they lost "authority" with clients. Pleck, *Domestic Tyranny,* 150, social workers did succeed in getting people certain needed resources.

32. Case 5,027 on Reel 135.

33. Case 5,040 on Reel 135.

34. Case 14,931 on Reel 205.

35. Case 52 on Reel 106. "A Client Evaluates," *The Family* 10:1 (March 1929), 15, at an unnamed agency a client reports on caseworker's actions. "She took a great interest in Richard. . . . She talked to us on the budget and learned us to work out one. . . . She followed each case in the family if medical attention was needed. . . . She brought books into the home. . . . She talked about Christmas and seen they were not left and had a tree. . . . She was truthful in all she said and done." Schneyer, "Mother and Children, Poverty and Morality," 226, female caseworkers protected and attempted to protect women from fathers and judges, and poverty and immorality. In my study of records, that occurred on occasion, but only as part of a complex dynamic.

36. Case 15,958 on Reel 215.

37. A discussion about the impact of wages and hours is in AC, *23rd Annual Report,* 1910, 12; also Bruno, General Secretary Reports, September 30, 1917, April 21, 1920; Letter, Bruno to A. E. Zonne, June 22, 1920, General Secretary Reports, Folder-8, Box 3; Minutes, Board Meeting, December 17, 1913, Folder 1–22–13 to 12–5–17; May 7, 1915; November 21, 1917, Folder 1–22–13 to 12–4–17, Box 5, FCS Collection. See also Wenocur and Reisch, *From Charity to Enterprise*, 36, 117, 118.

Annual reports ceased in 1916 as world war brought pressures to an overworked staff. After 1917 AC/FWA distinguished agency service as "major" or "minor," "active" or "inactive," but available records do not explain the classification nor indicate which cases were in what category. Between 1917 and 1926 casework staff increased from 15 to 30. Each had between 143 and 183 major and minor cases; but a growing percentage were minor. "Number of Families Served and Number on Staff, 1917–1926," Box 2, FCS Collection.

Richmond, "Paid Worker," National Conference of Charities and Correction, *Proceedings,* 1903, 560–66. Dorothy Becker, "Early Adventures in Social Casework," *Social Casework*, 44:3 (May 1963), 256. New York City COS proved its fiscal responsibility to donors by "skrimping" on salaries, thus creating high agent turnover. Lubove, *Professional Altruist*, 132–35, in the early 1920s the American Association of Social Workers determined almost half of 1,200 social workers nationally were college graduates, but with lower wages than elementary teachers. In 1928 the average social worker earned less than $1,800 annually, did casework in a large city, and had experience in other fields but not necessarily social work experience or a graduate degree. Ehrenreich, *Altruistic Imagination*, 81, from before World War I into the 1920s, social work salaries stagnated.

38. FWA, *Family Welfare Association in Action*, 48–50.

39. Richmond, *What Is Social Case Work?* 171, emphasized lack of "reciprocity" in cases. Pat Ayers and Jean Lambertz, "Marriage Relations, Money, and Domestic Violence in Working Class Liverpool, 191–1939, in Lewis, *Labour and Love*, 206, charity was considered a "one way" relationship ; Lewis, *Women In England,* 36, paternalism rather than contract framed relations between woman and welfare worker. Lubove, *Professional Altruist,* 23, over time workers' "superiority" based on "expertise" replaced their "moral" superiority to clients.

40. Michael Katz, "The History of an Impudent Poor Woman in New York City from 1918 to 1923," Paper Presented to Shelby Cullom David Center for Historical Studies, Princeton, January 11, 1985, 24. Explaining the circumstance of a poor woman and recipiency from a charity, Katz paraphrases an analysis of charitable giving from Gareth Stedman Jones, *Outcast London* (London: Oxford Press, 1971), 251–52, gifts imposed an obligation and the recipient had to express gratitude and humility in order to continue receiving.

41. Richmond, *Social Diagnosis* (New York: Russell Sage Foundation, 1917), 187–89, 196, 197.

42. Case 18,213 on Reel 235.

43. Case 360 on Reel 105.

44. Case 2,472 on Reel 120.

45. AC, *26th Annual Report*, 1910, 24. Many COSs acted similarly in response to exploitation of the lower class.

46. Heidi Hartmann, "Capitalism and Women's Work in the Home, 1900–1930" (Ph.D. Thesis, Yale University, 1974), 191–99; Susan Strasser, *Never Done: A History of American Housework* (New York: Pantheon, 1982), 248, 249, describes the theoretical efficiency of household budget keeping. Social workers held women to unrealistic expectations, Abramovitz, *Regulating the Lives of Women*, 151, 198; Ayers and Lambertz, "Marriage Relations, Money and Domestic Violence," 206, 207.

47. Gordon Hamilton, "Refocusing Family Case Work," in Lowry, *Readings in Social Work*, 87, 89, 93.

48. Case 15,541 on Reel 210. E. Wight Bakke, *The Unemployed Worker, A Study of the Task of Making a Living Without a Job* (New Haven, Conn.: Yale University Press, 1940), 29, 33, 371; to seek power over one's situation in natural; if employed this is "self-respect"; if on relief, such behavior is discouraged as lack of cooperation.

49. Case 14,972 on Reel 205.

50. Case 14,332 on Reel 200; Gordon, *Heroes of Their Own Lives*, 291, women were not passive recipients of social services.

51. Case 1,165 on Reel 114.

52. Case 1,332 on Reel 115. Others note that social workers recommended nurseries for child guidance and mothers routinely resisted, Mintz and Kellogg, *Domestic Revolutions*, 129; Lewis, "Working Class Wife and Mother and State Intervention," 110; Susan Mann, "Family, Class and State in Women's Access to Abortion and Day Care: The Case of the United States," in Dickinson, *Family Economy and State*, 237; Schneyer, "Mothers and Children, Poverty and Morality," 212.

53. Concern about the adequacy of working-class mothers and the relationship of this to mothers' pensions, juvenile delinquency, and neglect, is in Abramovitz, *Regulating the Lives of Women, 184, 206;* Gordon, *Heroes of Their Own Lives,* 114; Pleck, *Domestic Tyranny,* 148; Leff, "Consensus on Reform," 413; and Vandepol, "Dependent Children: Child Custody and Mothers Pensions," 230. Leslie Woodcock Tentler, *Wage-Earning Women, Industrial Work and Family Life in the United States, 1900–1930* (New York: Oxford University Press, 1979), 165–69, divorced and widowed women preferred work to charity to keep

charity workers outside of their child rearing. Relationship of neglect charges to women's class and marital status is in Linda Gordon, "Single Mothers and Child Neglect, 1880–1920," *American Quarterly* 37:2 (Summer 1985), 173–92.

54. NCCC, *Guide to Study of Charities and Correction* (Indianapolis: National Conference of Charities and Correction, 1908), 144–50; Owen Lovejoy, "Child Labor and Philanthropy," NCCC , *Proceedings,* 1907, 196.

55. Ellen Ross, "Labour and Love: Rediscovering London's Working-Class Mothers, 1870–1918," in Lewis, *Labour and Love,* 74–90, discusses the harmful impact of compulsory school laws on family economics.

56. 17,302 on Reel 225.

57. "Child Labor," *Monthly Labor Review*, XI:6 (December 1920), 129, 130. Minnesota State Commission of Labor and Industries investigated complaints of underage children working at hazardous locations.

58. Case 8,430 on Reel 105.

59. Minutes, Friendly Visitors Conference, February 26, March 5, 1913, and October 25, 1911, Folder-1, Box L.1, FCS Collection.

60. Case 707 on Reel 111 gives an example of a social worker encouraging a sickly child to work.

61. See Judith A. Baer, *The Chains of Protection: The Judicial Response to Women's Labor Legislation* (Westport, Conn.: Greenwood Press, 1978), and Alice Kessler-Harris, *Out to Work, A History of Wage-Earning Women in the United States* (New York: Oxford University Press, 1982),180–214. Debate about women in the work place preceded the struggle for protective legislation. See Edna Bullock, ed., *Selected Articles on the Employment of Women* (Minneapolis: N. W. Wilson, 1911), passim. Concern for women's dual roles appears in Women's Bureau publications, for example Caroline Manning, *The Immigrant Woman and Her Job,* #74 (Washington, D.C.: U.S. Department of Labor, 1930), 60–63.

62. AC, *21st Annual Report,* 1905, 21.

63. Fears about the effect of wives' work on husbands is in Violet R. Markham, "True Foundations of Empire; The Home and the Workshop," and Flora McDonald Thompson, "Truth about Woman in Industry," in Bullock, *Selected Articles on the Employment of Women*, 93, 106; Paul H. Douglas, "The Changing Basis of Family Support and Expenditure," in Margaret E. Rich, *Family Life To-Day, Papers Presented at a Conference in Celebration of the 50th Anniversary of Family Social Work in America*, 1927 (Boston: Houghton Mifflin, 1928), 105, suggested that working wives received better treatment from husbands.

64. Edward T. Devine, *Principles of Relief* (New York: Macmillan, 1904), 94, 95; Edward T. Devine, *Social Work* (New York: Macmillan, 1922), 127, 128.

Dorothy M. Brown, *Setting a Course: American Women in the 1920s* (Boston: G.K Hall Twayne,1987), 79, 99, a social work educator, Sophonisba Breckinridge, said poor women lacked the luxury of doing what they "preferred" at home *or* in the factory, as they were forced to do both.

65. Mimi Abramavitz, "The Family Ethic: The Female Pauper and Public Aid, Pre-1900," *Social Service Review* 59:1 (March 1985), 129–31, enforcing the family ethic for women, like enforcing the work ethic for men, also serves wider economic and political goals.

66. Case 1,780 on Reel 105.

67. Barbara Klaczynska, "Why Women Work: A Comparison of Various Groups—Philadelphia, 1910–1930," *Labor History* 17:3 (Summer 1974), 81, asserted women's experience prior to marriage was the clearest indicator of work after marriage.

68. Case 4,188 on Reel 130.

69. AC, *29th Annual Report,* 1913, 47; Minutes, Friendly Visitors Conference, February 12,1913, Folder-1, Box L.1, FCS Collection.

70. Case 685 on Reel 111.

71. Alice Kessler—Harris, *Out to Work, A History of Wage-Earning Women in the United States* (New York: Oxford University Press, 1982), 164, twentieth-century reformers understood that women worked for economic reasons.

72. Case 1,780 on Reel 150. Richmond and Hall, *A Study of Nine Hundred and Eighty-Five Widows Known to Certain Charity Organization Societies in 1910* (New York: Russell Sage Foundation, Charity Organization Department, 1913), 9, 21, 29, 30. Encouraging *female* boarders as a solution to sexuality suggests that COS discounted the possibility of same sex relations among women.

73. Richmond, "Married Vagabond," 1895 in Colcord and Mann, *Long View,* 69, 73. Also "War and Family Solidarity, 1918, *Ibid.*, 451. Edward Devine, *The Principles of Relief* (New York: Macmillan, 1904), 222, men of "weak character" used desertion to get emergency relief into their homes.

74. Colcord, *Broken Homes, A Study of Desertion* (New York: Russell Sage Foundation), 52, 53, 63, 106–40, 187, compared methods of casework to new "preventive family treatment."

75. Case 5,027 on Reel 135.

76. Agreement in Linda Gordon and Wini Breines, "New Scholarship on Family Violence," *Signs* 8:3 (Spring 1983), 519; Pleck, *Domestic Tyranny,* 136–40.

77. Case 1,039 on Reel 113. For similar attitudes in marriage counseling, see Pleck, *Domestic Tyranny*, 149, 162, 163; Schneyer, "Mothers and Children," 215; and Summers, "Home from Home," 59.

78. Karl de Schweinitz, *The Art of Helping People Out of Trouble* (Boston: Houghton Mifflin,1924),109, cautioned social workers to "interpret the man to himself" only if he would profit from this and asked for it and be "impersonal" as men were no doubt weary of judgments. Harsh criticism of social work methods by a Northwestern University sociologist, Ernest R. Mowrer studying case records from Chicago agencies in 1920, is in *Family Disorganization: Introduction to Sociological Analysis* (Chicago: University of Chicago Press, 1927), 60–62, 89, 177–87, 241; also his *Domestic Discord: Its Analysis and Treatment* (Chicago: University of Chicago Press, 1929), passim. See also Maurice J. Karpf, "Sociology and Social Work," in Fern Lowrey, ed. *Readings in Social Case Work*, 669–71.

79. Pearl C. Salsberry, "Experiments in Closed Cases," *The Family* 1:3 (May 1920), 4.

80. Case 14,901 on Reel 205 gives an example of an outspoken women accusing the agent of bringing "no good," only "grief" in the way her desertion was handled.

81. Case 10,010 on Reel 105; "Studies of Breakdowns in Family Incomes: Broken Families," *The Family*, 11:1 (March 1930),11, in a ten-year study of 165 families at Chicago agencies; 60 were judged self-supportive by case end.

82. Richmond, "Charity and Community," 1909, in Colcord and Mann, *Long View*, 188–95.

83. Breckinridge, *Family Welfare Work* , 49, found agents limited by their negative attitudes toward case families.

84. Glassberg, "Philadelphians in Need," 331, nineteenth-century charities "discovered" that recipients believed in the work ethic despite negative experiences with "opportunity" in American laissez-faire.

Conclusion

1. Competing political interests of individual family members is basic to the interpretation by Gordon, *Heroes of Their Own lives, The Politics and History of Family Violence, Boston 1880–1960* (New York: Viking, 1988), 295; see also Pleck, *Domestic Tyranny: The Making of American Social Policy against Family Violence from Colonial Times to the Present* (New York: Oxford University Press, 1987), 12, 128.

2. Differentiating between public and private spheres does little to explain the experience of working-class women, Jane Lewis, ed. *Labour and Love: Wom-*

en's Experiences of Home and Family, 1850–1940 (Oxford: Basil Blackwell, 1986), 1–3; Evelyn Nakano Glenn, "Racial Ethnic Women's Labor: The Intersection of Race, Gender and Class Oppression," *Review of Radical Political Economics* 17:3 (Fall 1985),102.

3. Lillian Rubin, *Worlds of Pain: Life in Working-Class Families* (New York: Basic, 1976), 6, questions the home as a refuge in a NIMH study of the contemporary working class.

4. Women's identification as wives and mothers stressed by Lewis, *Labour and Love: Women's Experiences of Home and Family, 1850 and 1940* (Oxford: Basil Blackwell, 1986) passim, and Lewis, *Women in England 1870–1950: Sexual Divisions and Social Change* (Bloomington: Indiana University Press, 1984); also Leslie Woodcock Tentler, *Wage-Earning Women, Industrial Work and Family Life in the United States, 1901–1930* (New York: Oxford University Press, 1979), passim.

5. Sheila Ryan Johansson, "Herstory as History: A New Field or Another Fad?" in Berenice A. Carroll, ed. *Liberating Women's History, Theoretical and Critical Essays* (Urbana: University of Illinois Press, 1976), 406, examines "status" in women's experiences. There were few choices in employment, and sex-differentiated wages were too low to create economic independence from men, family, or security in old age which means work brings most women little "status." Tentler, *Wage-Earning Women,* 24, 81, 147, 157, household work allowed women more authority, independence, and creativity than wage work.

6. Dorothy M. Brown, *Setting a Course: American Women in the 1920s* (Boston: G. K. Hall/Twayne, 1987), 2, "unnerving" changes are described for women's lives in the 1920s but little attention is given to poor women and poverty.

7. Steven Mintz and Susan Kellogg, *Domestic Revolutions, A Social History of American Family Life* (New York: Free Press, 1988), 135.

8. Depression in the Midwest was visible to AC/FWA staff as early as 1926, see Letter, Colcord to Otto F. Bradley, Council of Social Agencies, March 20, 1929, Box 1 Family and Children's Service Collection, Social Welfare History Archives, University of Minnesota. For Colcord's role nationally in policy change see Beverly Stadum "Joanna Carver Colcord," in Walter I. Trattner, ed. *Biographical Dictionary of Social Welfare in America* (New York: Greenwood, 1986), 189, 190.

9. "The Public and Private Family Agencies," in *Family Service, The Private Family Agency in Minneapolis in 1936*, n.p. Booklet, Minneapolis Collection, Minneapolis Public Library. For the influence of private charity work on 1930s public policy, see Stanley Wenocur and Michael Reisch, *From Charity to Enterprise, The Development of American Social Work in a Market Economy* (Chicago: University of Illinois Press, 1989), 155–57.

10. For an excellent critique of family biases built into original ADC and contemporary AFDC, see Mimi Abramovitz, *Regulating the Lives of Women: Social Welfare Policy from Colonial Times to the Present* (Boston: South End, 1988).

11. Ruth Sidel, *Women and Children Last, The Plight of Poor Women in Affluent America*, 100–114.

12. Sidel, *Women and Children Last,* 98, 99. Also "'Quiz' Helps Dispel Myths about Families in Poverty," *NASW* (National Association of Social Workers) *News* 33:7 (July 1988), 12.

13. Diana Pearce, "The Feminization of Poverty: Women, Work and Welfare," *Urban and Social Change* (February 1978), 28–36, first coined this phrase. An excellent statistical analysis is in Harrell R. Rodgers, Jr., *Poor Women, Poor Families, The Economic Plight of America's Female-Headed Households* (Armonk, N.Y.: M. E. Sharpe, 1986), 16–53.

14. Dorothy C. Miller, "Helping the Strong: Women Headed Families and Their Needs," paper presented at the National Women's Studies Association Annual Conference, Minneapolis, June 24, 1988; Miller also authored a larger study, *Helping the Strong: An Exploration of the Needs of Families Headed by Women* (Silver Spring: National Association of Social Workers, 1987).

Index